Enhancing Learning with Effective Practical Science 11–16

Also available from Bloomsbury

How Science Works, James D. Williams

Practical Work in Secondary Science, Ian Abrahams

MasterClass in Mathematics Education, edited by Paul Andrews and Tim Rowland

Enhancing Learning with Effective Practical Science 11–16

Edited by Ian Abrahams and Michael J. Reiss

Bloomsbury Academic
An imprint of Bloomsbury Publishing Inc

BLOOMSBURY
LONDON · OXFORD · NEW YORK · NEW DELHI · SYDNEY

Bloomsbury Academic
An imprint of Bloomsbury Publishing Plc

50 Bedford Square
London
WC1B 3DP
UK

1385 Broadway
New York
NY 10018
USA

www.bloomsbury.com

BLOOMSBURY and the Diana logo are trademarks of Bloomsbury Publishing Plc

First published 2017

© Ian Abrahams, Michael J. Reiss and Contributors, 2017

Ian Abrahams, Michael J. Reiss and Contributors have asserted their right under the Copyright, Designs and Patents Act, 1988, to be identified as Editors and Authors of this work.

All rights reserved. No part of this publication may be reproduced or transmitted in any form or by any means, electronic or mechanical, including photocopying, recording, or any information storage or retrieval system, without prior permission in writing from the publishers.

No responsibility for loss caused to any individual or organization acting on or refraining from action as a result of the material in this publication can be accepted by Bloomsbury or the author.

British Library Cataloguing-in-Publication Data
A catalogue record for this book is available from the British Library.

ISBN: HB: 978-1-4725-9228-6
       PB: 978-1-4725-9227-9
       ePDF: 978-1-4725-9229-3
       ePub: 978-1-4725-9230-9

Library of Congress Cataloging-in-Publication Data
A catalog record for this book is available from the Library of Congress.

Typeset by Integra Software Services Pvt. Ltd.

To John Barker and Robin Millar

Contents

Notes on Contributors x
How to Use This Book, *Ian Abrahams and Michael J. Reiss* 1

1 The Role of Practical Work in Science Education, *Ian Abrahams and Michael J. Reiss* 5

1.1 Introduction 6
1.2 Previous studies into the role of practical work 6
1.3 Five generic aims for the use of practical work 8
1.4 The role of practical work in enhancing the learning of scientific knowledge 8
1.5 The role of practical work in motivating students 10
1.6 The role of practical work in teaching laboratory skills 11
1.7 The role of practical work in developing scientific attitudes 12
1.8 The role of practical work in developing insights into and expertise of the scientific method 13
1.9 Current perspectives on the nature and purpose of practical work 14

2 Effective Practical Work: 'Hands on' and 'Minds on', *Ian Abrahams and Michael J. Reiss* 17

2.1 The 'hands on' and 'minds on' model that we advocate 18
2.2 Using the model in practice 20
2.3 Pre-training observations 22
2.4 Post-training findings 25
2.5 Conclusions and implications for undertaking practical work 27

3 Biology: Session Guides 11–14, *Indira Banner and Mark Winterbottom* 29

3.1 The structure of plant and animal cells 30
3.2 Investigating the effect of antiseptic on microbial growth 33
3.3 Effect of exercise on heart rate 36
3.4 Investigating respiration in plants and animals 38
3.5 Measuring forces exerted by different muscles 41
3.6 Investigating the effect of different nerve pathways on reaction times 43

- 3.7 Investigating variation within and between species 46
- 3.8 Extracting DNA from plant tissue 49
- 3.9 Determining the population size of a plant species on the school field 52
- 3.10 Investigation into how seeds are dispersed by the wind 54
- 3.11 Investigating responses of woodlice using choice chambers 56
- 3.12 Investigating photosynthesis by the presence or absence of starch in a leaf 59

4 Biology: Session Guides 15–16, *Indira Banner and Mark Winterbottom* 63

- 4.1 Investigating diffusion and surface area in agar blocks 64
- 4.2 Comparing the energy content of foods 66
- 4.3 Investigating the factors that promote decay 69
- 4.4 Investigating the effect of amylase on starch 72
- 4.5 Investigating the structure and function of the breathing system 75
- 4.6 Investigating *Daphnia* heart rate in response to caffeine 77
- 4.7 Investigating the presence and absence of light on photosynthesis using algal balls 79
- 4.8 Comparing stomatal density on leaves 82
- 4.9 Measuring transpiration rates from leaves in different conditions 85
- 4.10 Observing turgor and plasmolysis in onion cells 88
- 4.11 Root tip preparation and the mitotic index 91
- 4.12 Investigating the effects of evolution using a model 94

5 Chemistry: Session Guides 11–14, *Ann Childs and Elaine Wilson* 97

- 5.1 Separating the colours in black ink 98
- 5.2 Which is the most reactive halogen? 101
- 5.3 What substances cause hard water? 104
- 5.4 What salts are present in sea water? 108
- 5.5 What is the most reactive metal? 111
- 5.6 The difference between elements, mixtures and compounds 116
- 5.7 The extraction of metals from their ores using carbon 119
- 5.8 Plants as indicators 122
- 5.9 Diffusion of ions in solution – the case of lead(II) iodide 126
- 5.10 Using universal indicator to illustrate the process of neutralisation 129
- 5.11 Analysis of combustion products when a candle burns 132
- 5.12 The thermal decomposition of copper carbonate 136

6 Chemistry: Session Guides 15–16, *Ann Childs and Elaine Wilson* 139

- 6.1 What ions are present in an unknown ionic solid? 140
- 6.2 Transition metal ions as catalysts – which works best? 145
- 6.3 Modelling the formation of igneous rocks 148

- 6.4 How does the concentration of a reactant affect the rate of reaction? 152
- 6.5 How does changing the temperature of a chemical reaction affect its reaction rate? 155
- 6.6 Electrolysis of ionic compounds in solution 159
- 6.7 Electricity from pairs of metals 162
- 6.8 Making an iodine clock or a Landolt Clock 165
- 6.9 Cracking hydrocarbons 169
- 6.10 Emulsifiers 173
- 6.11 Making nylon rope 176
- 6.12 Thermometric titration 179

7 Physics: Session Guides 11–14, *James de Winter and Michael Inglis* 183

- 7.1 Measuring the speed of moving objects 184
- 7.2 Motion graphs 187
- 7.3 Relationship between force and extension for a helical spring 190
- 7.4 Observing the appearance of the Moon over time 193
- 7.5 Thermal conduction 196
- 7.6 Thermal insulation 199
- 7.7 Comparing the energy content of fuels 201
- 7.8 The law of reflection 203
- 7.9 The law of refraction 205
- 7.10 Filters and colours 207
- 7.11 Investigating the magnetic field around a bar magnet 209
- 7.12 Factors that affect the strength of a simple electromagnet 212

8 Physics: Session Guides 15–16, *James de Winter and Michael Inglis* 215

- 8.1 Circular motion 216
- 8.2 Efficiency and energy transfer 219
- 8.3 Personal power 222
- 8.4 Specific heat capacity 224
- 8.5 The pressure law 227
- 8.6 Estimating absolute zero/Charles law 230
- 8.7 Critical angle and total internal reflection 233
- 8.8 Finding the focal length of a lens and making a telescope 236
- 8.9 Potential difference and current characteristics for an Ohmic resistor 240
- 8.10 Resistance of a wire 243
- 8.11 Electromagnetic induction 246
- 8.12 Electrolysis 249

9 Additional Effective Practical Work, *Ian Abrahams and Michael J. Reiss* 253

10 Conclusions, *Ian Abrahams and Michael J. Reiss* 255

References 258
Index 262

Notes on Contributors

Ian Abrahams is Head of the School of Education and Professor of Science Education at the University of Lincoln, UK. Ian's interests lie in the areas of practical work, assessment of practical skills, the prevalence of scientific misconceptions and one-to-one academically asymmetrical mentoring. Prior to moving into Higher Education in 2007 he was a secondary school physics teacher and then subsequently a head of department. Ian has worked at the Universities of London, York and Leeds, collaborating with colleagues from Ireland, Israel, Germany, Singapore, South Korea and Turkey and has published and presented widely in his areas of interest.

Indira Banner is a lecturer in Science Education in the School of Education, University of Leeds. There she leads the PGCE Biology and is the deputy-lead for the Secondary PGCE. Visiting schools in the area is a great way for Indira to learn new ideas. She also spends some Saturdays teaching Master's programmes to newly qualified and more experienced school teachers. Before becoming a lecturer Indira completed a PhD in Plant Biology and after a few odd jobs here and there completed a PGCE at Leeds University and taught Science in a comprehensive school in Bradford for five years.

Ann Childs is an associate lecturer in Science Education at the Department of Education at Oxford University. As well as her professional work as a science teacher educator, her key research interest currently involves collaborative research with expert secondary science teachers into how they explain scientific concepts in secondary school science classrooms and the implications of this for teacher education (both ITE and CPD). Recently she has become director of an international masters in teacher education (science and mathematics) and her research interests now include teacher learning and curriculum development in a number of international contexts.

James de Winter is a PGCE physics tutor at the Faculty of Education, University of Cambridge, as well lecturing on the primary PGCE course. He currently also leads the country-wide teacher fellow and educational research programs for the Ogden Trust. Previously, for many years, he worked as a secondary school physics teacher and then for the Science Learning Network developing, writing and leading continuing professional development (CPD) courses regionally and nationally with a focus on supporting specialist and non-specialist teachers of physics.

Michael Inglis is a lecturer in the Centre for Studies in Science and Mathematics Education at the University of Leeds. He leads the Physics PGCE course and has a Doctorate in Education on student teachers' experiences of physics subject knowledge development. He taught physics in secondary schools in London and Hertfordshire, and spent two years supporting the professional development of science teachers and teacher educators in Ethiopia with Voluntary Service Overseas (VSO). Prior to becoming a teacher, Michael was a geophysicist in the oil industry.

Michael J. Reiss is Professor of Science Education at UCL Institute of Education, University College London. After a PhD and post-doc in evolutionary biology at the University of Cambridge, Michael trained to be a teacher. He taught science at secondary level for five years before returning to the University of Cambridge Department of Education as an academic. After six years there and six years at Homerton College, Cambridge, he moved to the Institute of Education, University of London in 2001. He is a Fellow of the Academy of Social Sciences and the former Director of Education at the Royal Society.

Elaine Wilson is a senior lecturer in education at the University of Cambridge and a Fellow of Homerton College. Elaine was a secondary school chemistry teacher in Bath and Cambridge and was awarded a Salters' Medal for chemistry teaching. Elaine teaches on the secondary science pre-service course and coordinates a 'blended learning' Science Education Master's course. She supervises Master's and Doctoral students in the Leadership academic group. She is active in Outreach work with schools and has been a Lead Teacher at Salters' Chemistry Camps.

Mark Winterbottom is a senior lecturer at the University of Cambridge prior to which taught in upper schools. His research interests are in classroom environment, teacher education and science education. Mark teaches on the Faculty of Education's PGCE and Master's courses, as well as undertaking teacher education and curriculum development work in Asia and the Middle East.

How to Use This Book

Ian Abrahams and Michael J. Reiss

> **Please read this short chapter before proceeding!**

The two of us, Ian Abrahams and Michael J. Reiss, as editors of this book and authors of several of its chapters, are passionate about school science education. One of the most distinctive features of secondary science teaching, compared to other school subjects, in many countries is the way in which students undertake practical work, often in dedicated science laboratories. Practical work is an integral and important part of both science teaching and science learning. As such, maximizing its effectiveness, as a means of developing or reinforcing conceptual understanding, is essential if students are to gain fully from the practical work that they do.

However, our experience, both as classroom teachers and through the research we have undertaken, is that all too often students do not learn from practical work what their teachers want them to. We will present evidence to substantiate this somewhat disheartening conclusion in Chapter 2, but our own judgement is consistent with much other research in showing that while many students enjoy practical work and learn certain skills from it – how to operate a microscope, conduct a flame test or measure the current at different points in an electric circuit, for example – it is too rarely the case that they learn the scientific concepts that their teachers want them to.

Students may be able to use a microscope to observe and accurately draw plasmolysed cells without understanding much (or even anything) about the differential permeability of cell membranes. They may be able to identify substances as a result of flame tests yet have no understanding of why the different colours that they observe are produced. They may be able to measure electric currents with great precision yet be unable to explain the difference between charge, current and potential difference. Others too have emphasized the need for 'the thinking behind the doing', in the language of Roberts and Johnson (2015).

This book is intended to help remedy this situation. The intention is that secondary science teachers, whether new to the classroom or with many years of experience, will be able to profit from it.

In Chapter 1 we review previous studies into the role of practical work and identify a range of aims that have been proposed for practical work. It might be supposed that one of the main purposes of practical work in school science would be help students better to learn science, that is, to acquire appropriate scientific knowledge and understanding effectively. In fact the literature shows that while this is a frequent aim of practical work, there is worryingly little evidence that this aim is more than occasionally met. It is to help remedy this state of affairs that this book has been written.

Chapter 2 is a vital chapter. It introduces a model for how science teachers can think of practical work and get their students to undertake it so that these students do acquire the scientific knowledge and understanding that we want them to. The fundamental driver behind this model is the belief that students need not only to engage practically with their hands in undertaking practical work, they need also to engage mentally with the scientific concepts that the practical is intended to help them learn. For this reason we distinguish between a 'domain of observables' (that which can be seen, heard, smelt or otherwise sensed) and a 'domain of ideas' (that which exists in the mind and requires conscious thought).

The model we advocate derives from earlier work that we undertook in a large-scale funded project called the 'Getting Practical: Improving Practical Work in Science' (IPWiS) project (Abrahams et al., 2014). We played a role in designing the approach but our main role was to evaluate the approach used in the project. This entailed us going into both primary and secondary classrooms and seeing students undertake practical tasks both before and after their teachers had had the training that the IPWiS project provided. The findings, which we present and interpret in Chapter 2, surprised us. They also helped us realize that while the training had some beneficial consequences, what was needed was written materials that made it a great deal clearer how practical work might be undertaken so as to promote scientific understanding.

Chapter 2 having introduced the model to help teachers get their students to undertake more effective practical work, Chapters 3–8 each provide twelve examples of session guides (essentially, lesson plans) for effective practical work. Chapter 3 does so in biology for teachers of 11- to 14-year-olds; Chapter 4 in biology for teachers of 15- to 16-year-olds; Chapter 5 in chemistry for teachers of 11- to 14-year-olds; Chapter 6 in chemistry for teachers of 15- to 16-year-olds; Chapter 7 in physics for teachers of 11- to 14-year-olds; Chapter 8 in physics for teachers of 15- to 16-year-olds. The biology chapters are written by Indira Banner and Mark Winterbottom, the chemistry ones by Ann Childs and Elaine Wilson and the physics ones by James de Winter and Michael Inglis.

Each of the twelve session guides in each of Chapters 3–8 explains the learning objectives for the practical and the procedure that students need to follow. An equipment list is provided along with things for the teacher to keep in mind and issues for discussion. Any health and safety issues are addressed. Note that health and safety legislation can vary from country to country. A key feature of the chapter is that each practical has an 'Effectiveness matrix' which clearly indicates what students should do and what they should learn, both while undertaking the practical and as a result of undertaking it.

It is these effectiveness matrices that emphasize the importance of the 'domain of ideas' as well as the 'domain of observables', our contention being, as we hope is increasingly evident by now, that too much time spent on practical work in secondary science lessons is occupied by the domain of observables, by teachers ensuring that students know what to do so that they observe what they ought to observe. But our contention is that observation is not enough. There is no automatic relationship between observation and understanding. A great deal of hard intellectual work needs to be undertaken by students if they are to understand what they observe in terms of the scientific models that their teachers want them to acquire. It is easy to hear that a bell gets fainter as the air is removed from a chamber that surrounds a bell and separates the bell from the class. It is another thing for a student to understand how this provides evidence that a material, such as air, is required for the transmission of sound.

While the effectiveness matrix lies at the heart of each of the 72 session guides, another feature that we emphasize is 'issues for discussion'. Many experienced teachers will find that these are the sorts of ideas that they regularly raise with students. That's great. However, we are well aware that the pressures of fitting science practicals into the timetable of a secondary school mean that it is all too easy for the time for meaningful discussion of the results of practical work to get squeezed. And we are not really talking here about getting students to draw up tables of results, produce graphs, consider anomalous findings and so on. We are thinking more of issues for discussion that are specific to each of these seventy-two practicals that enable students gradually to build up a scientific way of seeing the world. As Michael Young (2007) would emphasize, this is powerful knowledge – the sort of knowledge that learners can acquire, with good teaching, in school, whereas outside of school they are more likely to acquire everyday knowledge.

Accordingly, to facilitate students getting to grips with the scientific knowledge that each practical seeks to build, the ideas for discussion suggest a small number of key questions that teachers might raise with students. Of course, it is up to teachers how they might choose to use these questions. They could be posed in a whole class question-and-answer session or they might be given to pairs/small groups of students to discuss in class or they might be given as individual homeworks. There are arguments for each of these approaches and it may be that different approaches work best on different occasions. Mindful, in particular, that science teachers often teach outside their subject specialisms, the authors of Chapters 3–9 have provided one or more key responses to each issue for discussion.

Chapter 9 provides suggestions on how to move beyond the examples within the book so as to produce effective practical work for students in other areas of the science curriculum. Our hope is that the approach we have advocated here becomes internalized by teachers, so that it becomes second nature to them to ensure that students engage with the key ideas of science as well as develop their manipulative proficiency or other scientific skills.

Finally, Chapter 10 draws together the key arguments in the book. In particular, it addresses head-on a view that has been expressed by a number of leading science educators, namely that practical work in school science is overrated. This is not our view. However, it behoves the science education profession to find ways of demonstrating that school science practical work is worth it. Compared to most other subjects, secondary science in many countries enjoys considerable advantages, particularly through the provision of dedicated laboratories. In some countries class sizes are smaller in secondary science than in most other subjects, while support for science teachers may be provided by specialist technicians. None of this is inexpensive. School science practical work needs to prove its worth in cost–benefit analyses.

The role of practical work in science education

Ian Abrahams and Michael J. Reiss

1.1 Introduction (p. 6)
1.2 Previous studies into the role of practical work (p. 6)
1.3 Five generic aims for the use of practical work (p. 8)
1.4 The role of practical work in enhancing the learning of scientific knowledge (p. 8)
1.5 The role of practical work in motivating students (p. 10)
1.6 The role of practical work in teaching laboratory skills (p. 11)
1.7 The role of practical work in developing scientific attitudes (p. 12)
1.8 The role of practical work in developing insights into and expertise of the scientific method (p. 13)
1.9 Current perspectives on the nature and purpose of practical work (p. 14)

According to Plato, the world can be divided into the abstract world of ideas or thoughts and the concrete world of physical realities. He was not very successful in finding connections and relations between these two worlds. What Plato had forgotten was to include the laboratory, the missing link between the abstract world of thought and the concrete world of physical realities. The role of the laboratory is to connect the two worlds together. (Brodin, 1978, p. 4)

1.1 Introduction

Science education differs from almost all other subjects taught in school in that it involves practical lessons that are, generally speaking, undertaken in specifically designed and, in many cases, purpose built laboratories (White, 1988). We use the term 'practical lesson' to mean any lesson in which the students are involved in manipulating and/or observing real (as opposed to virtual) objects and materials, and it is this manipulation and observation that we will refer to as 'practical work'. Practical work in this sense is a broad category that includes, for example, 'recipe' (Clackson & Wright, 1992) style tasks (sometimes referred to as 'cook-book' tasks), experiments, investigations and discovery style tasks. In characterizing such activities *not* on the basis of where they are undertaken but on what is undertaken, it seems more appropriate to refer to them as 'practical work', rather than 'laboratory work' (or 'labwork'). That said, we recognize that in many countries, including England, most secondary school science practical work is undertaken in laboratories and so most of what we refer to as 'practical work' can also be thought of as being 'laboratory work'.

1.2 Previous studies into the role of practical work

In 1960 Kerr undertook the first extensive survey in order to inquire into the nature and purpose of practical work within the framework of the teaching of biology, chemistry and physics within grammar schools in England and Wales. The findings, which basically involved the teachers arranging ten suggested aims (purposes) for practical work in order of their perceived importance, are summarized in Table 1.1.

Table 1.1 Teachers' ten suggested aims (purposes) for practical work in order of their perceived importance (from Kerr, 1964, p. 27)

Pooled order of importance of aims of practical work

Ten aims of practical work	Teachers' rank ordering, 1 being most important Biology–B Chemistry–C Physics–P								
	Ages 11–14			Ages 15–16			Ages 17–18		
	B	C	P	B	C	P	B	C	P
To encourage accurate observation and careful recording	2	2	5	1	1	4	1	1	1
To promote simple, common-sense, scientific methods of thought	4	4	4	3	2	3	4	4	4
To develop manipulative skills	8	7	7	9	8	8	5	5	6
To give training in problem solving	9	9	9	8	9	9	9	7	8
To fit the requirements of practical examination regulations	10	10	10	10	10	10	8	8	10
To elucidate the theoretical work so as to aid comprehension	6	6	6	4	4	2	2	2	2
To verify facts and principle already taught	7	8	8	7	7	7	7	6	5
To be an integral part of the process of finding facts by investigation and arriving at principles	5	5	3	6	3	1	3	3	3
To arouse and maintain interest in the subject	1	1	1	5	5	5	10	10	9
To make physical phenomena more real through actual experience	3	3	2	2	6	6	6	9	7

While a direct comparison between the findings of Kerr (1964) and a subsequent study by Beatty (1980) (students aged 11–13 in England and Wales) is not possible since the latter study used an expanded list of twenty aims, a cautious comparison between the two studies can be made by comparing the order of importance of only those aims proposed by Kerr (1964) that are common to both studies. Bennett (2003) has suggested that despite a certain degree of variation between the studies in terms of teachers, subjects and student ages, there is a general consensus that most teachers perceived the most important aims of practical work as being:

- to encourage accurate observation and description;
- to make scientific phenomena more real;
- to enhance understanding of scientific ideas;
- to arouse and maintain interest (particularly in younger pupils);
- to promote a scientific method of thought.

(Bennett, 2003, pp. 78–79)

While other alternative lists have been proposed (Hodson, 1990; Kerr, 1964; Thompson, 1975; Woolnough & Beatty, 1980), they frequently share the same, or broadly similar, generic aims. Hodson (1990), for example, suggests that there are five primary aims for practical work:

- to motivate, by stimulating interest and enjoyment;
- to teach laboratory skills;
- to enhance the learning of scientific knowledge;
- to give insight into scientific method, and develop expertise in using it;
- to develop certain 'scientific attitudes', such as open-mindedness, objectivity and willingness to suspend judgement.

(Hodson, 1990, pp. 30–33)

While the lists proposed by Hodson (1990) and Bennett (2003) are not identical, they are, broadly speaking, similar and while accepting the arbitrary nature of any particular list, that proposed by Hodson (1990) provides a useful framework within which to consider the justifications for the use of practical work.

1.3 Five generic aims for the use of practical work

Despite the aspirations and expectations of those who advocate a central role for practical work in the teaching of science, the limited research that has been undertaken in this area has found it to be, as commonly used, no more effective in achieving *most* of these generic aims than other non-practical methods of teaching. It is to that research, and its implications for the five generic aims suggested by Hodson (1990), that we now turn.

1.4 The role of practical work in enhancing the learning of scientific knowledge

Research findings into the role of practical work in enhancing the development of conceptual understanding is, at best, ambiguous. For example, while Hewson and Hewson (1983) report a significant enhancement of conceptual understanding amongst students who had received a primarily practical-based instruction, compared to those who received a traditional, non-practical instruction, Mulopo and Fowler (1987) reported no significant difference in the level of conceptual understanding amongst students whether they had been taught using practical or traditional, non-practical methods. Indeed, Mulopo and Fowler report that the most significant factor in determining the extent of conceptual development was not the method of instruction but rather the student's level of intellectual development.

Indeed, reviews relating specifically to practical work (Chang & Lederman, 1994; Hofstein & Lunetta, 1982; Lazarowitz & Tamir, 1994; Watson et al., 1995) have shown that when outcomes are measured using pen and paper tests, the use of practical work offers no significant advantage in the development of students' scientific conceptual understanding. Given the central role of the laboratory, its high financial cost and the high aspirations that many teachers have regarding its value, such non-significant findings are disappointing if the development of conceptual understanding is seen as a prime function of practical work. Clackson and Wright (1992), rather negatively, suggest that:

> Although practical work is commonly considered to be invaluable in science teaching, research shows that it is not necessarily so valuable in science *learning*. The evidence points to the uncomfortable conclusion that much laboratory work has been of little benefit in helping pupils and students understand concepts. (p. 40)

Yager et al. (1969) argue that some academically able students may in fact consider laboratory work to be wasteful of their time, serving only to delay their pursuit of new theories and concepts. In contrast, Van den Berg and Giddings (1992) argue that such beliefs, if held by the students, would be a criticism of the form of specific practical tasks rather than constituting a criticism of practical work per se.

However, these findings seem, generally speaking, to reinforce Ausubel's (1968) assertion that 'In dividing the labour of scientific instruction, the laboratory typically carries the burden of conveying the method and the spirit of science whereas the textbook and teachers assume the burden of transmitting subject matter and content' (p. 346).

Hodson (1992) has claimed that it is necessary to introduce students to the relevant scientific concepts *prior* to their undertaking any practical work if the task is to be effective as a means of enhancing the development of their conceptual understanding. More recently, Millar (1998) has questioned whether the observation of specific phenomena within the context of a practical task can, unaided, lead to the development of conceptual understanding. In this context it has been proposed (Millar et al., 1999) that the function of practical work might be better understood in terms of a link, or bridge, between previously taught scientific concepts and subsequent observations.

One explanation (Tamir, 1991) suggested for the lack of research evidence to support the use of practical work as an effective means for developing students' conceptual knowledge is that, in contrast to teacher demonstration, its use can generate cognitive overload. Cognitive overload occurs as a consequence of simultaneous demands made of the students by practical work in that they need to apply intellectual and practical skills as well as prior knowledge (Johnstone & Wham, 1982).

Therefore, despite the frequent claims that one of the aims of practical work is to provide an effective means of developing conceptual understanding, the research findings suggest, at least when the outcomes are measured using pen and paper tests, that there is no significant advantage to its use.

1.5 The role of practical work in motivating students

Abraham (2009) has reported that what teachers frequently refer to as 'motivation' is, in a strict psychological sense, better understood as situational interest. The fact that situational interest is, unlike motivation or personal interest, unlikely to endure beyond the end of a particular lesson (Hidi & Harackiewicz, 2000; Murphy & Alexander, 2000) helps to explain why students need to be continuously re-stimulated by the frequent use of practical work. Once this fact is recognized, the reason why many pupils who claim to like practical work also claim to have little, if any, personal interest in science, or any intention of pursuing it once it is no longer compulsory (Abrahams, 2009) becomes clearer. For while these students *do* like practical work their reasons for doing so appear primarily to be that they see it as *preferable* to non-practical teaching techniques that they associate, in particular, with more writing (Edwards & Power, 1990; Gardner & Gould, 1990; Hodson, 1990; Hofstein & Lunetta, 1982). This helps to explain why, *despite* claims that students are said to prefer a laboratory-centred approach (Lazarowitz & Tamir, 1994; Pickering, 1987) and that its use encourages and motivates students to study science (Abrahams & Saglam, 2010; Arce & Betancourt, 1997; Kerr, 1964; Lazarowitz & Tamir, 1994), there is a broad consensus (House of Commons Science and Technology Committee, 2002; Millar & Osborne, 1998; Osborne & Collins, 2001; Osborne et al., 1998; Osborne et al., 2003) that far too many 'young people are, at age 16, closing off the option of entering a career in science or engineering at a time when the UK is suffering from a shortage of scientists and engineers' (House of Commons Science and Technology Committee, 2002, p. 23). Indeed, these issues are not limited to the UK and that '… it is obvious that the S&T sector in Europe (and other OECD countries) is facing a serious problem, [that is] the recruitment to the S&T sector' (ROSE, p. 28). In fact, this is happening despite the devotion of a significant proportion of science teaching time to the pursuit of practical work. Indeed, Bennett (2003) argued that there is little reason to doubt that the amount of time spent on practical work in the UK has not changed appreciably since the studies by Beatty and Woolnough (1982) and Thompson (1975) in which it was found that one third of the time allocated to science education, during 'A' level study (post compulsory education age 17–18), is devoted to some form of practical work (Thompson, 1975) with this rising to one half of science teaching time for students in the 11–13 age range (Beatty & Woolnough, 1982).

A study by Windschitle and Andre (1998) into pupil motivation and the influence of epistemological beliefs on learning found that practical work was primarily effective in motivating epistemologically more mature students and that in contrast the epistemologically less mature students found non-practical teaching styles more motivating. Other studies (Arce & Betancourt, 1997; Berry et al., 1999; Watson & Fairbrother, 1993) report that students are more frequently motivated by practical work in which they are allowed to exercise some degree of control over its design and which they find both challenging and rewarding, although Lazarowitz and Tamir (1994) suggest that the motivational effectiveness of such tasks can be reduced if they are perceived as too difficult.

1.6 The role of practical work in teaching laboratory skills

One of the difficulties in reviewing the literature that relates to the effectiveness of practical work in the teaching of skills is that the term 'skill' has been used to mean different things to different people in different studies (Bennett, 2003). Hofstein and Lunetta (1982) argue that many studies take too narrow a view of laboratory skills and consequently neglect to measure development in skill areas such as creative thinking, problem solving, general intellectual development, observing and classifying. Hodson (1990) distinguishes between 'craft skills' which are content specific – learning to read a micrometre, carrying out a titration – and content independent skills such as observation and manual dexterity which are generalizable to other contexts or disciplines, while Gott and Duggan (1995) question the appropriateness of using the term 'skill' to describe *any* content-independent processes. Dawe (2003) argues that content-independent skills are, because of their generalizability, of more value to *all* students, while content-specific skills are of value primarily to future scientists or technicians. However, Ausubel (1968) argues, with regard to problem-solving skills, that there is no reason to believe that even if they could be taught, in the context of one subject, that they could be transferred to other contexts or disciplines. Heaney (1971) reports that while a heuristic approach – in this context any approach to learning that employs a practical method – leads to the development of problem-solving skills, a more traditional 'didactic-with-demonstration' approach is actually detrimental to the development of problem-solving skills, a finding that has not been confirmed in any other study. Indeed, Millar (1989) and Millar and Driver (1987) argue that content-independent processes cannot be taught but are rather innate abilities that we all have a natural propensity to develop. Relatedly, a study by Boud et al. (1980) into students' perspectives about laboratory work reported that students themselves do not believe that their problem-solving skills improve as a consequence of undertaking practical work.

Similar uncertainty surrounds the effectiveness of practical work in the development of creative thinking. Hill (1976), using the Minnesota Test of Creative Thinking, reported an improvement in creativity after pupil involvement in practical work in chemistry. In contrast, Gangoli and Gurumurthy (1995), using an 'objective-type' test devised and standardized by Gurumurthy (1988), reported no evidence of improvement in creative thinking within their study.

Hofstein (1988) has pointed out that if the term 'skill' is interpreted narrowly to mean only 'manipulative skill', then practical work has, perhaps unsurprisingly, been found to have a measurable advantage over other non-practical types of instruction within science education (Gangoli & Gurumurthy, 1995; Kempa & Palmer, 1974). However, while not denying its relative effectiveness in this area, White (1996, 1979) and Clackson and Wright (1992) have questioned both the appropriateness and cost-effectiveness of its use as a means for developing content-independent manual dexterity, with White (1979) going so far as to claim that 'if skill in manipulation *per se* is the aim, not merely skill with scientific apparatus, there are cheaper and probably more efficient and effective ways of developing it. Needlework and fine woodwork are instances' (p. 762). Such criticism echoes that made about sixty years earlier in the *British Association Report* (1917) in which it was suggested that some purposes for undertaking laboratory work are of an intrinsically lesser value than others and that 'In the laboratory the development of dexterity and skill is only a secondary consideration' (British Association Report, 1917; quoted in Connell, 1971, p. 138).

1.7 The role of practical work in developing scientific attitudes

The term 'scientific attitude' is both broad and weakly defined within the literature. Indeed, it has been pointed out (Abrahams, 2009) that the term 'attitude' has been appropriated by different researchers to describe on the one hand 'scientific attitudes' and on the other hand 'attitudes towards science'. Aiken and Aiken (1969), discussing traits such as intellectual honesty, open-mindedness and curiosity, referred to them as 'the more cognitive scientific attitudes' (p. 295). In contrast, Hofstein and Lunetta (1982) use the term 'attitude' when discussing the development of 'favourable attitudes toward science' (p. 210). There has been relatively little research (Hofstein & Lunetta, 1982) to evaluate the effectiveness of practical work as a means of developing scientific attitudes although, in marked contrast, it has been pointed out (Simon, 2000) that there have been in excess of 200 studies into attitudes towards science.

Part of the explanation for this is to be found in terms of differences between the generic aims for practical work used by different researchers. Thus, while Shulman and Tamir (1973) place both attitude and interest towards science in the same generic category, Hodson (1990) places them in different generic categories and, as such, the term 'attitude' relates only to scientific attitudes and not to attitudes towards science.

Yet even when the term 'attitude' is used only with regard to scientific attitudes there is little evidence within the literature as to what constitutes scientific attitudes or, more importantly, how these are determined. Thus, while Henry (1975) suggests that scientific attitudes include the need to be (i) observant, (ii) careful, (iii) patient and (iv) persistent, Lazarowitz and Tamir (1994) suggest a much expanded list of scientific attitudes that includes 'honesty, readiness to admit failure, critical assessment of the results and their limitations, curiosity, risk taking, objectivity, precision, confidence, perseverance, responsibility, collaboration, and readiness to reach consensus' (p. 98).

However, from a study of seventeen senior biology laboratories (USA, age 17–18) Fordham (1980) reported that the pursuit of scientifically correct results meant that honesty, far from being a scientific attitude that was developed through the use of practical work, was frequently its first casualty insofar as 'If the experiment doesn't work we go to somebody else and get their results … it looks better when you get the results that you are supposed to … it's pretty obvious you won't get as good a mark as someone who got it to work' (p. 114).

Despite differences as to what might, or might not, be considered an appropriate scientific attitude, Gauld and Hukins (1980) have pointed out that the majority of the scientific attitudes that appear in the literature fall into three generic categories: (i) general attitudes towards scientific ideas, (ii) attitudes towards the evaluation of scientific ideas and (iii) commitment to a particular set of beliefs about science. From a more fundamental perspective Bennett (2003) has argued that despite the difference between scientific attitudes and attitudes towards science both are inextricably linked with behaviours, dispositions and beliefs, rendering a clear-cut distinction between them highly problematic.

In conclusion, Gardner and Gould (1990) claim, with regard to the development of scientific attitudes, that 'While students generally enjoy hands-on experience and the opportunity to work individually or in small groups, we cannot conclude that such experiences will, by themselves, bring about major changes in styles of thinking' (p. 151).

1.8 The role of practical work in developing insights into and expertise of the scientific method

Lazarowitz and Tamir (1994) have claimed that by undertaking practical work students develop an understanding of the nature of science, the way scientists work and, in particular, 'the multiplicity of scientific methods' (p. 98). Yet such a multiplicity of methods is often overlooked given the strength of the prevailing view (Bennett, 2003) of the scientific enterprise that is firmly embedded within a hypothetico-deductive (Popper, 1989) view of science. Millar (1989) has pointed out that even if the hypothetico-deductive view of science *is* an appropriate model for the scientific enterprise it does not accurately represent the nature of practical work as it occurs within the school laboratory.

Indeed, it has been claimed (Martin, 1979) that a large proportion of practical work undertaken within the school laboratory has been reflective of 'dubious or discarded philosophies of science' (p. 331), a reference to the now widely discredited inductive view (Millar 2004) that seeks to derive natural laws from observations. In the same context Layton (1990) has questioned the extent to which any philosophy of science has been systematically used to guide the nature of practical work in the school laboratory, noting that 'the philosophy of science has rarely been used in a systematic and deliberate manner as a prime source of objectives for student laboratory work' (p. 37).

Hodson (1989) has argued that the perceptions about both the nature of science and scientific method are shaped by the distorted manner in which textbooks portray the relationship between experiment and theory in that 'The actual chronology of experiment and theory is rewritten in text-books. This helps to sustain the myth that the path of science is certain and assigns a simple clear cut role to experiments' (p. 57).

It might be worth pausing briefly simply to clarify the difference between two contrasting views of science. The first of these is referred to as the inductive view and is one in which the starting point is experimental observation within which a local pattern might be discerned. By undertaking further experimental observations, over a larger sample, the initial local pattern might be found to be a more general one in the sense that it also holds with regards all of the observations in the larger sample. Such a general pattern might then lead to the formulation of a tentative hypothesis about the behaviour that would be experimentally observed in an even larger sample that could then be explored by undertaking an even larger and more diverse set of observations. If these subsequent observations all support the tentative hypothesis, this might lead to a general conclusion in the form of a theory. In contrast, the deductive view is one in which the starting point is an existing theory from which one, or more, scientifically testable hypotheses can be derived. Any of these hypotheses can be tested by comparing the observable behaviour predicted by the hypothesis with actual experimental observations. These experimental observations have the potential to either support or refute the hypothesis that, in turn, results in either in the refutation of, or further support for, the theory from which the hypothesis was derived.

Interestingly for teachers, Matthews and Winchester (1989) suggest that only if students are allowed to see that science is often less than certain and that the relationship between experiment and theory is not always unambiguous will they develop an understanding of scientific method. Lazarowitz and Tamir (1994) point out that such an approach will mean that 'the distorted image many students have of scientists (unusual persons wearing white gowns, working in isolation, and exhibiting extraordinary behaviour) may be discarded, and students may realize that scientists are ordinary persons' (p. 109).

1.9 Current perspectives on the nature and purpose of practical work

An increasing scepticism as to the effectiveness of the laboratory-centred approach to science teaching has led many researchers (Abrahams & Millar, 2008; Gagné & White, 1978; Hodson, 1996; Van den Berg & Giddings, 1992; Woolnough & Allsop, 1985) to question both the nature and purpose of practical work and how best to make its use most effective.

The current debate has served to highlight the fact that there still remains, despite the long history of debate, a wide range of differing views as to the nature and purpose of practical work. Just how wide this range is, and how it changes over time, can be seen by presenting a few of those positions that serve to mark out the boundaries within which most current views can be found.

In this respect Kreitler and Kreitler (1974) propose that the purpose of practical work is to provide a means of enabling students to gain direct experience with scientific concepts that in turn generate episodes that serve to give those concepts meaning. They reject as wholly unrealistic the suggestion that its purpose, even in part, is to aid in either the development of problem-solving skills or the generation of both curiosity and interest in science. In marked contrast, Woolnough and Allsop (1985) argue that the purpose of practical work has nothing at all to do with the development of conceptual understanding and go so far as to suggest a need to 'deliberately and consciously separate practical work from the constraint of teaching scientific theory … We will make no progress until we have cut this Gordian Knot' (pp. 39–40). While supporting this separation Hofstein and Lunetta (1982) go on to suggest that a main purpose of practical work, and one frequently overlooked, is in the development of creative thinking, problem solving, scientific thinking and general intellectual development as well as the effect it can have on students' attitudes to science.

When all these issues are taken together, along with the higher cost of building and maintaining school laboratories, the *prima facie* case for practical work no longer appears quite as self-evident as it did when the National Science Teachers Association asserted that:

> The time is surely past when science teachers must plead the case for school laboratories. It is now widely recognised that science is a process and an activity as much as it is an organized body of knowledge and that, therefore, it cannot be learned in any deep and meaningful way by reading and discussion alone. (1970, p. 3)

Despite strong beliefs amongst teachers regarding the value of practical work, the empirical results to date indicate that, other than as a means for improving manual dexterity, its long-term value is, at best, uncertain. Such uncertainty, Bates (1978) suggests, means that the onus of proof therefore still remains firmly on those who believe in its value in areas other than improving manual dexterity to prove their case:

> Teachers who believe that the laboratory accomplishes something special for their students would do well to consider carefully what those outcomes might be, and then to find a way to measure them for the answer has not yet been conclusively found: What does the laboratory accomplish that could not be accomplished as well by less expensive and less time consuming alternatives? (p. 75)

Yet Millar et al. (1999) optimistically point out that, despite these widely divergent views, most science educators recognize the educational value of practical work and would agree that it should constitute a significant proportion of the time spent in teaching science at school provided, as White (1996) argues, that the term 'educational value' remains loosely defined.

Effective practical work: 'hands on' and 'minds on'

Ian Abrahams and Michael J. Reiss

2

- **2.1** The 'hands on' and 'minds on' model that we advocate (p. 18)
- **2.2** Using the model in practice (p. 20)
- **2.3** Pre-training observations (p. 22)
- **2.4** Post-training findings (p. 25)
- **2.5** Conclusions and implications for undertaking practical work (p. 27)

The approach to practical work which we advocate and illustrate in this book is based on a fundamental principle – namely that students need to be helped to think about what they are doing and learning in a practical. As we will show below, the evidence from secondary science classrooms is that it is far too often the case that even students who are reasonably proficient at undertaking practical work have little understanding of why they are doing what they are doing or of what they are supposed to be learning from it.

Such practical work can still have some value. Students may develop certain skills and they may enjoy their science lessons. However, our belief is that practical work in school science can achieve much more than this.

2.1 The 'hands on' and 'minds on' model that we advocate

As we discussed in Chapter 1, practical work encompasses a broad range of activities that can have widely differing aims and objectives. The framework used here to determine the effectiveness of practical work is one that was developed and used by Abrahams and Millar (2008) in a previous study of the effectiveness of practical work. It draws on a model (Figure 2.1) proposed by Millar et al. (1999) for evaluating a practical task.

This model considers the effectiveness of a specific task *relative* to the aims and intentions of the teacher and, as such, the starting point (Box A) is the teacher's learning

Figure 2.1
Model of the process of design and evaluation of a practical task.

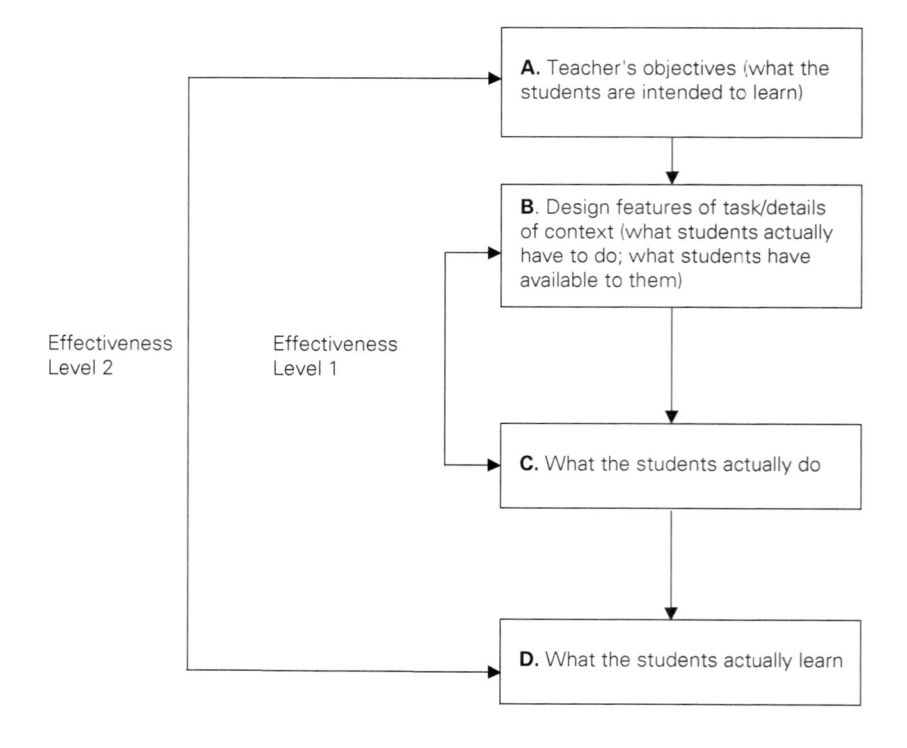

A. Teacher's objectives (what the students are intended to learn)

B. Design features of task/details of context (what students actually have to do; what students have available to them)

Effectiveness Level 2   Effectiveness Level 1

C. What the students actually do

D. What the students actually learn

objectives in terms of what it is they want the students to learn. After deciding what they want the students to learn, the next step (Box B) is for the teacher to design a specific practical task that, they believe, has the potential to enable the students to achieve the desired learning objectives. As the students might not do exactly what was intended by the teacher, the next step (Box C) considers what it is that the students actually do as they undertake the task. There are various reasons as to why the students might not actually do what their teacher intended; for example, they might not understand the instructions or, even if they do and adhere to them meticulously, faulty apparatus can prevent them from doing what was intended by the teacher. Alternatively, even if the task is carried out as the teacher intends and all of the apparatus functions as intended, the students still might not engage mentally with the task using the ideas that the teacher had intended them to use.

The final stage of the model (Box D) is thus concerned with what the students learn as a consequence of undertaking the task. This model allows the question of the effectiveness of a specific practical task to be considered at two separate levels. We can consider the effectiveness of the task (at level 1) in terms of the match – or alignment – between what the teacher intended students to *do* and what they actually do and the effectiveness of the task (at level 2) as being the match – or alignment – between what the teacher intended the students to *learn* and what they actually learn. 'Level 1 effectiveness' is therefore concerned with the relationship between Boxes B and C in Figure 2.1 (doing), while 'level 2 effectiveness' is concerned with the relationship between Boxes A and D (learning).

This model can therefore be used to address the following two questions:

1 Does the practical task enable the students to do the things the teacher intended them to do?
2 Does the practical task enable the students to learn what their teacher intended?

By combining this two-level model of effectiveness with a two-domain model of knowledge developed by Tiberghien (2000), in which there is a domain of observable objects and events (o) and a domain of ideas (i), it becomes possible to consider each of the two levels of effectiveness in terms of these two distinct domains.

These two levels of effectiveness, each of which can be considered with respect to the two distinct domains of knowledge, can be represented (Table 2.1) using a 2 × 2 effectiveness matrix.

Table 2.1 The 2 × 2 effectiveness matrix for practical work

A task is effective	in the domain of observables (Domain o)	in the domain of ideas (Domain i)
at level 1 (what students do)	If students can set up the equipment and operate it in such a manner as to undertake what the teacher intended.	If students can think about the task using the ideas and scientific vocabulary intended by the teacher.
at level 2 (what students learn)	If students can discover patterns within their observations/data and describe these; describe the procedure used and in future set up and operate similar equipment.	If students understand their observations/data by being able to link them, using the ideas and vocabulary intended by the teacher, with the correct scientific theory.

The effectiveness of any practical task can now be analysed and discussed in terms of two principal levels with each level being further divided into two domains. To illustrate the use of a 2 × 2 effectiveness matrix, consider its application to a practical task that was observed in which students study chromatographic separation of colours in dyes (Table 2.2).

Table 2.2 The 2 × 2 effectiveness matrix for a practical task involving an investigation of the chromatographic separation of colours in dyes

A task is effective	in the domain of observables (Domain o)	in the domain of ideas (Domain i)
at level 1 (what students do)	If students can construct a separation column to match the provided instructions; observe how a drop of dye placed on the filter paper spreads out as liquid seeps up the paper, so that several spots or streaks can be seen.	If students can talk about different substances moving up the paper at different speeds; several spots implying several substances; dyes as mixtures of substances.
at level 2 (what students learn)	If students can set up and use a chromatographic separation column. Students state that separated colours are different dyes that made up their initial dye; this can be used to separate a mixture of dyes into its components; that the pattern from an unknown dye can be compared with that of a known one to help identify the unknown one.	If students can state that different substances move up a chromatography column at different speeds; this can be used to see if something contains more than one substance; this can be used to separate the components substances in a mixture; that the chromatogram of an unknown sample can be compared with those of known samples to see if they contain the same component substances.

The four cells of Tables 2.1 and 2.2 are not independent as a task is unlikely to be effective at level 2:i unless it was also effective at levels 1:i, and, most likely, also at levels 1:o and 2:o. Such a framework provides an effective means of determining the effectiveness of any practical task in terms of the four cells of Table 2.1.

2.2 Using the model in practice

So that's our model for effective practical work. How useful is it in practice?

The model was used by us in an evaluation we undertook, with Rachael Sharpe, of the 'Getting Practical: Improving Practical Work in Science' (IPWiS) project (Abrahams et al., 2011). The project was led by the Association for Science Education (ASE), which created a package of continuing professional development (CPD) materials for it. These materials were designed by a consortium and were intended to help teachers reflect on and improve: (i) the clarity of the learning outcomes associated with practical work, (ii) the effectiveness and impact of the practical work, (iii) the sustainability of this approach within their schools, allowing for ongoing improvements and (iv) the quality, rather than quantity, of practical work used.

The IPWiS project, which ran for two years and involved 200 trainers, trained over 2000 teachers from both primary and secondary schools. The initial 200 trainers attended 'Train the Trainer' events. The project then used a cascade model in which these 200 trainers then ran training sessions themselves for schoolteachers in their own local areas who, in turn, it was hoped, would cascade down the training a further level within their own schools (primary) and departments (secondary). The course was designed for flexibility and the six-hour training could be delivered through a single (whole day) six-hour session, a pair of three-hour sessions (two half-day courses) or three two-hour sessions (twilight courses) with individual trainers deciding upon which approach to use in order to best meet the needs of their local teachers.

Some training courses were run for only primary or only secondary teachers while others hosted mixed groups and this again depended on the choice of the local trainer. Teachers working at both primary and secondary levels, and at all stages of their careers, attended the training sessions. All three secondary science main subject specialisms were represented by the secondary teachers. Technicians were also encouraged to undertake the training to enable them to better understand how practical work can be improved and to enhance the support they can offer teachers in practical lessons.

Permission was asked of ten primary teachers (students aged 5–11) and twenty secondary teachers (students aged 11–18), who had registered to undertake the IPWiS training, to observe two of their practical lessons, one prior to the training, in order to provide a benchmark of their practice, and another after the training was completed, to evaluate any changes in both their and their department's use of practical work. Ian Abrahams, Michael Reiss and Rachael Sharpe undertook audio-recorded observations of lesson and interviews that were carried out with the teacher before and after the lesson. The pre-lesson interview was primarily used as a means of obtaining the teacher's account of the practical work to be observed and of his or her view of the learning objectives of the lesson. The post-lesson interview collected their reflections on the lesson and its success as a teaching and learning event. Furthermore, when the opportunities arose, other members of the department were questioned about their knowledge and understanding of the IPWiS project. In addition to audio-recording all teacher–whole class discussions and instructions, conversations between groups of students, and between students and the researcher, were also recorded. These conversations, in addition to field notes that were made, provided insights into the students' thinking not only about the task(s) that they were observed undertaking, but also with regards to their recollections of other previous practical tasks that they had undertaken.

The schools within the evaluation were selected by the Association of Science Education as 'typical' primary and comprehensive secondary schools in England, in terms of size, with locations spread geographically. A reasonably balanced coverage of subject material and age ranges was achieved – see Table 2.2. While this book is concerned with secondary science teaching, the findings for the primary teachers of science proved to have great relevance for secondary science teaching and so are included in Table 2.3.

Table 2.3 Lesson observations by student age range and subject

School type	Student age range	Biology	Chemistry	Physics	Other (Earth Science)
Primary	5–7	2 (0)	1 (0)	5 (2)	0 (0)
	7–11	0 (2)	1 (1)	1 (3)	0 (0)
Secondary	11–14	4 (3)	3 (3)	6 (3)	1 (0)
	14–16	1 (0)	2 (1)	0 (0)	0 (0)
	16–18	1 (1)	1 (1)	1 (0)	0 (0)

Brackets indicate second round observations. Primary school 'science lessons' have been classified as biology, chemistry or physics so as to present an overview of the range of subject areas observed across all age ranges.

2.3 Pre-training observations

Primary schools

What emerged from the first round of observations was how well conceived, clear and productive practical science was in most of those primary schools visited. One possible explanation for this – an explanation which could strike some as paradoxical – might be that the lessons observed were, in all but one case, taught by teachers who were not science subject specialists in the sense that the term 'science subject specialists' is understood by secondary science teachers. Indeed, not only were the teachers not science specialists but some of them spoke to us about their own difficulties with scientific ideas and the meanings of certain scientific terms (Harlen & Holroyd, 1997). As a consequence of the difficulties they themselves encountered with some aspects of science, they appeared better able to empathize with the problems that their students faced when learning about new ideas in science, and the meaning of new scientific terms, than were many secondary subject specialists.

The primary teachers used practical tasks that were tightly constrained, of the kind that have been termed 'recipe' style (Clackson & Wright, 1992) as a means of ensuring that all of their students were able to see the desired phenomenon in the time available. Furthermore, by using relatively short practical tasks, embedded within a lesson rather than taking up the entire lesson, the teachers ensured that they had sufficient time to introduce students to, and fully discuss, new scientific terms and ideas in the way that it has been suggested (Abrahams, 2011) is necessary if teaching and learning are to be effective in developing conceptual understanding. Certainly our observations suggest that primary teachers see practical work as both a 'hands on' *and* a 'minds on' activity.

The findings of these baseline observations draw attention to characteristics of current good practice in the use of practical work in primary science teaching. They suggest an understanding of the need to ensure that practical work does not just involve 'doing' with observables but also requires students to think about, and engage with, scientific ideas and terms.

Secondary schools

The practical work that we observed throughout the twenty secondary schools was, generally speaking, effective in enabling most of the students, irrespective of their academic ability, to do what the teacher wanted them to do with observables and, in so doing, produce the required phenomena. While various factors contributed towards this effectiveness, two of the most noticeable were the use of 'recipe' style tasks, designed to reliably produce a particular phenomenon if those undertaking it adhered to the 'recipe', and the allocation of more time to the presentation, and clarification, of procedural instructions than did many of their primary colleagues.

Because a particular piece of practical work was likely to be considered as having 'failed' if the students were unable to produce the desired phenomena, teachers tended to focus their attention on ensuring that students were able to follow instructions in order to maximize the likelihood that they would all successfully produce the desired phenomena. Time constraints, and the fact that 'doing something with ideas' was not a necessary prerequisite for the successful production of phenomena, meant that when using 'recipe' style tasks teachers devoted relatively little whole class time to getting the students to do what they wanted them to do with ideas, that is, to think about the observables and phenomena they were seeing in a particular scientific way. Even when teachers did allocate time to getting the students to 'do things with ideas' the ideas were kept relatively simple to ensure that there was sufficient time not only to get the students to think about the observables and phenomena, using the intended ideas, but also to get them to produce the desired phenomena.

What emerged, as the following example illustrates, was that some tasks were observed to be little more than the unquestioning adherence to a 'recipe' in order to produce a phenomenon and/or data.

> Student: Yeah, so I'm just following the method that we've been given [indicates worksheet] and hopefully ... and we've got like the results table [points to pre-printed table on the worksheet] so we'll just get them [their results] down.

Practical work was found to be more effective in getting students to learn what the teacher intended about observables and phenomena than it was in getting them to learn about ideas. A possible explanation for this is that to be effective in getting students to learn what the teacher intended about observables and phenomena requires only that the students are able at some later time (such as in an examination) to describe qualitatively what they have seen, and/or be able to formulate simple relationships about observables. Given the observed effectiveness of practical work in enabling students to produce the desired phenomena it seems reasonable to expect that most students will be able to achieve what are essentially intellectually undemanding learning objectives.

Yet while some students were able to describe their observations, and/or formulate simple relationships about the data, during, or immediately after, the practical lesson, most were unable, without assistance, to recollect more than a few examples of the practical work that they had undertaken during their time at secondary school. Indeed, when asked, their recollections were found to relate primarily to practical tasks that were, in some sense, 'unusual'; furthermore, these recollections related almost exclusively to what had made that particular task – or something associated with it – unusual rather than to what the teacher might have intended them to learn and recollect.

For example, students recollected the burning of magnesium ribbon insofar as they remembered that it had been visually spectacular but there was no evidence that such 'memorable events' (White, 1979) provided any anchor point, or 'trigger', for associated scientific ideas that might have been learnt within the teaching sequence in which the practical lesson was embedded. Similarly, here is a short extract of a conversation one of us had with students during a lesson:

Researcher:	Can you remember any practicals you've done since you've been at school?
Student 1:	Yeah [talking to Student 2] do you remember in Year 7 [students aged 11–12], that collapsing can?
Researcher:	Collapsing can?
Student 2:	Oh yeah, they put it in something.
Student 1:	And put it in cold water.
Student 2:	Yeah.
Researcher:	What did you learn from that?
Student 1:	I don't know, I didn't learn anything, it was just quite funny.
Student 2:	When I did it, it didn't work [implode] for some strange reason.

In terms of getting students to learn about the ideas intended by the teacher, all of the observed practical lessons were either wholly or to a large extent ineffective. One way of helping to understand the reason for this is to think of the 'learning about ideas' as being the last step in a process that depends necessarily on the students having succeeded not only in doing and learning what the teacher intended about observables and phenomena but also in doing what the teacher intended with ideas. A failure adequately to achieve any one, or more, of these prerequisites adversely affects the students' ability to learn about the ideas intended by the teacher within that particular practical lesson. Indeed, the strong emphasis placed by the teachers on getting the students to 'produce the phenomena' resulted in them not including in their lesson plans the need to devote teaching time specifically to providing the conceptual 'scaffold' that is required to help with the development of the students' conceptual understanding.

2.4 Post-training findings

Doing with objects, materials and ideas

The overall impression to emerge from the observations of lessons after the teachers had completed their IPWiS training was that primary and secondary teachers continued to see the production of the intended phenomenon, and/or collection of the intended data, by the majority of students in their class, as being central to the success of a practical lesson. In this respect the continued widespread use of 'recipe' style tasks meant that in both primary and secondary schools practical work remained highly effective in enabling most of the students to successfully do what their teachers wanted them to, using the objects and materials provided.

While 'doing with objects and materials' is self-explanatory, 'doing with ideas' is less self-evident and refers to the process of using scientific terminology as well as thinking and talking about objects and materials, using theoretical entities or constructs that are not themselves directly observable. And while the overwhelming majority of the practical work we observed in our post-training visits, in both primary and secondary schools, was effective in enabling students to do what their teacher wanted them to do with objects and materials, primary teachers were, compared to their secondary colleagues, more effective in getting their students to 'do with ideas'. This was essentially as a result of teachers devoting whole class time to students' learning the meaning of the new scientific words or concepts rather than their teachers being more effective in getting the students to talk about objects and materials in terms of theoretical entities or constructs that are not themselves directly observable.

Primary school impact

The most notable finding to emerge from the post-training observations of primary school teachers was the extent to which there was a feeling that the IPWiS 'message' was nothing new and that primary teachers had been doing just what IPWiS was suggesting teachers do, in some cases, for many years. As one primary teacher explained:

> A lot of the stuff we'd already had training on before … I just feel that a lot of the stuff that was covered [on the IPWiS training] was things that on other science training [courses] I'd been on I'd already learnt.

Yet despite this, some of the primary teachers, as the following example illustrates, spoke of being more aware of the need to ensure that their practical lessons contained fewer learning objectives than might previously have been the case:

> It made me focus more on specific objectives. I think before [the IPWiS training] I would try to do too much in the whole lesson.

Overall the findings showed that while the IPWiS training had been effective in getting primary teachers to think more critically about some of the issues relating to the effectiveness of practical work, it had had little impact on their actual practice in terms of doing with objects, materials and ideas. This should not be seen as a criticism of either the primary teachers themselves or the IPWiS training, but rather reflects the fact that much of what IPWiS set out to achieve, certainly in terms of 'doing with ideas', was already taking place in primary science lessons.

Secondary school impact

The impact of the IPWiS training on secondary teachers varied considerably and this variation was seen to depend on not only who undertook the training, their role/seniority within the department and their enthusiasm for the project, but also the extent to which the aims of the project had active support from members of the school's Senior Management Team (SMT).

Upland Community College (their head teacher gave permission to use their name) clearly shows what can be achieved when conditions are close to 'ideal'. In this case it was the head of science who undertook the training, saw tremendous value in the material being delivered and returned to the school keen to implement the IPWiS project ideas across the department as a whole. The SMT within the school was fully committed to supporting the full-scale implementation of the required changes in the Science Department's schemes of work in order to bring them more into line with the ideas about the use of practical work as suggested by the IPWiS training. The SMT also provided time to enable a full and effective cascade of ideas to occur not only for the members of the school's own science department but also for the teachers of science in the school's feeder primary schools.

A very noticeable change in classroom practice evident as, compared with the first (pre-training) observation, the second lesson now only focused on a few, clearly identified, learning objectives, and was very much a 'hands-on' *and* 'minds-on' lesson. The structure of the lesson had also changed so that rather than the practical task taking up a large proportion of the lesson it was, in the post-training lesson, relatively short and embedded within the lesson and was only started *after* the students had engaged with the ideas that would enable them to understand their observations. Other members of the department showed in discussions that they too, as a result of the training being cascaded down to them, were familiar with the ideas of the IPWiS project. Not only did they talk positively about changes to the way that they now used practical work but they also said that they had begun to undertake regular peer observations of each other's use of practical work that were designed to help reinforce the IPWiS message within the department.

While Uplands shows what can be achieved, the impact in the other secondary schools was much less evident. While there were various reasons for this, including the seniority and role of the person undertaking the training, another particularly noticeable problem in getting the IPWiS 'message' heard in schools was the evident weakness of the cascade model of training used within the IPWiS project.

2.5 Conclusions and implications for undertaking practical work

Concentrating on the secondary schools, a number of findings emerged from the evaluation. The first is the fact that the IPWiS project did bring about changes in both the use and effectiveness of practical work. However, the extent of that change varied widely and while many secondary teachers appeared to understand the IPWiS project 'message' and *claimed* that it had changed their practice, our evaluation suggested that for most secondary teachers we observed their actual use of practical work remained relatively unchanged as a result of the training.

Secondly, despite the fact that many of the secondary teachers included the learning of scientific ideas amongst their learning objectives for practical lessons, there was little evidence to show that they recognized the need to *explicitly* plan how they wanted to get their students to learn about ideas. This was in marked contrast to the way in which their lesson plans, and recipe style tasks, typically made explicit what they wanted their students to do with objects.

Thirdly, the impact of the IPWiS project within a particular school was seen to depend upon who undertook the training, for example, whether they were a head of department or a newly qualified teacher (NQT), and the extent to which the school's SMT was supportive and proactive in wanting the IPWiS project ideas to be implemented.

The principal implication of all this is that while the IPWiS project was successful in raising secondary science teachers' *awareness* of how to improve the quality of the practical science work, more needs to be done to help secondary science teachers to get their students to think about the scientific ideas they are meant to be learning in lessons that centred on practical work. That is why we have written this book.

Each of the six chapters that follow has twelve session guides (essentially, lesson plans) for a particular practical. Three of these chapters are intended to be used with 11- to 14-year-old students (one chapter on biology, one on chemistry and one on physics) and three with 14- to 16-year-olds (again, one chapter on biology, one on chemistry and one on physics). Each session guide clearly explains the learning objectives for the practical and the procedure that students need to follow. An equipment list is provided along with things for the teacher to keep in mind and issues for discussion. Any health and safety issues are addressed. A key feature of these chapters is that each practical has an 'Effectiveness matrix' which clearly indicates what students should do and what they should learn, both while undertaking the practical and as a result of undertaking it.

Of course, it is not the intention that you, as the teacher, will get your students to undertake all these practicals. A whole range of factors will influence the practicals that you choose to use, including the curriculum that your students are following and your own preferences. In addition, some of the practicals included here for 11- to 14-year-olds may have been undertaken by students near the end of their previous phase of schooling – though the effectiveness matrix often means that students are encouraged to think about the practical work more than they may previously have done. Of course, if students have undertaken the practical or a similar one, their thoughts can be elicited. Even if they haven't, it is often a good idea to get students to talk about what they have already learnt that may be relevant and to think about what might happen in advance of undertaking the practical.

Although we have concentrated on the value of the effectiveness matrix, with its emphasis on students thinking about what they are doing as well as doing it and making observations, practical work can be used in other ways. For instance, it can be used to strengthen mathematical skills and skills of teamwork and communication. In addition, some practicals have cross-curricular potential, for example, in relation to geography.

The effectiveness matrices are based on Table 2.1. They have been designed to help (some readers may prefer the word 'require') students to think about what they are doing and what they are learning from undertaking the practical. Please note that while some practicals have entries in all four 'cells' of the effectiveness matrix, this is *not* always the case. In some cases, the practical has been designed so that only two or three cells are relevant.

Biology: Session Guides 11–14

Indira Banner and Mark Winterbottom

3

- **3.1** The structure of plant and animal cells (p. 30)
- **3.2** Investigating the effect of antiseptic on microbial growth (p. 33)
- **3.3** Effect of exercise on heart rate (p. 36)
- **3.4** Investigating respiration in plants and animals (p. 38)
- **3.5** Measuring forces exerted by different muscles (p. 41)
- **3.6** Investigating the effect of different nerve pathways on reaction times (p. 43)
- **3.7** Investigating variation within and between species (p. 46)
- **3.8** Extracting DNA from plant tissue (p. 49)
- **3.9** Determining the population size of a plant species on the school field (p. 52)
- **3.10** Investigation into how seeds are dispersed by the wind (p. 54)
- **3.11** Investigating responses of woodlice using choice chambers (p. 56)
- **3.12** Investigating photosynthesis by the presence or absence of starch in a leaf (p. 59)

3.1 The structure of plant and animal cells

Learning objectives

- To recognize the structure of plant and animal cells.

Procedure

To prepare microscope slides of animal cells and plant cells, students follow the procedure below:

- Animal cells: Each student should take a clean cotton bud and scrape the inside of one of their cheeks. This is then wiped onto the middle of a glass slide. Carefully add one drop of methylene blue indicator and lower a cover slip onto the drop, being careful not to trap air bubbles.

- Plant cells: Each student should take a layer from half an onion, and carefully peel the thin membrane from its underside. Breaking the layer and gently pulling apart the two halves can make it easier to find the membrane, which is one cell thick. Cut a 5 mm square section of the membrane and lay it on a microscope slide. Add a drop of iodine solution to the membrane and carefully lower the cover slip onto the drop, being careful not to trap air bubbles.

Figure 3.1
Onion epidermal cells (photograph by Claire Simpson and Stef Lesnianksi)

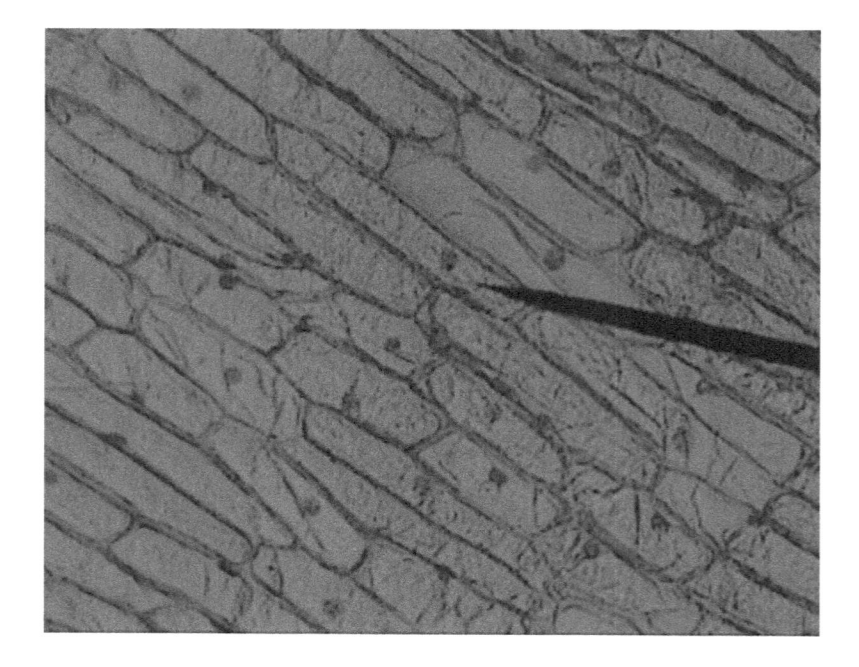

To observe the cells, students use a light microscope. Place a slide onto the stage of the microscope and carefully adjust the coarse focus knob on the lowest magnification so that it is close to the slide. Looking down the microscope, turn the knob towards you, so that the lens raises, until the image is almost in focus. Then use the fine focus knob to adjust the image so that it is sharp. Once the cells are in focus, students can gradually increase magnification by rotating the objective lenses to higher power, using the fine focus knob to focus the new image. Students should draw what they see (see Figure 3.1).

Effectiveness matrix

	Domain of observables	**Domain of ideas**
What students do	Students can: • Make onion cell and cheek cell slides. • Use a microscope to observe the structure of both types of cell. • Draw both types of cell.	Students can talk about: • Cheek cells occurring separately and having a roughly circular shape and each with a dark structure inside it (nucleus). • Onion cells occurring together in a wall-like structure and each with a dark structure inside it (nucleus). • The observable differences between the types of cell.
What students learn	Students can later: • Make a microscope slide of living material. • Use a microscope to observe living material. • Draw a microscope specimen.	Students can later talk about: • The structure of a plant cell and an animal cell. • The similarities and differences between the two.

Keep in mind

Air bubbles are easily mistaken for cheek cells. It can be helpful to project an image from a microscope onto a whiteboard or have photographs to show your students to help them locate the correct structures. Students can find it hard to focus the microscopes. Printing secret messages in 4-point font to be read by microscope, or observing newspaper, wool or hair can be very engaging in familiarizing students with microscope use.

Issues for discussion

What makes the plant cell shape so different from the animal cell? *The cellulose cell wall which gives the plant cells their fixed shape. Animal cells do not have cell walls.*

Why do you think the structure of the animal and plant cell is different? *This is because of the function of the parts of the cell so plant cells have a cell vacuole and cell wall to help maintain their shape which helps the whole plant to maintain its shape. Some plant cells have chloroplasts to absorb light needed for photosynthesis.*

Why can't you see chloroplasts in these onion cells? *This is because the onion bulb does not photosynthesize (as it is found underground). The leaves of the plant photosynthesize.*

In what other plant cells will you not find chloroplasts? *You would not find chloroplasts in the root cells of most plants because they do not photosynthesize as they are usually in the dark.*

Health and safety

Students must wear goggles and gloves while making the slides. Iodine solution is harmful to eyes. If skin comes into contact with methylene blue, wash immediately. Ingestion of methylene blue requires immediate medical attention. All students should wash their hands after use.

Used cotton buds should be placed in containers of disinfectant and disposed of appropriately.

Cover slips especially, but also glass slides, are fragile and easy to lose. Take care when handling these.

Microscopes should always be carried with two hands. If using microscopes with mirrors to reflect the light, be careful that students don't reflect the Sun directly into their eyes.

Equipment

Students should work in pairs and between them have:

    A light microscope

    Methylene blue stain

    Iodine solution

    2 microscope slides and cover slips

    1 pair of fine forceps

    2 cotton buds

    Disinfectant

    Onion (cut into 1–2 cm^2 pieces)

    Safety goggles

3.2 Investigating the effect of antiseptic on microbial growth

Learning objectives

- To learn how the growth of microorganisms can be regulated to different extents by different antiseptics.

Procedure

Nutrient agar plates should be prepared for each student. These can be inoculated by a broth but it is more interesting for students if they can collect samples of bacteria using cotton buds from around the classroom (e.g. keyboard of computer, door handle, desk or floor) and inoculate the plates with these. Small discs can be made using a hole-punch on filter paper which may be best prepared before the practical. Using clean forceps take a small disc and dip it into an antiseptic product, such as hand wash, tea tree oil, or washing up liquid. Three discs with different antiseptics and one in distilled water for a control can be equally spaced on the plate (see Figure 3.2). The plate can then be covered, and secured using two or three pieces of sticky tape from top to bottom of the plate. The plates should then be carefully labelled, turned upside down so that any condensation does not collect on the surface of the agar, and left to grow at room temperature. Plates can be observed the following week.

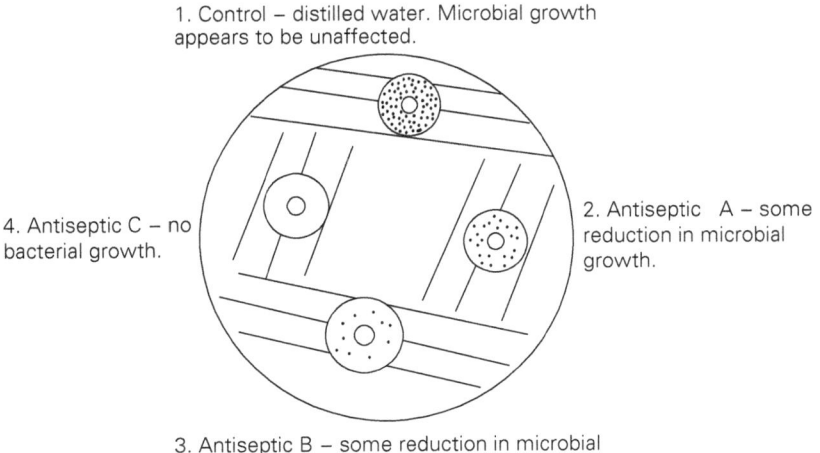

1. Control – distilled water. Microbial growth appears to be unaffected.

2. Antiseptic A – some reduction in microbial growth.

3. Antiseptic B – some reduction in microbial growth. More effective than in 2.

4. Antiseptic C – no bacterial growth.

Figure 3.2 Diagram to show possible outcome from the experiment

Effectiveness matrix

	Domain of observables	Domain of ideas
What students do	Students can: • Take appropriate safety precautions. • Collect samples of bacteria from around the classroom using cotton buds.	Students can talk about: • Microbial growth on the majority of the agar plate. • The lack of microbial growth around the disinfectant disks.
What students learn	Students can later: • Use safe and appropriate aseptic techniques for different investigations with microorganisms, for example, in the study of microbial action in food decay.	Students can later talk about: • Microbial growth being controlled by antiseptics. • Why the agar plates are not incubated anaerobically or at 37 °C. • How aseptic techniques are used to make sure that the agar plate is not contaminated by microorganisms from the environment.

Keep in mind

Labelling should be done neatly at the side of the plates and not on the top or bottom so that results are not obscured by pen. Plates should be stored upside down so condensation does not fall onto the agar surface. Plates should not be completely sealed nor stored at 37 °C to avoid encouraging the growth of potentially harmful microbes. Encourage aseptic techniques: washing hands; only opening the agar plate cover a small amount; not breathing on the agar; working near to the Bunsen burners, using sterile forceps (these can be sterilized in a hot Bunsen flame as long as they are allowed to cool afterwards).

Issues for discussion

Why do we use agar to grow microbes? *The agar is actually called nutrient agar as it contains nutrients and water which are needed for microbial growth.*

Why was one disc dipped only in distilled water? *This was to act as a control in case it was an effect of moisture on the microbes that prevent them from growing (as much).*

Why should aseptic techniques be used? *Aseptic techniques reduce the chances of the agar plate being infected by microbes from the atmosphere.*

Which antiseptic was the most effective in this test and how do you know? *Students should observe a ring around the paper disc where the antiseptic liquid has diffused through the agar. This ring might have a reduced number or type of microbes in it.*

Health and safety

Bunsen burners can be used to help create an aseptic environment where students are working. These should be on the yellow flame and students should be careful to tuck in ties, tie back long hair and wear safety goggles at all times.

When students secure the lids on the agar plates it should not be a complete seal to make sure that the environment on the plate is aerobic and not anaerobic. The plates should not be incubated at 37 °C. Do not open the plates after growth but dispose of them after autoclaving.

Equipment

Per student:

    1 nutrient agar plate

    1 pair of clean forceps

    1 or 2 cotton buds

Available for the class:

    A beaker of antiseptic liquid to dispose of cotton buds

    Small discs of filter paper (at least 4 per student)

    A range of antiseptic liquids for use in investigation

    Distilled water

    Waterproof labelling pens

3.3 Effect of exercise on heart rate

Learning objectives

- To understand the effect of exercise on heart rate.

Procedure

Students should measure their heart beats for 30 seconds and record their heart rate per minute. They should then exercise vigorously for 30 seconds (e.g. running on the spot or performing star jumps). They then measure their heart rate again immediately when they stop the exercise. This is repeated for exercise of different durations, for example, 1 minute, 2 minutes and 4 minutes. Heart rate can be plotted against duration of exercise on a line graph. This can be extended by asking students to predict how exercising at different intensities might have an effect on heart rate or by measuring the speed of recovery of heart rate to pre-exercise levels.

Effectiveness matrix

	Domain of observables	Domain of ideas
What students do	Students can: • Find their pulse. • Count heart beats for 30 seconds before and after exercise and calculate heart rate per minute.	Students can talk about: • The difference in heart rate before and after exercise. • How heart rate increases with increased duration of exercise.
What students learn	Students can later: • Design and carry out an investigation to find out how different intensities of exercise affect heart rate. • Design and carry out an investigation to find out how quickly the heart rate recovers after different lengths or intensities of exercise.	Students can later talk about how: • More exercise requires more energy and so increased respiration. • Increased respiration means that more oxygen is needed. • Oxygen is carried in the blood. The heart beats faster to increase the blood supply.

Keep in mind

Students sometimes find it hard to find their pulse in their wrists. The carotid artery in the neck can be easier to find. It helps if all students start and stop at the same time so the class teacher times the exercise periods. The practical works much better if students exercise vigorously – this is worth encouraging, bearing in mind the points under health and safety. It is helpful if students have a results table in their books to note down pulse rates as they are going along. Remember they have to calculate pulse rate per minute.

Issues for discussion

What do you notice about your pulse rate? *The pulse rate increases with increasing duration of exercise.*

Why does your pulse rate increase as you do more exercise? *The pulse rate increases so that there is more blood being pumped around the body. This is needed for increased energy to be released in respiration for the increased movement during exercise. Increased respiration needs more oxygen and products of digestion which are carried to all cells of the body in the blood.*

Other than increased heart rate what else happens to you when you exercise a lot? *You might feel warm and sweat; you might find it hard to breathe and pant (breathe quickly and heavily) a lot when you have finished; you might feel aches in your muscles. This is because of the increased respiration in your cells.*

Will your pulse rate keep increasing if you exercise more? *No, the heart rate will have a maximum rate above which it won't increase. If you are not then getting enough oxygen for aerobic respiration your cells will respire without as much oxygen as they need (anaerobic respiration), you may feel some aches, as mentioned previously, called cramp, and you might have to pant when you stop.*

Health and safety

Make sure that there is space for students to exercise and that floor space is clear. Be aware of students who might have asthma or other health issues. There may also be students who feel embarrassed or uncomfortable doing this.

Equipment

    Stopwatch for the teacher
    Graph paper to plot graph

3.4 Investigating respiration in plants and animals

Learning objectives

- To understand that the process of respiration releases carbon dioxide into the atmosphere.
- To understand that animals and plants do this all the time.

Procedure

Students should work in pairs. Each pair will set up five boiling tubes; two have *Cabomba* submerged in hydrogen carbonate indicator and two have woodlice sitting on a breathable plug made of some kind of mesh above the indicator. The fifth tube should contain indicator only and all should have air tight bungs. For one *Cabomba* and one woodlouse, cover the tubes with opaque paper or foil. Leave the tubes in a rack, preferably overnight (see Figure 3.3). Then remove any paper and observe the colour of the indicator.

Figure 3.3
Diagram to show the experimental set-up

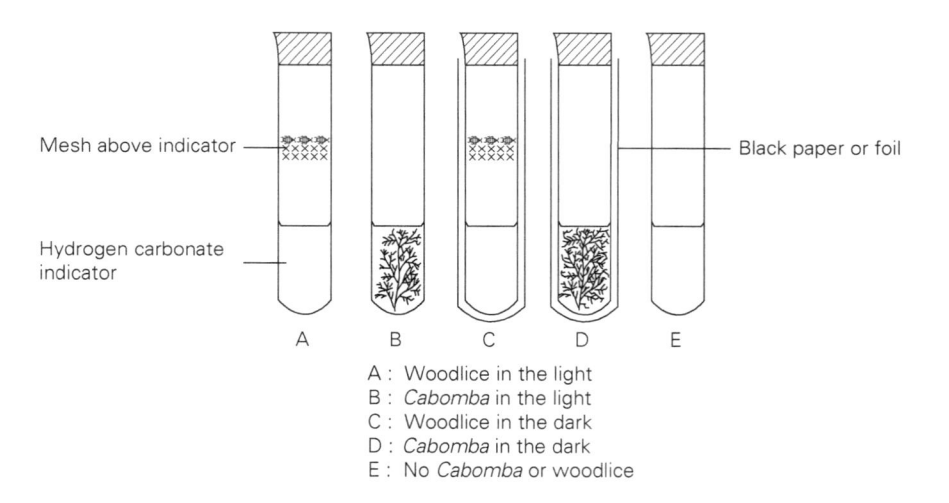

A: Woodlice in the light
B: *Cabomba* in the light
C: Woodlice in the dark
D: *Cabomba* in the dark
E: No *Cabomba* or woodlice

Effectiveness matrix

	Domain of observables	Domain of ideas
What students do	Students can: • Set up the five boiling tubes to make sure that the experiment is repeatable and reliable. • Observe and compare the colour of the indicator in the boiling tubes after a given time.	Students can talk about: • The colours of the indicator in each of the five boiling tubes in relation to the presence or absence of light and whether they contain plants or animals.
What students learn	Students can later: • Test for carbon dioxide in a different experiment, using hydrogen carbonate indicator. • Set up an experiment to investigate respiration safely and so that animals are kept alive.	Students can later talk about: • Plants in the dark make the indicator go yellow because they are respiring but not photosynthesizing. • Plants in the light make the indicator go dark pink to purple, depending on light intensity, because they are photosynthesizing more than they are respiring. • Animals in the light and dark make the indicator go yellow as they are respiring but not photosynthesizing.

Keep in mind

Cabomba is a tropical pond weed and therefore should not be put in an external pond after use. Make sure students treat the woodlice with respect and put them back into their normal habitat as soon as possible after the experiment.

It is a common misconception that plants photosynthesize during the day and respire only at night; it is important that students understand that plants, like animals, respire all the time.

Issues for discussion

What do the colours of the hydrogen carbonate indicator show? *The concentration of carbon dioxide in the atmosphere or solution; when it is high the indicator goes yellow and when it is low the indicator goes purple.*

If plants respire all the time, like animals, why is the colour of the indicator in the *Cabomba* in the light different from the woodlice in the light? *It is different because plants also photosynthesize in the light so the release of carbon dioxide by respiration in the plants is masked by the uptake of carbon dioxide during photosynthesis.*

What would happen to the colour of the indicator if we breathed into it using a straw?
The indicator would go yellow as we breathe out air with a higher concentration of carbon dioxide than the air that we breathe in.

Health and safety

After handling the living organisms, students should wash their hands, especially before eating.

Equipment

Per pair of students:

    5 boiling tubes and bungs

    2 small pieces of mesh or gauze to separate woodlice from indicator below them in the boiling tube

For the class:

    Hydrogen carbonate indicator

    Woodlice (ideally several for each student)

    Cabomba (this can be cut into pieces that will fit into each boiling tube)

    Foil or thick black paper to put around boiling tubes depending on ambient light

3.5 Measuring forces exerted by different muscles

Learning objectives

- To learn that muscles pull on bones to exert a force.
- To understand that the biceps and triceps work antagonistically.

Procedure

By using a 100 N force meter students can measure the force exerted by the triceps and biceps (a 50 N force meter may be enough). Working in pairs, one student should hold the force meter vertically, by gripping one end. The second student should hold the other end of the force meter with their dominant arm. The arm needs to be bent and the student should try to straighten the arm downwards for a measure of the force exerted by the triceps. Then the first student should hold the force meter horizontally, by gripping one end and the second student should hold the other end of the force meter with a straight arm and try to bend the arm to move upwards, so the hand moves towards the shoulder (see Figure 3.4). Each pair of students does this three times for each muscle. Then repeat this with the non-dominant arm and compare the results.

Figure 3.4 Diagram to show how to use a force meter to measure the force exerted by the biceps

Keep in mind

You could use spring balances if there are no force meters and explain the relationship between mass and force (on earth). Some students will be able to pull a higher force than others but this shouldn't cause problems. If students work in pairs only one student in each group has to measure the forces exerted by their muscles.

Effectiveness matrix

	Domain of observables	Domain of ideas
What students do	Students can: • Measure the force exerted by their biceps and triceps. • Compare forces exerted by their left and right arms and by their triceps and biceps in each arm.	Students can talk about: • The biceps and triceps each exert a force. • Different muscles exert different forces. • The muscles in one arm may exert more force than the muscles in the other arm.
What students learn	Students can later: • Use a force meter to reliably measure the force exerted by objects.	Students can later talk about: • How muscles often work in antagonistic pairs. • That many muscles generate movement by pulling on a bone to exert a force. • In most people, the arm in which muscles are used more can exert a bigger force.

Issues for discussion

What errors might there be in this data? *Force meters are not very accurate or it is hard to see the reading clearly; the student might be using other muscles linked to the arm to try to pull the meter.*

Why are the muscles in the arm which is used more often able to exert a higher force than the other arm? *This is because with repeated use muscles get stronger.*

Where else in your body might you find antagonistic muscle pairs? *Try to encourage students to think of the similar movements in their legs. They do not need to be able to name the muscles there though.*

Health and safety

Encourage students to do this carefully in order to isolate the triceps and biceps as much as possible; this will minimize any possible strain injury by students using their backs, for example.

Equipment

Per pair of students:
   100 N force meter

3.6 Investigating the effect of different nerve pathways on reaction times

Learning objectives

- To understand that there are different nerve pathways in the human body.
- To be able to calculate and compare means of sets of data.

Procedure

Working in pairs one student drops the ruler and the other student catches it as soon as s/he can. The ruler should be dropped from the same position each time so that the bottom of the ruler is level with the catcher's thumb and forefinger (see Figure 3.5 - Scenario 1). The distance of the ruler falls before the student catches it is a measurement of the reaction 'time'. This should be repeated to allow a mean to be measured.

The procedure should then be repeated with the catcher's eyes closed and the bottom of the ruler just touching the thumb of the catcher so that s/he can feel when it is dropped rather than see it (see Figure 3.5 - Scenario 2).

Figure 3.5 Experimental set-up

Scenario 1: Completing the experiment with eyes open

Scenario 2: Completing the experiment with eyes closed

Effectiveness matrix

	Domain of observables	Domain of ideas
What students do	Students can: • Measure the distance dropped before the ruler is caught. • Repeat ten times and calculate mean distances dropped. • Compare means of distance when eyes were open and eyes were closed.	Students can talk about: • The variation in measurements within and between data sets of eyes open and eyes closed. • The response time with eyes open is faster than with eyes shut.
What students learn	Students can later: • Use this method to investigate the effect of other variables on reaction time. • Compare different sets of data using their means. • Plan experiments that include repeating measurements for greater reliability.	Students can later talk about: • How the distance for the nerve impulse to travel from the eye to the brain is less than that from the finger tip to the brain and therefore the reaction time is faster when eyes are open. • How variation in a data set is caused by other variables which have not been accounted for (e.g. practice).

Keep in mind

Metre rules can be used since 30 cm rulers can be missed completely. However, 30 cm rulers are easier to catch and the fact that they do not measure all reaction 'times' can be a point of discussion. This practical is ideal for students to think about reliability. It is possible to transform the distance measures into times using the equation of motion $s = 0.5\ gt^2$, where s is distance in metre, g is acceleration due to gravity (equal to 9.8 m per second per second) and t is time in seconds.

Issues for discussion

Why are the results longer for when eyes are closed than when open? *When eyes are open the nerve pathway is from the eyes to the brain and back to the fingers. However, when the eyes are shut the pathway is from the finger tips to the brain and back to the finger tips. The latter pathway has a longer distance and therefore it will take longer to catch the ruler.*

Imagine if you touched something hot with your finger; you would move it away very quickly. That is called a reflex action. How can reflex actions be so fast? *This is because the nerve pathway goes from the finger tips to the spinal cord and back to the muscles controlling the fingers without going all the way to the brain. This makes the reflex action very fast.*

What other reflex actions are there? Why do we have reflex actions? *Students might answer: blinking in dust, narrowing pupils in bright light, sneezing etc. Reflex actions are to protect the body from harm.*

Health and safety

Do not allow the students to use the rulers for sword fights.

Equipment

30 cm rulers

3.7 Investigating variation within and between species

Learning objectives

- To understand that there is variation within a species (intraspecific) and between species (interspecific). Usually variation within a species is less than between species.

Procedure

Each pair of students should have at least eight leaves from two different species of plants. They then measure each leaf with a tape measure or ruler (length and/or breadth) (see Figure 3.6). Measurements should be written in a table and displayed as a scatter graph. Students should look at the range of measurements of each variety and compare measurements within and between the species. For an extension, they can calculate mean values of the measurements from each species and compare these.

Effectiveness matrix

	Domain of observables	Domain of ideas
What students do	Students can: • Measure accurately the maximum length or breadth of a sample of leaves from two species of plants. • Record the data in a table and display as a scatter graph.	Students can talk about: • The differences in the measurements within each species. • The differences in the measurements between the two species.
What students learn	Students can later: • Use a ruler or callipers accurately to measure biological material. • Present suitable data on a scatter graph.	Students can later talk about: • How the scatter graph shows the differences within and between groups. • That there is variation within and between groups.

Keep in mind

It is ideal to use two species of plants with leaves that are generally different in size from each other although with some overlap. Tree leaves can be used or plants from the school field like dandelion and plantain. Try to make sure leaves are simple in shape, that is, made up of one single shape (like beech leaves) rather than in leaflets (like horse chestnut leaves). This is a good practical activity for encouraging careful measurement, recording and graph drawing. Make sure students have thought about the axes on the graph in terms of labelling and length.

Issues for discussion

What do students notice about the patterns on the graphs? *This depends on the plant species that have been selected but they might show that the points on the graph of the leaves of one species are relatively close together and slightly separate from the points on the graph of the other species.*

Are all the leaves of one species the same size? *The leaves will vary in size within each species as well as between each species. The difference in the size of the leaves in one species may be due to the age of the leaves, whether the leaves are from different individuals within a population or the growing conditions (see next question).*

What causes the variation within the variety and between varieties? *Variation is caused by genetic inheritance and environmental factors. So, for example, dandelion leaves may grow taller than plantain leaves due to their genes, but this will vary according to the amount of sun and rain, the soil type and structure, the presence or absence of other competing species or grazing etc.*

Health and safety

Wash hands after handling plant material.

Equipment

Per pair:

    1 ruler or pair of callipers

Available for the class:

    Two species of leaves (try to make sure that the leaves are of slightly different size, for example, dandelion and plantain work well)

Graph paper

Figure 3.6
Image to show measurement of leaves (photograph by Indira Banner)

3.8 Extracting DNA from plant tissue

Learning objectives

- To see a sample of DNA.
- To recognize that DNA is found in plant cells.
- To understand the basic process of DNA extraction and its purpose.

Procedure

Students should take about 50 g of thawed frozen peas and mash them using a spoon or fork in a beaker. Mix this thoroughly with a solution containing 90 ml distilled water, 10 ml cheap washing up liquid, to break down the cell membrane, and 3 g salt, to release the DNA and allow the DNA to coalesce. This should be left at 60 °C for exactly 15 minutes before cooling in an ice bath for 5 minutes, stirring frequently. Filter using a coffee filter in a funnel. Pour 10 ml of filtrate into a boiling tube, add 2–3 drops of protease and mix well. Pour ice-cold ethanol very carefully down the side of the boiling tube until it forms a layer on top of the pea extract. Leave for 5 minutes. DNA should precipitate out into the cold ethanol layer (see Figure 3.7).

Figure 3.7 Experimental set-up (photograph taken by Claire Simpson)

Effectiveness matrix

	Domain of observables	Domain of ideas
What students do	Students can: • Use detergent, ice-cold ethanol and proteases to extract DNA from plant cells. • Observe DNA from plant cells.	Students can talk about: • Why they are using detergent, cold ethanol and a protein enzyme (protease) to help extract the DNA from the cells. • The differences between DNA double helix diagrams and models and real DNA.
What students learn	Students can later: • Measure mass and volumes of liquids accurately. • Extract DNA from different plants.	Students can later talk about: • How plants as well as animals have DNA in their cell nuclei. • How the process of DNA extraction needs to first release the DNA from the nucleus so that it can be isolated.

Keep in mind

You can use various different plant materials in a similar way. Onions tend to work well but are rather smelly. Don't use kiwifruit or strawberries as the precipitate tends to contain a lot of pectin. RNA is also common in the precipitate in addition to the DNA. There are many protocols available on the Internet. Because there is a lot of 'wait time', ensure students have something to do or think about during the wait.

Issues for discussion

Why might we want to extract DNA from humans? *Students may have a range of answers and these can include paternity testing and looking for markers of disease. Sensitivity is needed when discussing these issues in case students are personally affected by them.*

Health and safety

Ethanol is usually chilled in the freezer and if so the ethanol must be in a sealed container so that vapour cannot escape and potentially ignite. Students must not eat the source fruit or vegetable.

Equipment

Students should work in pairs and between them have:
- A small beaker of peas (about 50 g)
- 2 medium beakers
- 1 spoon or fork (to mash the peas)
- Distilled water
- 1 measuring cylinder (100 ml or larger)
- A small amount of salt (3 g)
- 1 coffee filter paper and a funnel
- 1 boiling tube

Available for the class:
- Water bath at 60 °C
- ice-cold ethanol
- Mass balance

3.9 Determining the population size of a plant species on the school field

Learning objectives

- Understand the need for, and process of, random sampling.

Procedure

Each student should be introduced to some common species that might be found on the school field using a basic key or field guide. In pairs or small groups students should then randomly position 10 quadrats on the school field and count the number of individuals of a particular species in the quadrats. These numbers should be recorded and a mean number calculated. Students should measure (if possible) or be given the area of the school field (or a smaller area such as the football pitch, as appropriate). An estimate of the population size of the whole field can then be calculated.

Effectiveness matrix

	Domain of observables	Domain of ideas
What students do	Students can: • Identify some common plants using a simple key. • Randomly position 10 quadrats in the sample area. • Calculate an estimate of the population size.	Students can talk about: • The variety of plant species on the school field. • How to take random samples. • How to calculate an estimate of population size.
What students learn	Students can later: • Calculate an estimate of the population size of a different species using random sampling. • Use a key to identify different common plant species such as trees.	Students can later talk about: • The value of taking random samples. • How estimates of population sizes are affected by non-random distributions.

Keep in mind

Species like dandelion and plantain are easy to identify and count, whether in flower or not. Others that are commonly seen are daisies and clover, as well as grass. It is worth discussing random sampling before undertaking the practical. You may want to give students random number tables. You may want to discuss estimating percentage cover with students bearing in mind this cannot be used to look at population numbers.

Issues for discussion

Why is it important to sample randomly? *It is important to do this to try to get a representative sample and avoid biased sampling.*

How might sampling be biased? *Biased sampling might result from: choosing areas that have a lot of dandelions, not many etc., even if trying not to do that; throwing the quadrat as this will be limited to the distance the quadrat can be thrown; not covering the whole area of the field, for example by staying close to a path.*

Why is it important to find out about populations of species? *This might be used for surveying an area to look at the impact of an activity (e.g. impact of playing football on the dandelion population of the field) or to survey an area as a part of planning whether to undertake a development on that land (e.g. are there rare plants which means that the development should be undertaken somewhere else?).*

How might you design a key to help other students identify plants on the field?

Health and safety

If you are not going off-site then health and safety considerations are only to do with being outside; encourage students to take enough clothing to be warm but not too much; think about sun burn. Make sure students walk carefully around the site and are in view.

Equipment

Per group:
   1 quadrat
   A basic key and/or field guides (these can easily be made from images on the Internet)

Available for the class:
   Long tape measures or trundle wheels
   Random number tables

3.10 Investigation into how seeds are dispersed by the wind

Learning objectives

- To understand how some seeds are adapted to being dispersed by the wind.

Procedure

Students should work in pairs. Each pair should take one each of three different types of seeds, for example, parsnip and *Osteospermum* (wind-dispersed) and seeds that are dispersed another way, for example, animal-dispersed, like tomato seeds. Choosing a safe height that also allows enough time for seeds to disperse, students should release seeds of the different species and measure the horizontal distance that each seed travels from the point it was dropped. This is best done outside (if there is a breeze) or, if inside, with a fan on low power to simulate the wind; otherwise even wind-dispersed seeds are likely to fall without travelling far. When students have released and measured the distance travelled by 10 seeds per species they should calculate the mean, range and median for each species and compare these.

Effectiveness matrix

	Domain of observables	Domain of ideas
What students do	Students can: • Release seeds from different species at the same height and measure the distance travelled. • Calculate the range and median distance travelled per species. • Draw a bar chart (with distance on the y-axis) to show the distance the seeds of each species have travelled.	Students can talk about: • The fact that different seeds travel different distances. • There is variation in the range within and between the distance travelled by seeds of different species. • There is variation in the medians between species.
What students learn	Students can later: • Carry out the same practical but using different variables (e.g. height seeds are dropped, size or mass of seed or wind strength).	Students can later: • Discuss how some seeds are adapted to wind dispersal. • Suggest explanations as to why seeds travel different distances. • Propose ways in which the seeds of other species are dispersed.

Keep in mind

The fruit from sycamore and ash trees are winged and these are an excellent resource if they can be found; they should be kept for future use. There are also many variants of this method which means students are able to decide on variables, should that be desired. For greater accuracy, use a plumb bob or similar to allow the horizontal measurements to be made from below the vertical drop.

Issues for discussion

Apart from in the wind, in what other ways are seeds dispersed? *Seeds can be dispersed in a number of ways, for example, when animals defecate after eating the fruit that the seeds are in; by sticking to an animal's fur or feathers and later falling off; by propulsion, when seeds are forcibly ejected.*

What might be an advantage and a disadvantage of wind dispersal compared to animal dispersal? *An advantage of wind dispersal stems from the fact that fruits are expensive to the plant in terms of resources; if animals eat the fruit of the plant they might also eat the buds and leaves of the plant which means it wouldn't easily be able to make as many seeds. A disadvantage of wind dispersal is that many seeds end up in places where they have no chance of germinating.*

Why do seeds need to be dispersed rather than grow near to their parent tree? *If individuals grow too close to the parent, then they might compete for resources such as light and space; dispersal also allows a plant to colonize new habitats.*

Health and safety

It might be advisable (for the practical to work well) for students to release seeds from a height above their reach, in which case great care should be taken if students stand on chairs or desks.

Equipment

Available to the whole class:

- Seeds that are adapted for wind pollination such as *Osteospermum* and parsnip (sycamore or ash if available)
- Seeds dispersed by animals, e.g. tomato seeds
- Electric fan(s) set to low power
- Metre rules for measuring height and distance

3.11 Investigating responses of woodlice using choice chambers

Learning objectives

- To learn that woodlice respond to different environmental conditions.

Procedure

Students should work in pairs. Each pair should set up a choice chamber, half in the light and half in the dark. This can be done easily using thick black paper to cover half of the chamber (see Figure 3.8). Students should place a given number of woodlice in the choice chamber and then count the number of woodlice in the light and in the dark after 5 minutes. Depending on time available, repeat this about five times at 2-minute intervals. Students should calculate the mean average number of woodlice in the light and in the dark. Mean percentages can be shared with the class for further discussion.

Figure 3.8
Experimental set-up (photograph taken by Claire Simpson)

Effectiveness matrix

	Domain of observables	Domain of ideas
What students do	Students can: • Handle woodlice with care. • Set up a choice chamber with different conditions in different areas and record the number of woodlice in different areas of the choice chamber after 2 minutes. • Repeat this a number of times and calculate mean number of woodlice in each area and record this on a chart.	Students can talk about: • How woodlice will move across the different areas of the choice chamber changing the number of woodlice in each area. • What they predict will happen based on what they know about the habitat of woodlice.
What students learn	Students can later: • Use invertebrates in experiments with a good ethical attitude. • Carry out an experiment to investigate animals' responses to different environmental conditions (e.g. humidity). • Calculate the mean value of a set of numbers and choose an appropriate way to display the data.	Students can later talk about: • How woodlice choose to be in the dark more than the light to reduce water loss by evaporation. • How woodlice are negatively phototactic. • The need to repeat observations to minimize error and the effect of anomalies in the data.

Keep in mind

Woodlice should be treated with respect and returned to their normal habitat as soon as possible after the investigation. Mean values could be converted to a percentage to share data with the class for further discussion.

Issues for discussion

Why might you expect woodlice to choose the dark (or damp) area over the light (dry) one? *Woodlice prefer dark and damp habitats to reduce water loss by evaporation.*

For what other reason might having a habitat under stones and fallen trees be good for woodlice? *Such areas may be high in the food that woodlice eat and they are hidden from predators.*

What other animals might prefer these conditions? *Some other animals that live in similar habitats are earthworms, slugs and snails. This is also to help reduce loss of water by evaporation.*

Do plants prefer these conditions? *Some plants prefer damp conditions to reduce water loss but not dark conditions as most need light for photosynthesis.*

What is the advantage of using class data rather than using the results from one choice chamber? *The class set of data, as it is made up of many different observations, is likely to reduce the effect of error or anomalies.*

Health and safety

There are no health and safety issues associated with this investigation.

Equipment

Per pair of students:
- 1 choice chamber or Petri dish with black paper over one half
- Several woodlice (ideally about 6–8 per pair)
- 1 stop clock
- 1 or 2 calculators

3.12 Investigating photosynthesis by the presence or absence of starch in a leaf

Learning objectives

- To learn that starch is found in leaves because it is one of the end products of photosynthesis.
- To understand that if plants can't photosynthesize, the store of starch in the leaf is used up.

Procedure

Put one plant in the dark for 48 hours prior to the lesson and one in the light. During the lesson students should work in pairs. Students should take a leaf (or part of a leaf) from each of the two plants. The leaves should be kept separate from each other throughout the procedure. Place each leaf in a small beaker of boiling water for about a minute. Then put the leaf into a boiling tube and add enough ethanol to cover the leaf. Place the boiling tube into an 80 °C water bath and leave for 5 minutes. After this remove the leaf from the boiling tube using forceps and rinse under cold water. Place the leaf on a white tile so it is spread out and add a few drops of iodine solution to cover the leaf. After a few minutes a blue/black colour indicates the presence of starch. Students should compare leaves from both plants (see Figure 3.9).

Effectiveness matrix

	Domain of observables	Domain of ideas
What students do	Students can: • Safely extract chlorophyll from leaves (e.g. of pelargoniums). • Use iodine solution to test a leaf for starch. • Observe that a blue/black colouration is present in a leaf that has been kept in the light but it is yellow/brown in a leaf that has been kept in the dark.	Students can talk about: • Why they are using boiling water and ethanol. • Why there is the difference in colour between the leaf that has been kept in the dark and the leaf that has been kept in the light.
What students learn	Students can later: • Use the test for starch to determine presence or absence of starch in different materials (e.g. foods). • Use this method to predict and test where photosynthesis occurs in variegated leaves (e.g. of spider plants).	Students can later talk about: • How starch an insoluble compound is made up of many sugar molecules, which is why it is found in leaves. • If a pelargonium plant is left in the dark for 48 hours it cannot photosynthesize and uses up its store of starch.

Keep in mind

Students are always told that the end product of photosynthesis is sugar and yet when we test to see if plants can photosynthesize in the light and dark we test for starch. Students may not realize the relationship between sugars and starch and why we are testing for starch in the leaf.

The procedure is quite complicated and students need to think about what they are doing at each stage and why.

Variegated spider plant leaves can be used to aid students' understanding about the relationship between the presence of chlorophyll and starch content.

Issues for discussion

Why are we testing for starch? *Because the glucose that is formed in photosynthesis is soluble and so it is converted into starch, which is insoluble, for storage.*

What happens to the starch if there is no photosynthesis? *The starch is converted to glucose and used in respiration.*

What might plants need sugar for? *Sugar is needed for respiration in plants for all the life processes. Sugars can also be used to make other compounds needed for different structures in the plant.*

In the procedure what do boiling water, ethanol and iodine solution do? *The boiling water breaks down the cell walls and disrupts the cell membranes, so that the cell contents can be extracted. The ethanol dissolves the chlorophyll so that we can see the colour change more clearly. The iodine solution tests for the presence of starch by going blue/black when starch is there.*

What would a variegated leaf look like after completing this procedure (e.g. a spider plant leaf)? *A variegated leaf would be blue/black where it had previously been green and stained yellow by the iodine solution where it had previously been white. This is because photosynthesis does not take place where the cells do not have chlorophyll.*

Health and safety

- It is important to wear safety goggles throughout the practical task and until everyone has cleared away.
- Ethanol is highly flammable – when using ethanol all naked flames should be extinguished.
- To warm the ethanol it is best to use water bath or boiling water in beakers from a kettle (rather than a Bunsen burner).
- Iodine solution – harmful to eyes and stains clothes.

Equipment

For the class:

   Two plants – one of which has been in the dark for 48 hours (pelargoniums work well)
   Kettles for boiling water
   Water baths (at 80 °C)

Per pair of students:

   2 small beakers
   2 boiling tubes
   1 pair of forceps
   Iodine solution
   Ethanol
   1 white tile

Figure 3.9 Experimental set-up (photograph taken by Claire Simpson)

Biology: Session Guides 15–16

Indira Banner and Mark Winterbottom

4

- **4.1** Investigating diffusion and surface area in agar blocks (p. 64)
- **4.2** Comparing the energy content of foods (p. 66)
- **4.3** Investigating the factors that promote decay (p. 69)
- **4.4** Investigating the effect of amylase on starch (p. 72)
- **4.5** Investigating the structure and function of the breathing system (p. 75)
- **4.6** Investigating *Daphnia* heart rate in response to caffeine (p. 77)
- **4.7** Investigating the presence and absence of light on photosynthesis using algal balls (p. 79)
- **4.8** Comparing stomatal density on leaves (p. 82)
- **4.9** Measuring transpiration rates from leaves in different conditions (p. 85)
- **4.10** Observing turgor and plasmolysis in onion cells (p. 88)
- **4.11** Root tip preparation and the mitotic index (p. 91)
- **4.12** Investigating the effects of evolution using a model (p. 94)

4.1 Investigating diffusion and surface area in agar blocks

Learning objectives

- To understand that diffusion is faster when surface area:volume ratio is higher.

Procedure

Students should work in pairs. Each pair can be given or can prepare themselves at least three blocks of agar which have been made up with sodium hydroxide and phenolphthalein: for example, 0.5 cm^3, 1 cm^3 and 2 cm^3 in volume. Students should place the blocks in 0.1 M hydrochloric acid for 5 minutes. During this time students can calculate the surface area to volume ratios of the blocks and draw a table to show the results of the investigation. After 5 minutes the blocks should be removed, cut in half and the volume of the undiffused (unchanged) part in the middle calculated. This can then be used to calculate the diffused volume.

Effectiveness matrix

	Domain of observables	Domain of ideas
What students do	Students can: • Calculate surface area and volume and surface area to volume ratios of different-sized blocks of agar. • Calculate the volume of the coloured cube in each block and subtract this from the total volume of the cube to find the volume through which the acid has diffused. • Calculate the percentage of the total volume through which diffusion has occurred.	Students can talk about: • Smaller blocks have a larger surface area to volume ratio and larger blocks have a smaller surface area to volume ratio. • Greater percentage of a smaller block experiences diffusion in a given time.
What students learn	Students can later: • Calculate the surface area to volume ratio of a cube. • Calculate percentage diffusion.	Students can later talk about: • Diffusion is more effective when there is a large surface area to volume ratio. • In an organism with a large enough surface area to volume ratio, diffusion through the external surface is sufficient to support life. • Organisms with a small surface area to volume ratio have developed adaptations to increase their surface area.

Keep in mind

Students may find it difficult to calculate and understand the concept of surface area to volume ratio. It might be useful to give students small plastic cubes prior to the experiment to check students' understanding in this area.

Issues for discussion

Where is the concept of surface area to volume ratio seen in living organisms? *Many examples including gas exchange systems (and digestive systems in animals) where small organisms can take in oxygen through their skin, whereas larger organisms (with a relatively small surface area), for example, humans, have lungs which have a large surface area to volume ratio. Leaves are very thin so that gases can diffuse effectively in and out of them. It is also seen with relation to temperature so that animals in hot areas may have larger ears so heat energy is lost to the atmosphere more easily (e.g. desert foxes), whereas animals in cold areas have smaller ears (e.g. arctic fox).*

Health and safety

Blocks contain the alkali sodium hydroxide and students are using hydrochloric acid so they should wear goggles. The 0.1 M hydrochloric acid is dilute but students should take care if moving about with it; should any spill, they should wash the acid off their skin immediately.

Equipment

Each pair of students should have:
- Agar jelly to cut into blocks (at least three different sizes)
- A fine knife (it does not have to be sharp)
- 200 ml 0.1 M hydrochloric acid
- 3 or 4 small beakers for the agar blocks
- Ruler

4.2 Comparing the energy content of foods

Learning objectives

- To understand that oxidation of different foods releases different amounts of energy.
- To be able to evaluate data, identifying sources of energy loss.

Procedure

Students should work in pairs. Each pair should find the masses of a variety of foods and note these in a table. Students should then measure out a volume of water that about half fills the boiling tube and note its temperature. One piece of food should be set alight using the blue flame on a Bunsen burner set nearby to the students' workstation. A mounted needle is used to hold the food (see Figure 4.1). The burning food is then placed directly under the boiling tube to heat the water. If the flame burning the food is extinguished it can be re-lit until the food will not burn anymore. At this point the temperature of the water should be measured again and noted. This is repeated for all foods. The water should be changed for each new piece of food, taking care to measure the volume of water each time. The students then calculate the energy in the food:

$$\text{Energy in food (per gram)} = \frac{\text{volume of water heated (ml)} \times \text{change in temperature (°C)} \times 4.2}{\text{mass of food (g)}}$$

where 4.2 is the specific heat capacity of water which is the energy in joules (J) needed to increase the temperature of 1 ml of water by 1 °C.

The students' calculations for the energy in their samples should then be compared with the energy values on the packaging, which is often displayed per 100 g.

Effectiveness matrix

	Domain of observables	Domain of ideas
What students do	Students can: • Find the mass of different foods and measure a volume of water using a measuring cylinder. • Measure the temperature before and after heating, and calculate the temperature change of the water. • Calculate the energy released by the piece of food and compare their findings to the nutritional information on the packet of food.	Students can talk about: • How the temperature of the water increases by different extents with different foods. • How some energy heats the water, but some energy is released into the surroundings. • How to calculate the energy released using the specific heat capacity of water.

	Domain of observables	**Domain of ideas**
What students learn	Students can later: • Take accurate measurements using a balance and a measuring cylinder. • Use a calorimeter to measure and calculate the energy released by a material.	Students can later talk about: • How different foods release different amounts of energy. • Why their findings differ from the nutritional information on the packet of food. • Why they controlled variables such as the distance between the burning food and the water.

Keep in mind

Try to choose foods that might burn – highly processed corn-based crisps work well. It is from these that, sometimes, globules of fat can be seen dropping from the sample. You can also use crackers. Other foods work best dried, for example, bread and cheese.

Before starting the practical students may want to draw up a results table in their books showing food stuff, mass, volume of water, starting and end temperature of the water, change in temperature and two final columns where they can calculate the energy released by their food. They will calculate energy per gram of food and it is likely that the nutritional information will be energy per 100 g.

Be careful that discussions around (un)healthy food and diet are handled sensitively.

Issues for discussion

How and why do the students' values differ from the packaging? *The students' values will be lower than those on the packaging due to not all the chemical energy in the food being used to heat the water. The food may not have completely burnt; some of the food may have broken off or fat may have been lost in drips (this is often visible from crisps); energy from the burning food is not all heat energy; some is light energy. The heat energy will heat the atmosphere as well as the water so not all of it will be measured.*

Given these issues, how did students make sure that this experiment was as reliable as possible? *Students should place the burning food the same distance from the boiling tube every time. Students should use the same volume of water every time which has the same or similar starting temperature.*

You might also wish to have a discussion about a balanced diet and/or food labelling.

Health and safety

Students tend to enjoy burning food and they must make sure they are aware of the safety precautions needed. They must wear goggles and tie back their hair as they are using Bunsen burners. They should stand with chairs tucked under the desk in front of them. Food must be burnt over a heat-proof mat. Students should be careful to make sure the handle of the mounted needle does not heat up or catch light. Do not use nuts, or food containing nuts (risk of allergies), and check if any members of the class have any other allergies.

Equipment

Students should work in pairs. Each pair should have:

- 2 pairs of goggles
- A clamp, boss and stand
- Boiling tube
- Thermometer
- Samples of some foods (not nuts)
- Wooden-handled mounted needles or tongs to hold the food as it is burning
- 1 Bunsen burner and measuring cylinder between two pairs
- Several sets of mass balances around the room (as many as possible)
- The packages that the food came in with its nutritional information

Figure 4.1
The equipment (photographs taken by Claire Simpson and Stef Lesnianski)

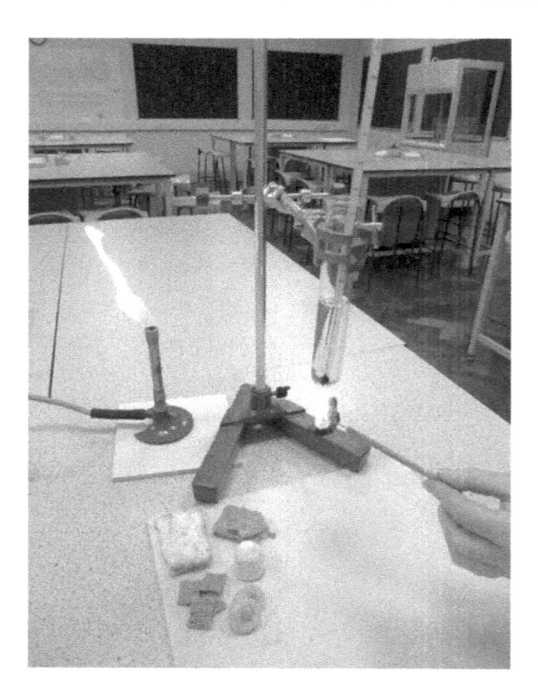

4.3 Investigating the factors that promote decay

Learning objectives

- To learn what conditions are needed for decay.
- To understand why these conditions are needed.
- To explain how preserving food tries to prevent these conditions.

Procedure

Students should work in pairs. Each pair should take four test tubes and place the same number of peas (about 8–10) in each one. Each test tube should then be placed under certain defined conditions, for example, distilled water, salted water, oil and no liquid (see Figure 4.2). A bung should be placed on each test tube. Students should decide how to record their data. These might be as drawings or descriptions. The test tubes should be left for a week or two weeks for students to make and record observations on several occasions. The experiment could easily be extended by placing test tubes of peas in a fridge, a freezer, near a heater or in the sunlight and in a cool place in the laboratory.

Figure 4.2
The experimental set-up (photograph by Claire Simpson)

Effectiveness matrix

	Domain of observables	Domain of ideas
What students do	Students can: • Set up test tubes with peas in a range of conditions, keeping all other conditions the same.	Students can talk about: • Which peas they expect to decay and which to be preserved. • The extent of decay of peas in different conditions. • Using qualitative data to draw conclusions.
What students learn	Students can later: • Set up an investigation with controlled conditions. • Test for other conditions that might affect decay, such as pH.	Students can later talk about: • Why decay is affected by temperature, water and oxygen. • The importance of decay in cycling materials through an ecosystem.

Keep in mind

It might be hard for students to link the decay of food with decomposition of materials, such as dead animals and leaves, in the environment outside. The environment in the lab will not be completely consistent. Students could be made aware of, or asked to think about, what would happen if test tubes were left near a heater, in sunlight or in permanent shade.

Issues for discussion

How is decay affected by atmospheric conditions? *The presence of oxygen speeds up decay as many organisms that cause decay need oxygen. Water is needed for decay as the organisms that cause decay need water. There will be an optimum temperature at which decay occurs; very low temperatures or high temperatures will slow down or prevent decay.*

What are some of the ways that food is preserved to reduce the effect of these conditions? *Examples might include: food is packed in a vacuum or under oil so that there is no oxygen present; food may be dehydrated like pasta, coffee and peas so there is no water present; food may be frozen or heat-treated (e.g. ultra-heat treatment UHT milk) to kill microorganisms or slow down their activity.*

Why is decay useful for the functioning of ecosystems? *Without the decay process then dead organisms would not 'rot away'. The decomposition of dead organisms or parts of organisms (e.g. leaves) recycles nutrients (e.g. carbon and nitrogen) back into the soil to be used again by growing plants.*

Health and safety

Students should not eat the peas. Some students may be allergic to mould that grows, so keep bungs on test tubes.

Equipment

Each pair needs (depending on what conditions are being investigated):

    4 test tubes with bungs

    A small beaker of thawed frozen peas or fresh peas

    A small beaker of oil

    Water

    Access to a fridge

4.4 Investigating the effect of amylase on starch

Learning objectives

- To understand that some enzymes break down large molecules into their constituent smaller molecules.
- To understand that food needs to be digested in order to be absorbed by the human body.

Procedure

Students should carry out the experiment in pairs (see Figure 4.3). Each student should set up a model gut using a piece of Visking tubing. The Visking tubing can be sealed at the bottom by tying a knot in it. Starch solution and amylase solution are added inside the tubing. The tubing is then sealed at the top by tying a knot in it. The tubing should then be rinsed with distilled water to make sure no starch or amylase solutions are on the outside of the tubing. Alternatively, tubing can be tied in a knot at the bottom and attached at the top by an elastic band to the sawn-off barrel of an old syringe, as shown on the Nuffield Foundation Practical Biology website http://www.nuffieldfoundation.org/practical-biology/investigating-effect-amylase-starchy-foodstuff.

The tubing is then placed in a small beaker of distilled water. The liquid outside the tubing can be tested more easily than that inside, so can be tested at 5 or 10 minute intervals, if desired, for starch and glucose. This can be done using a spotting tile for starch with iodine solution and following a procedure using Benedict's solution to test for reducing sugars. The solution inside of the tubing can be tested for starch and glucose towards the end of the practical. Be careful that the pipettes are rinsed through with distilled water after each use. The longer time the tubing can be left, for example, for 25–30 minutes, the more likely there will be clear results. A slightly higher temperature than room temperature will increase the rate of diffusion without denaturing the amylase solution, so the beaker could contain warm water or the beakers could be placed in a water bath at about 40 °C.

Effectiveness matrix

	Domain of observables	Domain of ideas
What students do	Students can: • Set up a model gut using Visking tubing. • Test for the presence of starch and glucose.	Students can talk about: • The ways in which the experiment is an effective and not so effective model for the human gut. • How the liquid outside the Visking tubing, in the beaker, tests positive for glucose and negative for starch. • How the solution inside the Visking tubing tests positively for glucose and for starch.
What students learn	Students can later: • Carry out food tests for starch and glucose. • Use Visking tubing in other experiments as a model for a membrane in living organisms.	Students can later talk about: • The role of amylase in the digestion of starch to glucose. • How small molecules like glucose can diffuse across selectively permeable membranes and large molecules like starch cannot. • How digestion is needed so that nutrients from food can be absorbed into the blood.

Keep in mind

Visking tubing needs to be soaked in water to soften it before use. Students need to be careful that the starch solution is not present on the outside of the tubing by rinsing it thoroughly after it has been sealed.

Issues for discussion

How does the Visking tubing support learning about the process of digestion? *Students might talk about how only the smaller digested molecules of glucose move through the Visking tubing, and not the larger starch molecules, as happens with diffusion into the blood from the gut.*

What are the limitations of Visking tubing as a model for the gut? *Students might talk about the size and colour of the gut being different from the tubing (which are not important differences) and the absence of blood vessels in the model (which is an important difference).*

What other membranes could be modelled by Visking tubing? *Students might talk about animal cell membranes and the absorption by diffusion of small digested molecules from the blood into cells. They should be encouraged to think of plants too and the process of osmosis that causes water to enter plant cells across the plant root cell membrane from the soil.*

Health and safety

Iodine solution is harmful to the eyes and so goggles should be worn throughout this experiment. Testing for glucose using Benedict's solution involves boiling water, either from a kettle or over a Bunsen burner, and care should be taken when students are doing this, especially if they are carrying beakers of hot water around the room.

Equipment

Per pair of students:
- 2 pairs of goggles
- 1 section of pre-soaked Visking tubing
- 1 small beaker
- (Warm) water

For the food tests:
- 2 pipettes
- Spotting tile
- Small bottle of iodine solution
- 1 medium beaker
- 3–4 test tubes
- Small bottle of Benedict's solution

Available for the class:
- Kettle (if Bunsen burners or water baths are not used)

Figure 4.3
Experimental set-up (photographs by Stefan Lesnianski and Claire Simpson)

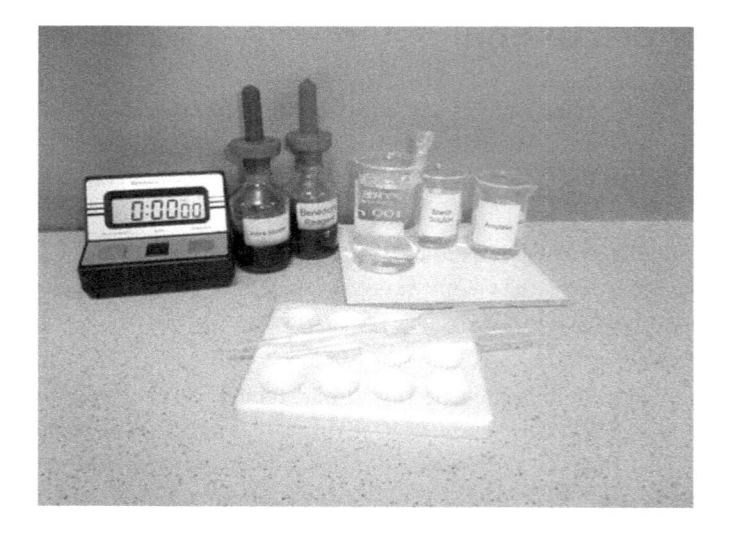

4.5 Investigating the structure and function of the breathing system

Learning objectives

- To understand the adaptations of the breathing system for gaseous exchange.
- To learn how to dissect animal tissue safely and carefully.

Procedure

Students should work in groups of four. Each group should have access to one pair of lungs. It is helpful for students to first observe the teacher inflating a pair of lungs with air using a small air pump and note any changes in size and colour. It is also beneficial for students to watch the teacher complete the dissection if time allows.

Students should be asked to feel the weight and texture of the lungs before cutting into them. Sharp scissors work well for the students to cut down the trachea noting the texture and shape of the cartilage rings. Students should then follow one bronchus and then one bronchiole as far as possible, noting how far into the lungs the cartilage rings are present. A small piece of lung tissue can be removed and placed in a beaker of water to observe what happens before and after squeezing the tissue under the water.

Effectiveness matrix

	Domain of observables	Domain of ideas
What students do	Students can: • Observe the visible features of the breathing system and relate its structure to their own bodies. • Use a pair of scissors to cut open the trachea, a bronchus and a bronchiole as far as possible, and feel and describe their texture.	Students can talk about: • The way the lungs enlarge when inflated. • The C-shaped rings of the trachea, bronchi and bronchioles. • The way lung tissue feels spongy and floats in water, and that air bubbles emerge when you squeeze it under water.
What students learn	Students can later: • Safely and carefully dissect animal tissue.	Students can later talk about: • The elastic and spongy nature of the lungs caused by millions of alveoli which allow the lungs to take in a lot of air. • The expansive network of bronchioles that quickly carries air to the alveoli. • The C-shaped cartilage rings prevent collapse of the trachea, bronchi and bronchioles.

Keep in mind

It can be difficult to get hold of uncut lungs. Well before the day of the practical, contact a good butcher or try going directly to an abattoir. The animal tissue used should be lamb to avoid offence that might be caused if using pig or cow lungs. Some students may have ethical objections to dissection or feel ill at the sight of the tissue or blood. It is important to respect these feelings. All students should be respectful in their attitude towards using animal tissue in the laboratory.

Issues for discussion

What is the purpose of the C-shaped rings in the trachea, bronchi and bronchioles? *The C-shaped rings are to stop the tubes from collapsing, thus cutting off the air supply.*

How does lung tissue behave in water and why? *The lung tissue floats in water before it is squeezed; when it is squeezed under water, bubbles of gas are given off and the tissue may sink. This indicates the enormous capacity of the lung tissue for holding air.*

What structures give the lung tissue this spongy feel and why are they necessary? *The lung tissue is made up of millions of alveoli which are microscopic thin-walled sacs where gas exchange between the lung and the blood vessels takes place.*

Health and safety

Students must wash their hands after touching the tissue. Some students might wish to wear gloves; consider avoiding latex gloves in case of allergy. The tissue must be disposed of appropriately. It is best to avoid scalpels and instead use scissors for cutting the tissue; however, these must be sharp. Consider requiring students to wear safety goggles. CLEAPPS recommends that a lung is inflated inside a plastic bag.

Equipment per group

1 pair of lungs between a group of 4, if possible

2 pairs of scissors

1 large beaker of water

Gloves, if wanted

4.6 Investigating *Daphnia* heart rate in response to caffeine

Learning objectives

- To understand the effects of stimulants on heart rate.

Procedure

Each student should have a cavity slide and select a large *Daphnia*, transferring it to the slide by pipette and immediately adding enough of the pond water to just cover it. Placing the *Daphnia* on a small spread-out piece of cotton wool helps to keep the *Daphnia* still. Using low power on a light microscope students should count the heartbeats over a 20-second period and repeat this 3–4 times. The heart beat may be about 300 beats per minute so students might need a clicker or they can draw a pencil dot on paper for every beat and count them afterwards.

Then add a small quantity of dilute caffeine solution and repeat the experiment.

Effectiveness matrix

	Domain of observables	Domain of ideas
What students do	Students can: • Use a pipette to place a *Daphnia* onto a cavity slide. • Use a microscope to count the number of heart beats per minute of a *Daphnia*.	Students can talk about: • How heart rate in beats per minute can be calculated from the number of heart beats in a given time. • How the heart rate is higher when the concentration of caffeine is higher.
What students learn	Students can later: • Use a microscope to make observations on living material. • Use a similar method to measure the effect of different stimulants on a living organism.	Students can later talk about: • How stimulants increase the heart rate of living organisms. • Caffeine as a stimulant.

Keep in mind

Students should treat the *Daphnia* with respect and return them to the central tank as soon as possible after completing the experiment.

Heat from a lamp may raise the temperature of the *Daphnia* and have an effect on heart rate.

Issues for discussion

To what extent can your conclusions be applied to humans? *Students have to appreciate that they have to be careful in extrapolating the findings to humans as the physiology of the* Daphnia *is very different from that of humans. However, it might help them to think about the effect of stimulants on animals more widely.*

How does caffeine affect humans? *Caffeine generally does make humans' heart rates faster. Some people feel more alert when this happens so they drink coffee when they are tired if they want to remain awake.*

What other things makes the heart beat faster in humans? *Adrenaline, which is a hormone found in humans and released at times of fear, makes the heart beat faster; it helps to make the body ready for action by causing the heart to pump more blood to the skeletal muscles. Exercise also makes the heart beat faster.*

What is the outcome of faster heart rate in humans and when or why might that be advantageous? *A faster heart rate increases the volume of blood being pumped from the heart which means that the cells in the body are supplied with more oxygen and sugar for respiration so that they can release more energy if needed. This is important if doing exercise or for running away from a frightening situation.*

Health and safety

Undiluted caffeine is harmful if ingested so the solution should be made to be a similar strength to cola or coffee drinks.

If the *Daphnia* comes from an outside pond, ensure students wash their hands after the experiment.

Equipment

Per pair of students:

   1 light microscope

   1 *Daphnia*

   1 cavity slide or small petri dish

   1 pipette

   A small piece of cotton wool

Available to the group:

   Dilute caffeine solution

4.7 Investigating the presence and absence of light on photosynthesis using algal balls

Learning objectives

- To know that carbon dioxide is taken up during photosynthesis.
- To know that photosynthesis needs light to occur.
- To understand that hydrogen carbonate indicator can be used to test for the occurrence of photosynthesis by showing the presence or absence of carbon dioxide.

Procedure

This procedure is adapted from the Science and Plants for Schools (SAPS) website.

Students should work in pairs. If time allows, it works well if students can make the algal balls from part way through the method, as this will let them see that the algal balls are plant material 'trapped' inside the jelly-like balls (see Figure 4.4). It is also an engaging start to the practical. Otherwise the algal balls can be prepared by the technician. To find out how to make the algal balls please go to http://www.saps.org.uk/secondary/teaching-resources/235-student-sheet-23-photosynthesis-using-algae-wrapped-in-jelly-balls.

Depending on the size of the bottles, students should place about 15 algal balls in each of two small bottles with lids. As long as the number of balls is the same in each of their two bottles, the exact number doesn't matter. Students should then add red hydrogen carbonate solution indicator to each bottle so it is full to the brim. This is to try to exclude any air from being in the bottle. The red colour shows that the indicator has been exposed to atmospheric levels of CO_2. When the lids are secured tightly, students should cover one bottle completely with black paper or aluminium foil to exclude the light and secure this with sticky tape. Both bottles should be placed in an area that gets direct sunlight or (preferably) in front of a lamp. Students will be looking for a colour change in the indicator solution after about 30 minutes.

Effectiveness matrix

	Domain of observables	Domain of ideas
What students do	Students can: • Set up the experiment to have two bottles that are almost exactly the same, apart from one has a covering to exclude light. • Record any colour changes in the indicator after 30 minutes.	Students can talk about: • How, in the presence of algal balls and light, the hydrogen carbonate indicator turns from red to purple and in the absence of light, hydrogen carbonate indicator turns from red to yellow.

Effectiveness matrix (continued)

	Domain of observables	Domain of ideas
What students learn	Students can later: • Use this method to test the effect of other variables on photosynthesis, for example, carbon dioxide concentration or light intensity or quality. • Use hydrogen carbonate indicator to demonstrate the occurrence of photosynthesis in aqueous plants.	Students can later talk about: • How a yellow colour indicates presence of carbon dioxide in the solution, and a purple colour indicates absence of carbon dioxide in the solution. • How a purple colour indicates occurrence of photosynthesis, and a yellow colour indicates the absence of photosynthesis. • How light is required for photosynthesis to occur.

Keep in mind

Students need to understand that the algae in the algal balls are alive and are an example of a photosynthesizing organism.

Students can make the algal balls themselves, although this might take an extra lesson.

Issues for discussion

What processes are happening in the plants that are in the light? *The key thing is that students appreciate that the plants are respiring and photosynthesizing as well as undergoing the other life processes.*

What could you do to increase the rate of photosynthesis? *This could lead to various ideas such as: warm the water; change the pH to the optimum; increase the carbon dioxide concentration; increase the light intensity.*

How else could you use the algal balls to investigate photosynthesis? *There could be a number of investigations, for example, to measure the effect of different intensities or wavelengths of light on photosynthesis, or different numbers of algal balls.*

Health and safety

Students should follow good laboratory practice, washing their hands at the end of the experiment.

Equipment

Per pair of students:

    About 30 algal balls

    2 small bottles with lids

    1 small bottle of hydrogen carbonate solution (red)

Available for the class:

    Lamps

    Black paper or foil

    Sticky tape

Figure 4.4
Algal balls (photograph by Claire Simpson)

4.8 Comparing stomatal density on leaves

Learning objectives

- To understand why stomata are not distributed evenly on a leaf.

Procedure

Students should work in pairs; each pair takes a leaf or part of a leaf from a plant (pelargoniums work well). Varnish or 'second skin' should be painted on to the leaf in two or three places and no bigger than about 1 cm^2. These can be on just the underside of the leaf or on both sides of the leaf as required. Once the varnish is dry students use a mounted needle and forceps to gently peel off the varnish which will have an imprint of the leaf surface which can be observed under a microscope (see Figure 4.5).

Students make a slide from the peel by placing it on a glass slide and covering it with a cover slip.

To measure the density of stomata on the leaf, students should count the number of stomata they can see in one field of view. They then calculate the area they are observing by using an eyepiece graticule (see 'Keep in mind' on the next page) to find out the radius (r) of the circle in view and substituting this in the equation area = πr^2. The density is the number of stomata in a defined area.

Effectiveness matrix

	Domain of observables	**Domain of ideas**
What students do	Students can: • Make a stomatal peel and use the microscope to count the number of stomata visible within the field of view. • Measure the radius of the field of view and calculate the area. • Calculate the density of stomata on different parts of the leaf.	Students can talk about: • The different densities of stomata in different parts of the leaf (e.g. there are more stomata on the underside of the leaf, and on the green areas of a variegated leaf).
What students learn	Students can later: • Compare stomatal density of leaves between different species. • Use this technique to visualize other microscopic details on a surface.	Students can later talk about: • How fewer stomata on the upper side of a leaf help to reduce transpiration and how plants open and close their stomata in order to control transpiration. • How stomatal density is higher in areas where photosynthesis is happening in order to supply carbon dioxide.

Keep in mind

The eyepiece graticule should have been calibrated for each magnification on a microscope using a stage micrometre so that students know the length of one division on the eyepiece graticule scale. Clear nail varnish is often used to make stomatal peels but occasionally this can damage the leaf it is painted on. Water-based varnishes can also be bought from DIY stores and used effectively. The SAPS and Nuffield websites recommend using medical 'second skin', which is also effective. Spider plants and pelargoniums are often found in school laboratories and can be used to take stomatal peels (this also allows the comparison of a monocotyledonous and a dicotyledonous plant).

Issues for discussion

How and why does the number of stomata differ between the upper and lower sides of a leaf? *For most leaves the number of stomata on the upper side of the leaf will be lower than the number on the underside. This is to reduce water loss by evaporation (transpiration) from the upper side of the leaf which is more exposed to heat from the Sun.*

How might plants from different habitats differ in their stomata? *Stomata normally occur at reduced densities in desert plants. Some plant species have developed a photosynthetic system that allows them to open the stomata at night to allow diffusion of carbon dioxide into the plant where it is stored for use during the day (Crassulacean acid metabolism).*

Health and safety

Students should be careful when using glass slides and cover slips, which are easy to break. Mounted needles and forceps can also be sharp.

Equipment

Each pair of students needs:
- Part of a leaf
- 1 white tile
- 1 glass slide with cover slip
- 1 mounted needle
- 1 pair forceps
- Access to varnish or 'second skin'
- 1 microscope with an eyepiece graticule

Figure 4.5
(a) The equipment.
(b) Removing the peel from the underside of a leaf (photographs taken by Claire Simpson)

4.9 Measuring transpiration rates from leaves in different conditions

Learning objectives

- To understand that transpiration rate varies with different environmental conditions.
- To learn how to set up and use a potometer and understand what it is measuring.

Procedure

Students should complete the practical in pairs. Each pair should be given a cutting from a plant (woody cuttings from bushes often work well) with several leaves on it. The cut end of the stem of this (but not the leaves) is placed under water and cut about 2 cm from the end, using scissors. This is to try to avoid any air bubbles being present in the xylem of the stem. The potometer is then assembled under water (see Figure 4.6). The type of potometer will make the procedures here slightly different. Basically, the woody stem should be pushed through a small hole in the bung and sealed with petroleum jelly. This bung should be firmly placed on a small jar or conical flask of water so the bottom of the stem is submerged so it can take up water. This is connected to a graduated tube which is linked to a beaker of water. A separate reservoir of water can be opened to push the air bubble to an appropriate starting position so its subsequent movement can be observed (this can also be done by a syringe). The whole apparatus can be placed on a balance to measure water loss to the atmosphere as loss of mass.

In order to measure the rate of water loss, students should measure the loss of mass and/or movement of the air bubble in the capillary tubing over a given time as the plant transpires water. The students can then change the environmental conditions around the cutting (e.g. by placing fans, heaters, lights near them) and measure the rate of transpiration in different conditions.

Effectiveness matrix

	Domain of observables	Domain of ideas
What students do	Students can: • Use a potometer on a balance to observe water loss from a leaf. • Record readings from the balance and/or from the graduated tubing. • Calculate the rate of water loss using the data from the balance and/or graduated tubing.	Students can talk about: • Why the bubble in the potometer moves and why the mass of the cutting goes down. • How the speed of these changes is higher in certain environments, for example, bright light or windy conditions.

Effectiveness matrix (continued)

	Domain of observables	Domain of ideas
What students learn	Students can later: • Use two ways to measure transpiration rate. • Take a reading from a graduated scale from the bottom of the meniscus.	Students can later talk about: • How the decreasing mass of the cutting and the movement of the bubble in the graduated pipette are measures of loss of water from the leaf. • Why there is more photosynthesis in bright light (more stomata are open so transpiration rate is higher).

Keep in mind

Students may need reminding, or to be taught, that to measure the volume accurately the reading must be taken from the bottom of the meniscus of water. Remind students that because the flow of water is unbroken, we can calculate water uptake into the leaf as equal to water loss from the leaf. Students may need to be reminded that in most plants the roots take up the water which can be tens of metres away from the leaves in tall trees. The rate of transpiration may be faster in a cut stem than in a rooted plant due to the water being taken directly into the xylem in the cut stem. It can be difficult to avoid air getting into the system so students should not be too surprised if some results are not what they expected.

Issues for discussion

How do different conditions affect water loss from the leaf? *Bright light increases transpiration rate because more stomata will open; windy conditions increase transpiration rate because diffusion from the leaf to the air surrounding the leaf is faster.*

How might adaptations to plants living in hot and/or windy conditions help control water loss from the leaves? *Stomata on the lower side of the leaf; rolled up leaves to reduce evaporation; lowering the surface area to volume ratio of the leaves to make diffusion slower (e.g. cactus); fewer stomata.*

Health and safety

Students should be careful with glassware, especially when putting the bung firmly in place. Students should also take care when cutting the stem under water as, if woody, it could be hard to cut and scissors will need to be sharp.

Equipment

Each pair needs:

A potometer

A stem with several leaves to increase possible transpiration (best to avoid waxy leaves which will reduce it)

A sensitive balance

Access to fans, hair dryers, heaters, lights

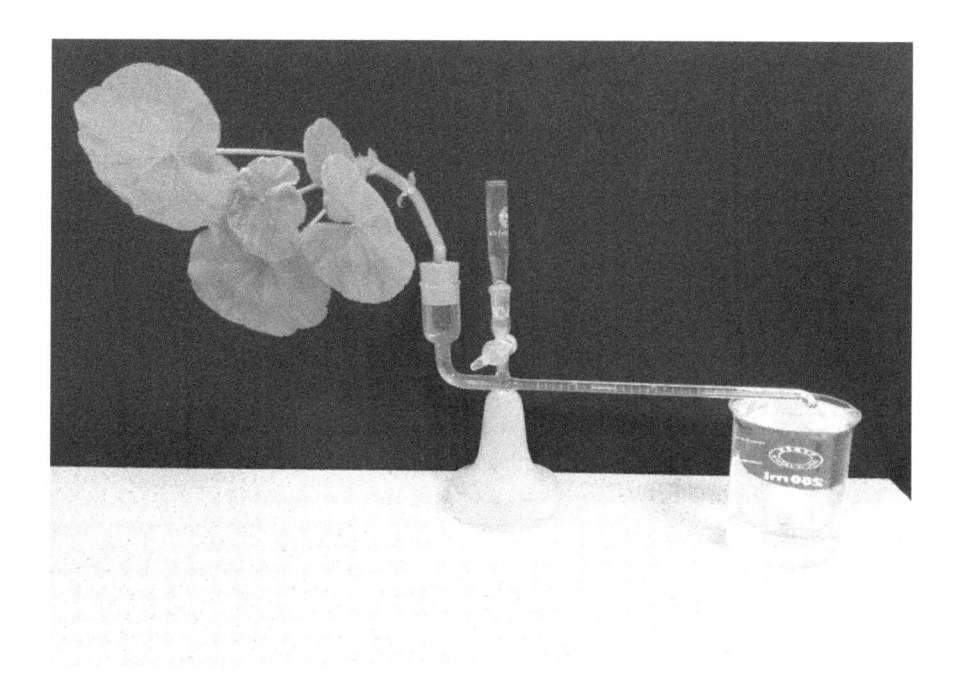

Figure 4.6 An example of a simple potometer (photograph taken by Claire Simpson)

4.10 Observing turgor and plasmolysis in onion cells

Learning objectives

- To understand the effect of increasing solute concentration on turgor in plant cells.
- To recognize plasmolysed and turgid cells.

Procedure

Students should work in pairs. Each pair should take a small piece of onion and cut about 1 cm^2 from it. Students should take a single layer of cells, lay it on a slide and place one or two drops of distilled water onto the layer. Carefully lower a coverslip over the layer to minimize air bubbles. Observe the cells through a microscope, starting with the low power lens (see Figure 4.7a). Then take another 1 cm^2 layer of cells from the onion. Make a new slide in the same way except this time place one or two drops of salt water (e.g. 2 per cent) onto the layer before lowering the coverslip. Repeat with a more concentrated salt solution (e.g. 5 per cent) (see Figure 4.7b). Students could be asked to make a range of salt solutions from 0 to 5 per cent salt concentration.

Use a microscope to compare the cells to those mounted with distilled water.

Students should count the number of plasmolysed cells they can see in one view under the microscope and work this out as a percentage of the total number of cells in that view. Plasmolysed cells are recognized by observing that the cytoplasm has come away from the cell wall. Turgid cells are recognized when there is not a visible gap between the cytoplasm and the cell wall.

Figure 4.7
(a) Onion cells before plasmolysis (turgid).
(b) Onion cells after plasmolysis (photographs taken by Stef Lesnianski and Claire Simpson)

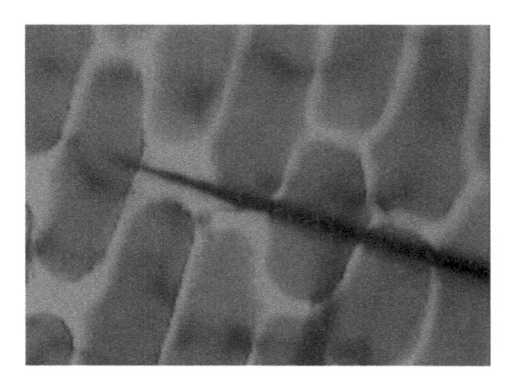

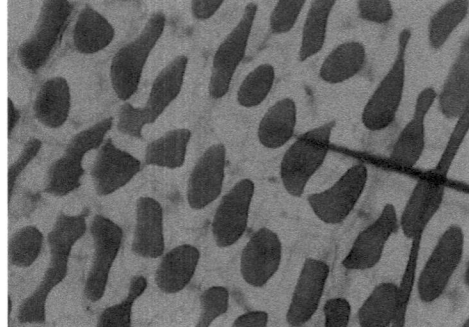

Effectiveness matrix

	Domain of observables	Domain of ideas
What students do	Students can: • Prepare an onion microscope slide. • Prepare different dilutions of salt solutions. • Use a microscope to count plasmolysed cells and calculate the percentage of plasmolysed cells.	Students can talk about: • How changing concentration can change the number of plasmolysed cells. • The relationship between solution concentration and the percentage of plasmolysed cells.
What students learn	Students can later: • Make a microscope slide and use it to investigate processes in cells. • Make solutions of different concentrations from a stock solution, for example, sucrose solutions.	Students can later talk about: • How water molecules diffuse across differentially permeable membranes by osmosis. • Osmosis as the net diffusion of water molecules from an area of high water concentration to an area of low water concentration. • If a cell is placed into a solution with a low concentration of water, then water will move out of the cell by osmosis and the cell will plasmolyse, whereas if a cell is placed into a solution with a high concentration of water, then water will move into the cell by osmosis and become turgid.

Keep in mind

It is very important that students are able to use microscopes effectively to observe microscopic structures. It is worth checking that they are seeing what is intended, perhaps by showing a similar photograph or using a microscope camera to show a suitable example from the class. Students should be using key words here but they may need help with meaning, spelling and/or pronunciation.

Issues for discussion

What will happen to the cells in the salt solution if they were then placed in distilled water (this can be done as an addition to the practical by drawing out salt water using filter paper and replacing it with distilled water)? *Students should observe that plasmolysed cells that were in the salt water solution start to become more turgid due to water diffusing into the cells from the distilled water, by osmosis.*

Why does plasmolysis happen? This occurs when the solute in the solution surrounding the onion cell is more concentrated than the cytoplasm so water moves out of the cytoplasm and into the surrounding solution by osmosis. This causes the cell membrane to move away from the cell wall and the cell vacuole to shrink. The reverse is true when the cell is placed in distilled water; the cell vacuole expands and the cytoplasm presses against the cell wall and the cell is said to be turgid.

Health and safety

As with any microscope work students should always carry the microscope with two hands and use the equipment with care.

   Glass slides and cover slips are easily lost or broken.

   Students may have access to sharp knives or scalpels to cut the onion piece.

Equipment

Per pair of students:

   A small piece of onion (red onions are better as there is a natural dye in the red epidermal cells)

   Knife to cut the onion

   Microscope

   Microscope slides and cover slips (enough to match the number of different concentrations of salt solution)

   Mounted needle for careful placing of cover slip

   Distilled water

   Sodium chloride solutions (ranging from 1 to 5 per cent salt concentration)

4.11 Root tip preparation and the mitotic index

Learning objectives

- To prepare a root tip squash and observe cells undergoing mitosis.
- To calculate the mitotic index and use this to think about how much time cells spend in mitosis.

Procedure

Students should work in pairs. Students should each have access to one or two growing root tips from garlic cloves or onions. Each pair should use a scalpel to cut off about 1 cm of the root from the tip. This should be placed in ethanoic acid in a watch glass for about 10 minutes to fix the cells. During this time they should warm a small volume (no more than about 20 ml) of hydrochloric acid in a water bath at 60 °C in a small beaker. Rinse the root tips in cold water for a few minutes before placing them in the beaker of warm hydrochloric acid for 5 minutes, to soften the root by breaking down the cell walls which also allows more effective uptake of the stain. Then rinse the root tips again in cold water for a few minutes.

The root tips should be carefully removed from the water and placed on a glass slide using a mounted needle. The students should cut off and keep the 2 mm closest to the tip and dispose of the rest. Then the stain is added and left for a few minutes to have greater effect. The tissue can be broken up with the mounted needle before the cover slip is placed over the root tips to squash them. This needs to be done carefully to try to reduce air bubbles and so the cover slip does not break. A few layers of paper towel can be placed over the coverslip before pushing down on it with the thumb. View the slide under a light microscope, preferably at high power, and count the number of cells undergoing mitosis and those that are not (see Figure 4.8).

This is not a straightforward procedure, and students should be told that all of them may not be able to find cells undergoing mitosis.

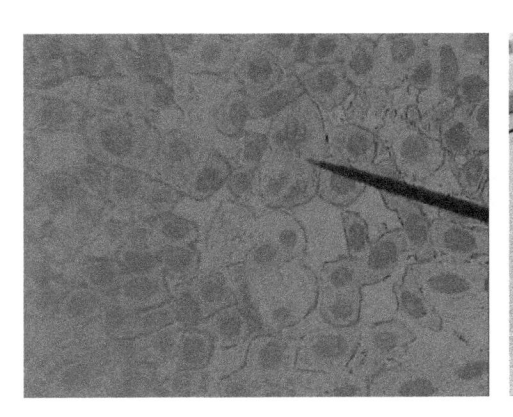

Figure 4.8
(a) Garlic root tip squash showing mitosis in some cells (photograph by Stef Lesnianski and Claire Simpson).
(b) Experimental set-up (photograph by Claire Simpson)

Effectiveness matrix

	Domain of observables	Domain of ideas
What students do	Students can: • Prepare a root tip squash. • Use the microscope to count the number of cells undergoing mitosis.	Students can talk about: • How cells are at different stages of the cell cycle, including mitosis. • How the mitotic index can be calculated. • The proportion of cells (a) undergoing mitosis, and (b) interphase.
What students learn	Students can later: • Make a microscope slide of a sample using a stain. • View a microscope slide at high power.	Students can later talk about: • How chromatids separate during mitosis and how daughter cells are formed. • The purpose of mitosis for growth and repair. • How the proportion of cells undergoing mitosis provides an estimate of the proportion of time each cell spends in mitosis.

Keep in mind

Some students may need extra support in calculating the mitotic index if they are not confident in mathematics. The mitotic index (MI) is calculated from the number of cells in the field of view as:

MI = number of actively dividing cells observed/total number of cells observed

Students need reminding about how cells typically look at the different stages of mitosis and when not undergoing mitosis.

For an additional task: Can students recognize cells undergoing different phases of mitosis?

Issues for discussion

Why isn't every cell in a visible stage of mitosis? *Not all cells are actively dividing all of the time. Interphase is when cells are carrying out other processes including growing in size. During interphase, the DNA also replicates in preparation for mitosis. This is by far the longest phase and so the majority of cells will be seen at interphase.*

Why can we see what is happening to the chromosomes during mitosis but not during interphase? *During mitosis, the DNA in the chromosomes is condensed and the chromosomes coil and this has the visual effect of thickening the chromosomes so that they become visible.*

Why do root cells divide by mitosis? *This type of cell division enables the growth of the organism and the repair of worn-out or damaged cells. All daughter (new) cells have the same genetic material as the parent cell.*

Health and safety

Goggles must be worn at all times as warm 1.0 M hydrochloric acid is hazardous. Students will also be using ethanoic acid (which is flammable and corrosive) and a stain, for example, toluidine blue, which may not be hazardous but will stain clothes.

Scalpels or sharp knives must be handled with care, especially when being carried.

Equipment

Students should work in pairs. Each pair has:

- 2 root tips cut about 1 cm from the end
- Scalpel
- Watch glass
- Small bottle of ethanoic acid
- Small beaker of distilled water
- Small beaker of 1 M hydrochloric acid
- Mounted needle
- Slide and cover slip
- Stain (e.g. toluidine blue)
- Microscope

There should be access to:

- Water bath at 60 °C

4.12 Investigating the effects of evolution using a model

Learning objectives

- To understand the changes in a population due to predation over time.
- To understand weaknesses and strengths of this investigation as a model for evolution.

Procedure

Students should work in pairs. Each pair counts equal numbers of dyed rice grains of two different colours (e.g. sixty of each colour) which are placed in a tray of dyed vermiculite. One colour of the rice grains should be the same colour as the vermiculite and one a contrasting colour. In a given time (e.g. 30 seconds) one student should remove as many rice grains as possible, using the forceps. After the given time students should count the number of rice grains of each colour removed and calculate the number of each colour that is left. The number of missing rice grains should be replaced by adding them to the vermiculite mixture (in this example, to make a total of 120 grains), by adding equal numbers of grains of the two colours. The number of rice grains of each colour in the mixture should be noted. If the number of rice grains to be added is an odd number then the students should be asked to round up to the next number to make it even. The procedure should be repeated twice more and the final numbers of both colours counted.

Students should be encouraged to think about the model and how each element (rice and vermiculite) and procedure relates to evolution: rice represents prey; vermiculite represents the habitat; the student removing the rice grains represents predation; and each cycle represents a new generation with the added rice grains representing reproduction. However, the number of grains added is not proportional to the number of grains left at each cycle. This means that the numbers of the differently coloured rice grains and their proportions will be different at the start of each cycle.

Effectiveness matrix

	Domain of observables	Domain of ideas
What students do	Students can: • Remove as many rice grains as possible in a given time from the mixture and count the grains of each colour, recording this in a table. • Follow the procedure 3 times and make an accurate record of the number of differently coloured rice grains in the population at the end of each cycle.	Students can talk about: • How those grains of rice (colour 1) which are the same colour as the vermiculite are harder to see and those (colour 2) which are in contrast to the colour of the vermiculite are easier to see. • How there are more colour 2 rice grains removed than colour 1 rice grains. • How the proportion of colour 1 rice grains increases and how the proportion of colour 2 rice grains decreases with each stage of the model.
What students learn	Students can later: • Use a similar method to investigate other population changes. • Follow a complicated procedure using a table to manage data collection.	Students can later talk about: • How this model represents prey being removed from a population, for example, like caterpillars being eaten by birds. • How each stage of the model represents another generation. • How individuals who are less well camouflaged will experience more predation than those who are better camouflaged and how the better camouflaged individuals are more likely to survive and breed to pass on their genes.

Keep in mind

This is quite complex in that students must complete a table with several calculations in it. Students might need help to design the table and to manage the data recording process.

Issues for discussion

Why is this a good model for evolution? *This models a relationship between predator and prey. This shows that camouflage is an effective way of reducing predation as the population of the rice grains of the same colour of the vermiculite should increase in size as the contrasting coloured rice decreases. The fact that the populations change over time is modelling evolution.*

Why is this a poor model of evolution? *This does not allow for any other features in a predator–prey relationship, for example, movement of the prey to avoid the predator or the influence of other populations. It is also unlikely that the same number of each population would be produced every cycle (generation).*

Health and safety

There are no health and safety issues associated with this practical so long as students don't eat the rice.

Equipment

Per pair of students:

- A small tray or Petri dish of vermiculite, dyed a bright colour (e.g. green)
- A small handful of rice dyed the same colour as the vermiculite
- A small handful of rice dyed a contrasting colour to the vermiculite
- A pair of forceps
- Stop clock

Adapted from the Nuffield Foundation Practical Biology protocol

Template for a results table:

	Number of grains removed		Number of grains added		Percentage of grains of each colour	
	Colour A	Colour B	Colour A	Colour B	Colour A	Colour B
Start					50	50
Cycle 1						
Cycle 2						
Cycle 3						

Chemistry: Session Guides 11–14

Ann Childs and Elaine Wilson

5

5.1 Separating the colours in black ink (p. 98)
5.2 Which is the most reactive halogen? (p. 101)
5.3 What substances cause hard water? (p. 104)
5.4 What salts are present in sea water? (p. 108)
5.5 What is the most reactive metal? (p. 111)
5.6 The difference between elements, mixtures and compounds (p. 116)
5.7 The extraction of metals from their ores using carbon (p. 119)
5.8 Plants as indicators (p. 122)
5.9 Diffusion of ions in solution – the case of lead(II) iodide (p. 126)
5.10 Using universal indicator to illustrate the process of neutralisation (p. 129)
5.11 Analysis of combustion products when a candle burns (p. 132)
5.12 The thermal decomposition of copper carbonate (p. 136)

5.1 Separating the colours in black ink

Learning objectives

- To be able to describe and explain how chromatography can be used to separate mixtures.
- To be able to calculate R_f values for the components from the separation of mixtures.

Procedure

Paper chromatography is the simplest method to use to demonstrate the principles of chromatography using soluble inks. Black ink is particularly good because it is often made of a number of different coloured inks. A line about 1 cm from the bottom of the filter paper is drawn using a pencil and ruler and a spot of soluble black ink is made on the filter paper on that line. The filter paper is placed in a beaker with a small amount of water in such a way that the water level is *below* the pencil line on the filter paper. The upper end of the filter paper is bent over to hold it in place (see Figure 5.1). The water is then left to rise up through the filter paper, which separates the colours in the ink.

Figure 5.1
How to set up a chromatogram

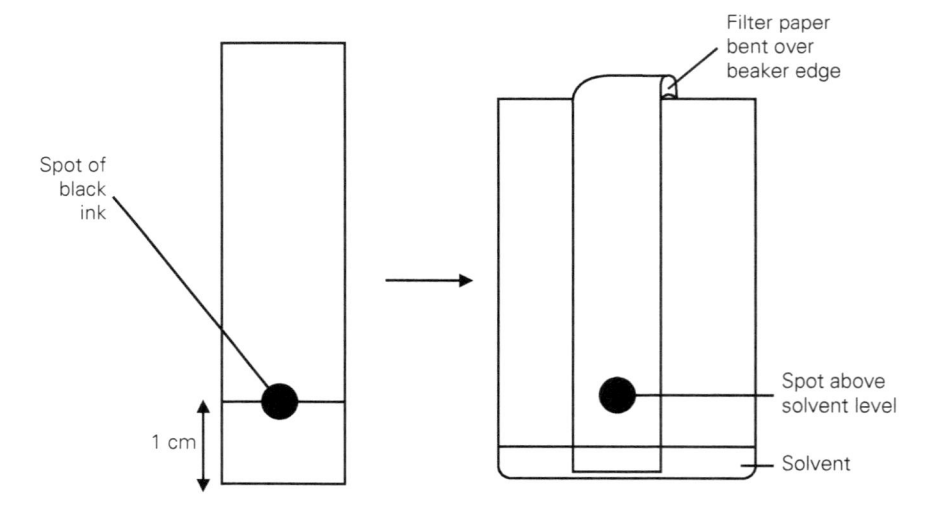

Variation on this method

(i) *Forensic science variation*

A scenario could be created where teachers show students a forged cheque and students are asked to provide evidence from the experiment to eliminate various suspects. Each group is given a piece of filter paper with a spot of ink extracted from the cheque. Students then put spots of ink from the suspects on the pencil line. They then place their filter paper in the beaker (see Figure 5.1) and this will be used to eliminate various suspects and provide evidence in court, amongst other evidence, of who might be the forger. The suspect most likely to be the forger is identified by the pen that has the same separation pattern as the ink from the forged cheque (confirmed by calculating R_f values).

(ii) *Food colours*

Food colours can be separated into different colours. A good example is the food colour in a brown smartie. This is best done by putting a circular piece of filter paper on a beaker. The brown smartie is placed on the centre of the filter paper and a drop of water is added to the smartie and then drops are added very slowly. The water dissolves the brown food dye which then spreads out in a circle on the filter paper and the different colours (green/yellow outer ring, red inner ring) can be distinguished.

Effectiveness matrix

	Domain of observables	Domain of ideas
What students do	Students can: • Carry out the procedures as described above to separate the colours in black ink.	Students can talk about: • State the different colours of the different inks present in the ink under test. • Explain how chromatography can separate the different colours in inks (i.e. because different colours in the ink mixture travel at different rates as the water rises up the filter paper).
What students learn	Students can later: • Carry out further investigations to investigate the mixtures of colours in other inks and food dyes.	Students can later talk about: • Why the different components in the mixture of the ink under test travel at different rates (i.e. different colour inks have different affinities with stationary phase (paper) and mobile phase (water)). Those with a strong affinity to the stationary phase travel the least difference and those with the greatest affinity to the mobile phase (water) travel further. • Determine R_f values for the different components of a mixture.

Keep in mind

There needs to be some explanation accompanying this experiment about why the components separate. The calculation of R_f values can be used in the forensic science example to show which two inks are the same because they will be made up of components with the same R_f values. Although this can also be determined by observation, the use of R_f values makes the method more accurate. The R_f value = distance moved by the compound/distance moved by the solvent. The R_f value of a particular compound is always the same – if the chromatography has been carried out in the same way. This allows industry to use chromatography to identify compounds in mixtures (http://www.bbc.co.uk/schools/gcsebitesize/science/add_edexcel/covalent _compounds/seperationrev2.shtml). Other techniques such as gas chromatography in forensic science as well as how the principles of gas chromatography are similar to the paper chromatography example can be discussed.

Issues for discussion

For the example of the basic separation of one coloured ink, for example black ink, a discussion about which colours travel fastest and which slowest and why can be held.

For the forensic science example, a discussion about how the technique has enabled the identification of the pen which was used for the forgery and the use of R_f values to make this identification more secure.

Health and safety

Laboratory goggles should be worn by all students during the practical.

Students should be told that they should not eat the smarties in the laboratory.

Equipment

250 cm³ beaker

Filter paper (both rectangular and circular)

Pencil

Ruler

Chemicals

Variety of black water-soluble felt-tip pens

Other pen colours

Smarties (brown ones work best)

5.2 Which is the most reactive halogen?

Learning objectives

- To explore the trends in reactivity in Group 7 – the halogens.
- To be able to predict the results for fluorine and astatine.

Procedure

Chlorine water, bromine water and iodine solution (two drops of each) are put on to a spotting tile as shown in Figure 5.2.

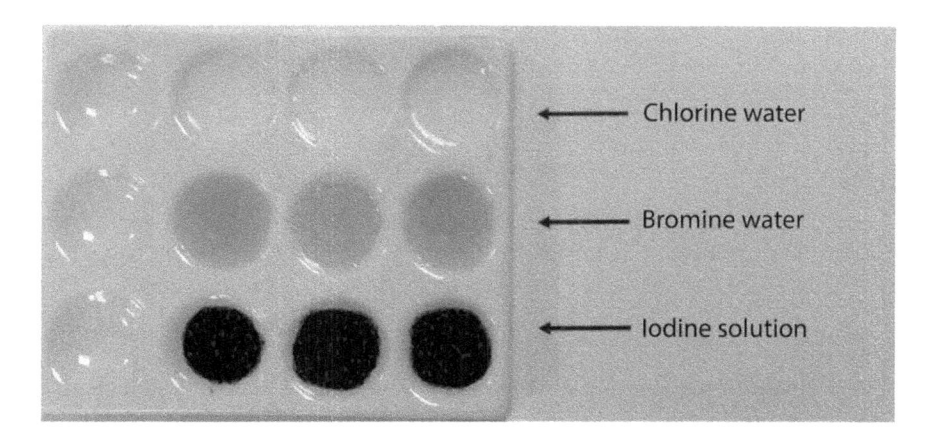

Figure 5.2 Spotting tile with aqueous solutions of elemental halogens

To each are added solutions of potassium chloride, potassium bromide and potassium iodide. Students can note down the colour changes in the following table. These reactions can also be done in test tubes.

	Potassium chloride solution	Potassium bromide solution	Potassium iodide solution
Chlorine water			
Bromine water			
Iodine solution			

Effectiveness matrix

	Domain of observables	Domain of ideas
What students do	Students can: • Set up and carry out the experiment as described, either in test tubes or on a spotting tile.	Students can talk about: • Why some reactions result in halide ions being displaced to form the elemental halogen and some do not, drawing on their understanding of the reactivity of the halogens.
What students learn	Students can later: • Set up and carry out a similar set of displacement experiments for different metals and their metal salt solutions to determine the order of reaction of these metals (see displacement reactions of metals and metal salts).	Students can later: • Predict, using their understanding of the reactivity of the halogens, what would happen if fluorine and astatine were also included.

Keep in mind

As in the case of the displacement reactions for metals, students need to understand what constitutes a reaction here. Reactions are indicated by the following colour changes:

$$Cl_2(aq) + 2KBr(aq) \rightarrow Br_2(aq) + 2KCl(aq)$$

The light yellow colour of the chlorine water changes to an orange solution as elemental bromine is formed.

$$Cl_2(aq) + 2KI(aq) \rightarrow I_2(aq) + 2KCl(aq)$$

The light yellow colour of the chlorine water changes to a brown solution as elemental iodine is formed.

$$Br_2(aq) + 2KI(aq) \rightarrow I_2(aq) + 2KBr(aq)$$

The orange colour of the bromine water changes to a brown solution as elemental iodine is formed.

Issues for discussion

Ask students to explain, using their understanding of the reactivity of halogens, why some reactions occurred and some did not. *Get students to write word and chemical equations for the reactions where displacement occurred.*

Ask students to predict what will happen if fluorine and sodium fluoride and astatine and potassium astatide were used in the experiment. *Get students to write word and chemical equations for the reactions which occurred.*

Health and safety

Laboratory goggles should be worn by all students.

Chlorine water – (low hazard) but chlorine gas which can escape from this solution is hazardous and so chlorine water should have a HARMFUL label – see the CLEAPSS Hazcards and recipe book.

Bromine water (toxic, irritant, harmful) – see the CLEAPSS Hazcards and recipe book.

Iodine solution – (harmful if concentration is equal to or greater than 1 mol dm^{-3}, if less than 1 mol dm^{-3}, then the solution is low hazard) – see the CLEAPSS Hazcards and recipe book.

0.1 mol dm^{-3} solutions of:

Potassium chloride (low hazard) – see the CLEAPSS Hazcards and recipe book

Potassium bromide (low hazard) – see the CLEAPSS Hazcards and recipe book

Potassium iodide solutions (low hazard) – see the CLEAPSS Hazcards and recipe book

Equipment

For each group:
  Test tube rack/test tubes *or* spotting tile
  Plastic dropping pipettes

Chemicals

Chlorine water
Bromine water
Iodine solution

0.1 mol dm^{-3} solutions of

Potassium chloride
Potassium bromide
Potassium iodide

5.3 What substances cause hard water?

Learning objectives

- To carry out tests to distinguish between hard and soft water.
- To identify the ions which cause hard water.
- To explain why some areas of the United Kingdom have hard water and other areas do not.

Procedure

Stage 1: What is the difference between hard water and soft water?

(i) Students take two test tubes in a test tube rack and fill one to 2 cm height with a sample of hard water and the other to 2 cm height with a sample of soft water (distilled or deionized water). Three to four drops of soap solution are added to each test tube, a stopper added and the mixture is shaken vigorously.

(ii) Optional – students put about 20 cm^3 of hard water into an evaporating basin and 20 cm^3 of two samples of soft water (one distilled water and one sodium chloride solution) into two other evaporating basins. The evaporating basins are either left for a few days for the water to evaporate or kept on a tripod and gauze on a heat-resistant mat and the water evaporated using a Bunsen burner (different groups could be given different samples of water to evaporate).

Results from (i) are intended to establish that the addition of soap solution to hard water forms scum and very little lather and the addition of soap solution to soft water produces no scum and larger amounts of lather. Results from (ii) will show that

- Hard water contains dissolved substances which cause it to be hard.
- Some soft water contains no dissolved substances and some soft water does contain dissolved substances, but that these substances do not cause the water to become hard.

Stage 2: What substances cause hard water?

Students are given five solutions and they test each one for hardness as described in stage 1: sodium chloride solution; calcium chloride solution; magnesium chloride solution; sodium sulphate solution; magnesium sulphate solution.

This stage of the experiment should establish that it is calcium (Ca^{2+}) ions and magnesium (Mg^{2+}) ions which cause the hardness in water. The use of sodium chloride and sodium sulphate solutions, which will both be soft and lather well, should help students to conclude that it is the Ca^{2+} and Mg^{2+} ions which cause hardness not the chloride (Cl^-) or sulphate (SO_4^{2-}) ions. Word equations showing the formation of scum, magnesium and calcium stearate can be introduced.

Effectiveness matrix

	Domain of observables	Domain of ideas
What students do	Students can: • Carry out the experiments in stages 1 and 2.	Students can: • Explain how to carry out tests to distinguish hard and soft water. • State that calcium (Ca^{2+}) ions and magnesium (Mg^{2+}) ions dissolved in water cause the water to be hard.
What students learn	Students can later: • Plan and carry out tests on a range of samples of water to distinguish if they are hard or soft. • Test for calcium (Ca^{2+}) ions or magnesium (Mg^{2+}) ions. See p. 41 for details (see Section 6.1) to determine which ion is causing the water to be hard.	Students can later: • Explain and write a word equation to show how scum is formed when soap solution is added to magnesium (Mg^{2+}) ions and calcium (Ca^{2+}) ions. • State that chloride (Cl^-) ions or sulphate (SO_4^{2-}) ions do not cause hardness and explain how the evidence from the experiment demonstrates this. • Explain why water in a particular area (either their own water or commercially bottled water) is hard or soft because of the rock formations in the area from which the water is sourced.

Keep in mind

(i) This experiment is very flexible and can form part of an investigation where pupils can bring in samples of water from their homes or from visits/trips and test them for hardness. In addition, when they have done work on Section 6.1 (see experiment p. 141), if their water sample is hard they can test it to see if calcium (Ca^{2+}) ions or magnesium (Mg^{2+}) ions are causing the hardness.

(ii) Iron(II) (Fe^{2+}) ions and Iron(III) (Fe^{3+}) ions also cause water to be hard but are less commonly the cause of hard water. However, iron(II) sulphate solution and iron(III) nitrate solutions could also be included. If iron(III) nitrate solution is included, then potassium or sodium nitrate solutions would need to be added to eliminate the nitrate ion as a source of hardness.

(iii) The water samples can be linked to the local geography and rock formations to explain why the water is hard or soft. Maps can be displayed on laboratory walls as an ongoing project for a science club, for example and as students collect water samples and test them they can be added to the map. In addition, commercially branded bottled water can be tested from a range of sources. Students could be asked to read the labels and predict from the substances in the water if the water will be hard or soft. These could also be added to the map.

(iv) Students can carry out further work in distinguishing permanently hard from temporary hard water (http://www.nuffieldfoundation.org/practical-chemistry/testing-hardness-water).

Issues for discussion

What is observed when soap solution is added to hard and soft water?

What is scum? What is the word equation for the formation of scum?

Which ions cause hard water?

What chemical test can you do to distinguish between calcium (Ca^{2+}) ions and magnesium (Mg^{2+}) ions?

Why is the water in your area hard/soft?

Is sea water hard or soft? (for links to the experiment see Section 5.4, p. 105)

Health and safety

Laboratory goggles should be worn by all students.

As the hard water solution evaporates, it will begin to spit when almost all of the water has evaporated. Therefore, ask students to turn off the Bunsen burner when there is still a little solution in the evaporating basin and let the rest of the water evaporate off without the Bunsen burner as a heat source.

0.1 mol dm^{-3} solutions of:

Sodium chloride, calcium chloride, magnesium chloride, sodium sulphate, magnesium sulphate (low hazard) – see CLEAPSS Hazcards and recipe book.

Soap solution – see CLEAPSS Hazcards and recipe book.

Stage 1:

Equipment

For each group:

2 test tubes and two stoppers

Plastic dropping pipettes for soap solution

Test tube rack

Two evaporating basins

Bunsen burner

Tripod

Gauze

Heat-resistant mat

Chemicals

Soap solution

Sample of hard water (e.g. magnesium sulphate solution, 0.1 mol dm^{-3})

Two samples of soft water (one distilled water and one containing a salt that does not cause hardness, for example sodium chloride, 0.1 mol dm^{-3})

Stage 2:

Equipment

For each group:

6 test tubes

Stoppers

Test tube racks

Plastic dropping pipettes for soap solution

Chemicals

0.1 mol dm^{-3} solutions of sodium chloride solution, calcium chloride solution, magnesium chloride solution, sodium sulphate solution, magnesium sulphate solution

Soap solution

5.4 What salts are present in sea water?

Learning objectives

- To name the different salts present in sea water.
- To explore the different solubility of the salts in sea water.
- To identify the different ions present in sea water (extension).

Procedure

Stage 1:

Sea water is put into an evaporating basin and left to evaporate slowly over a week (to make this even more impressive, top up with sea water a few times). Figure 5.3 shows how the salts in sea water deposit (in an ideal situation). The most soluble salts are the last to crystallize and so form the inner core in the evaporating basin.

Figure 5.3
Diagram of an evaporating dish to show the deposition of salts from sea water

Note: If you are in a school which cannot get sea water, then a solution of sea water can be made (see chemicals below to explain how). In addition, some aquaria sell sea water crystals or these can be bought on the Internet.

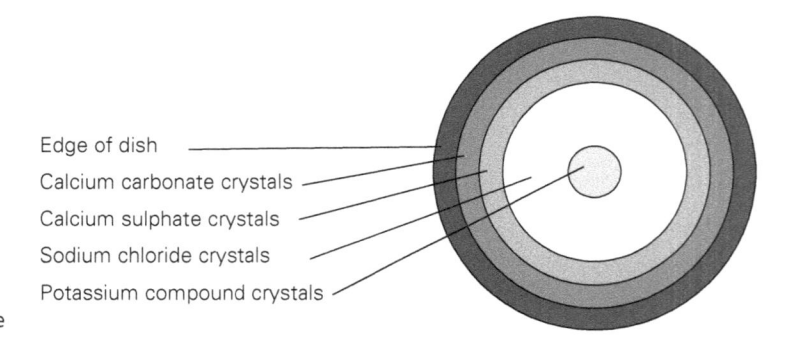

- Edge of dish
- Calcium carbonate crystals
- Calcium sulphate crystals
- Sodium chloride crystals
- Potassium compound crystals

Stage 2: Extension – verifying the ions present in the different bands

See Section 6.1 practical for details about how to test for the positive and negative ions in each band that has crystallized. Different groups could be given different compounds from the different bands produced in stage 1 to test.

Effectiveness matrix

	Domain of observables	Domain of ideas
What students do	Students can: • Follow the instructions to get a good banding of different chemicals crystallizing from the sea water.	Students can: • Explain that sea water is made up of different salts and not just sodium chloride.
What students learn	Students can later: • Carry out tests for ions successfully to identify and verify the ions present in the different bands produced by different samples of sea water.	Students can later: • Explain how the solubility of the different salts produces the different bands in the evaporating dish. • Use the evidence from their tests to show which ions are present in the different bands.

Keep in mind

Many students may think that sea water contains only sodium chloride and so this experiment will challenge that preconception. The crystallization of the salts may not produce perfect bands and so there will be some overlap of ions between bands.

Issues for discussion

Before starting the experiment, students can be asked about what they think sea water contains. After the experiment and the testing of the different bands, questions can be asked about:

What ions does each band contain? How do they know?

What compound is most soluble in sea water? Why?

Which is least soluble? Why?

If they have done the experiment to determine the ions which cause hard water, there could be a discussion about whether sea water is hard or soft.

In addition, students could discuss or be asked to research how salt is crystallized from brine industrially and about the different commercial uses of the salts present in sea water. In the experiment students may not get well-differentiated bands. So, a discussion can be held about why their experiment did not produce good differentiation and how good separation is achieved in industry so that the different components do not contaminate each other.

Health and safety

Laboratory goggles should be worn by all students.

Potassium chloride (low hazard) – see CLEAPSS Hazcards and recipe book.

Sodium chloride (low hazard) – see CLEAPSS Hazcards and recipe book.

Calcium sulphate (low hazard) – see CLEAPSS Hazcards and recipe book.

Calcium carbonate (low hazard) – see CLEAPSS Hazcards and recipe book.

See Section 6.1 practical for details.

Equipment

For each group:

Evaporating basin

See Section 6.1 practical for equipment needed to test for cations and anions.

Chemicals

Sea water (either sea water or commercially made sea water from the Internet). If a solution of salt is made up, it is advisable to look up relative proportions of each salt. The predominant salt is sodium chloride, making up over 50 per cent of most samples of sea water; the other salts are in smaller proportions.

See Section 6.1 practical experiment for equipment needed to test for cations and anions.

5.5 What is the most reactive metal?

Learning objectives

- To explain, using the reactivity series of metals, why some metals will displace other metal ions from their solutions and others will not.

Procedure

Samples of metals:

Magnesium ribbon (small 1 cm lengths).

Zinc foil or granules.

Lead foil cut into small squares.

Iron filings.

Copper foil cut into small squares or copper turnings.

Are reacted with a range of solutions (0.1 mol dm^{-3}) of the salts of these metals:

Magnesium sulphate solution.

Zinc sulphate solution.

Iron(II) sulphate solution (The solution is oxidized slowly by air and so should be stored in a sealed container in cool conditions – the solution should be a pale green colour; if it is more yellow, then oxidation may have taken place.)

Lead(II) nitrate solution.

Copper(II) sulphate solution.

These series of reactions can be carried out in the following two ways:

(i) In tests tubes.
(ii) On spotting tiles.

There are advantages and disadvantages of both.

Test tubes	Spotting tiles
Advantages • There is no cross-contamination of solutions as each experiment is conducted in a separate test tube.	**Advantages** • Small amounts of the metals and their salt solutions are used. • The spotting tile allows students to see all of the experiments at once. • Disposal is easier – all solutions and metals can be washed into a large container or beaker.

Test tubes	Spotting tiles
Disadvantages • Larger amounts of solution are used. • Large numbers of test tubes are used if each group does all the combinations (although groups can be allocated to do some of the combinations and then results are shared between groups).	**Disadvantages** • Solutions can often mix together on the tile and cross-contaminate each reaction. • The students have to label their spotting tiles clearly or they can be confused about which metal/metal ion combination is on each 'spot'.

Students could be asked to fill in a table below and predict if a reaction will occur using the reactivity series of metals before trying it out.

	Magnesium sulphate		Zinc sulphate		Iron(II) sulphate		Lead(II) nitrate		Copper(II) sulphate	
Magnesium	Prediction	Result	Prediction	Result	Prediction	Result	Prediction	Result	Prediction	Result
Zinc	Prediction	Result	Prediction	Result	Prediction	Result	Prediction	Result	Prediction	Result
Iron	Prediction	Result	Prediction	Result	Prediction	Result	Prediction	Result	Prediction	Result
Lead	Prediction	Result	Prediction	Result	Prediction	Result	Prediction	Result	Prediction	Result
Copper	Prediction	Result	Prediction	Result	Prediction	Result	Prediction	Result	Prediction	Result

Effectiveness matrix

	Domain of observables	Domain of ideas
What students do	Students can: • Carry out the experiment as described either in test tubes or on spotting tiles.	Students can talk about: • Why some reactions result in metal ions being displaced and some do not, drawing on their understanding of the reactivity series of metals.
What students learn	Students can later: • Set up and carry out a similar set of displacement experiments for different halogen solution with their halide salt solutions to determine the order of reaction of the halogens (see Section 5.2).	Students can later: • Predict using the reactivity series what will happen when pairs of metal and metal ions are reacted. • Explain their prediction using their understanding of the reactivity series of metals. • Explain why some combinations predicted to react do not do so (i.e. because the two metals are very close together in the reactivity series of metals).

Keep in mind

This practical can be used to establish a reactivity series from the metal/metal ion combinations used in the reaction. In practice this is challenging because metals that are close together in the reactivity series often do not react and this can be potentially confusing. Therefore, this experiment focuses on the power of the reactivity series of metals to predict which pairs will react and which will not and then asks students to test their predictions.

It is important to establish with students what constitutes a reaction. Students will often see small bubbles on the surface of the metal in the salt solution and record this as a positive reaction. This is the metal reacting with H^+ ions in some of the salt solutions to form hydrogen gas on the surface of the metal. A possible way around this is to do one worked example as a class demonstration such as copper and silver nitrate. Students could first be asked to predict from the reactivity series of metals if copper will displace silver from silver nitrate solution. The reaction could then be demonstrated in a test tube with a coil of copper wire lowered into dilute silver nitrate solution (or use a combination such as an iron nail in copper(II) sulphate solution if silver nitrate solution is not available). Initially, a grey sludge of silver forms on the copper wire but as the reaction proceeds, a very fine and sparkling thread of silver metal forms. Furthermore, the solution turns from colourless to blue, indicating the presence of Cu^{2+} ions in solution (see Figure 5.4). The modelling of this one example shows that students are looking for the formation of a metal (on the surface of the original metal) and this is what indicates that a reaction has taken place. It also models how to use the reactivity series of metals to predict the outcome of combinations of metals and metal ions in solution before students undertake other combinations themselves.

Issues for discussion

Why some metals do not displace the metal ion from its solution when predicted to do so?

Discuss other combinations and get students to predict if a reaction will occur or not.

If other displacement reactions, such as the thermite reaction (aluminium and iron(III) oxide), have been demonstrated, discuss how the principles from this experiment link and apply to that reaction.

Discuss links to the extraction of metals from their ores and link to the experiment such as copper(II) oxide and carbon, iron(III) oxide and carbon.

Health and safety

Laboratory goggles should be worn by all students.

0.1 mol dm^{-3} solutions of:

Lead(II) nitrate (toxic) – see the CLEAPSS Hazcards and recipe book.

Copper(II) sulphate – see the CLEAPSS Hazcards and recipe book.

Magnesium sulphate (low hazard) – see the CLEAPSS Hazcards and recipe book.

Zinc sulphate – see the CLEAPSS Hazcards and recipe book.

Iron(II) sulphate (irritant) – see the CLEAPSS Hazcards and recipe book.

Silver nitrate – see the CLEAPSS Hazcards and recipe book.

Magnesium ribbon (low hazard).

Lead foil (toxic, dangerous for the environment) – see the CLEAPSS Hazcards and recipe book.

Copper wire and copper foil (low hazard).

Zinc foil or granules (low hazard).

Iron filings (low hazard).

Equipment

For each group:

Spotting/dimple tile method	Test tube method
• Spotting tile – if students do all the experiments, they will need a tile with twenty dimples/depressions; however, if different groups of students are allocated different combinations and then results are pooled, smaller tiles can be used. • Plastic dropping pipettes (must be washed clean of salt solutions between each experiment). • Felt-tip pen or other means of labelling the dimples on the spotting tile.	• Twenty test tubes (fewer if different groups of students are allocated different combinations and then results are pooled). • Test tube rack. • Plastic dropping pipettes (must be washed clean of salt solutions between each experiment). • Felt-tip pen or other means of labelling.

Chemicals

0.1 mol dm^{-3} solutions of:

Magnesium sulphate solution

Zinc sulphate solution

Iron(II) sulphate solution

Lead(II) nitrate solution

Copper(II) sulphate solution

Iron filings (a pinch)

Lead foil cut into small squares (1 cm length)

Magnesium ribbon (1 cm length)

Zinc foil or granules

Copper foil cut into small squares or copper turnings

For the demonstration

Copper wire 20 cm (wind this around a pencil and draw out into a coil)

Silver nitrate solution (0.1 mol dm^{-3})

Test tube

Test tube rack

Figure 5.4
Copper coil coated in crystals of silver metal – note the colour of the solution is now blue due to the presence of Cu^{2+} ions in solution.

5.6 The difference between elements, mixtures and compounds

Learning objectives

- To describe the differences between elements, mixtures and compounds.
- To explain the differences between elements, mixtures and compounds.

Procedure

The first step is to produce a mixture of the two elements iron and sulphur. This can be done as a demonstration to the whole class on a sheet of white A4 paper. Start with two separate piles of sulphur and iron and emphasize that these are elements and get students to note the appearance of each element and then to mix them together at the centre of the paper. Again get the students to describe the appearance of the mixture. Take a spatula of this mixture and put it on another piece of paper. Use a magnet wrapped in paper to show that this mixture can be separated, in this case by using a magnet because of the magnetic properties of iron. It can be helpful to have two different colours of plastic beads which join together to model iron atoms and sulphur atoms. When the beads are mixed it can be seen that the iron and sulphur can be pulled out as there are no bonds between the atoms and then, after reaction, the beads can be joined together to model the chemical bonding in iron(II) sulphide (FeS). The Royal Society of Chemistry guidelines for this experiment suggest that students are given ignition tubes already one quarter full of the iron and sulphur in a 7:4 mixture (0.125 moles of each solid). The students need to plug the ignition tube with mineral wool. This is essential to prevent sulphur vapour from escaping as it can catch fire and combust to form sulphur dioxide gas (see CLEAPSS Hazcards and recipe book). The ignition tube, held by a test tube holder, is heated strongly in a Bunsen burner with the air hole open. It is important that the mixture is heated until it just begins to glow red and then the Bunsen burner is immediately switched off so that students can see the red glow spread throughout the mixture. The hot ignition tube can then be left on a heat-resistant mat to cool down. Once cool, it is possible to break open the ignition tubes to show the appearance of the product, iron(II) sulphide. The ignition tubes can be broken open using a pestle and mortar and this is best done by the teacher wearing protective gloves. However, ignition tubes are very hard and so the teacher could also demonstrate the reaction in a test tube and only break this tube open. It is an important part of the practical to show that the compound iron(II) sulphide is non-magnetic because this emphasizes the key chemical point that two elements have reacted together to form a compound in which the elements are chemically combined with chemical bonds between iron and sulphur atoms.

Effectiveness matrix

	Domain of observables	Domain of ideas
What students do	Students can: • Set up the equipment, for example set up the Bunsen burner on a heat-resistant mat and heat the iron and sulphur in the ignition tube safely without igniting the sulphur vapour.	Students can: • Discuss the fact that the product formed is different from both the original elements (it is now a black solid) and cannot be separated using a magnet and is therefore a compound.
What students learn	This quadrant is intentionally blank in this task.	Students can later talk about: • How the key difference between a mixture and a compound is that the atoms of iron and sulphur in iron(II) sulphide are chemically bonded and so cannot be separated using a magnet. In the mixture, the atoms are not chemically bonded and so can be separated using a magnet. (See suggestion of use of models to help this explanation).

Keep in mind

When the magnet is passed over the reaction products, quite often there is some unreacted iron left in the reaction products which is attracted to the magnet. This is usually because, even though a stoichiometric mixture of 7:4 has been used, some sulphur escapes as described above and this leaves unreacted iron. As part of the follow-up to this experiment, this issue should be discussed.

A really good teacher demonstration that reinforces the points about the difference between an element and a compound is the reaction between aluminium and iodine (details from http://www.nuffieldfoundation.org/practical-chemistry/reaction-between-aluminium-and-iodine). Aluminium iodide is very different in appearance from its constituent elements. Where this demonstration is not so good is emphasizing the difference between a mixture and a compound. When aluminium and iodine solids are mixed, there is no easy way to show how they can be separated as is the case with the iron and sulphur example. However, this point could be discussed and students could be asked about how they could separate a mixture of aluminium and iodine.

Issues for discussion

What is the difference between the elements iron and sulphur?

What is the difference between the mixture of iron and sulphur and the compound iron(II) sulphide?

Take this in stages – comparisons both on appearance of the elements, mixture and compound and on whether, for the mixture and compound, elements can be separated.

Why is it possible to separate the iron from the sulphur in the mixture?

Why is it not possible to separate the iron from the sulphur in the compound iron(II) sulphide?

What was observed during the experiment which showed a chemical reaction was taking place? (The same can be asked of the aluminium and iodine reaction if this is demonstrated.)

Why was there some unreacted iron still present in the products?

Health and safety

Laboratory goggles should be worn by all students.

Use small ignition tubes with students since this limits the amount of the iron and sulphur mixture that is used.

Ensure the ignition tubes have small plug of mineral wool in them to prevent the sulphur escaping and combusting to produce sulphur dioxide gas.

Emphasize to students that, after the reaction has taken place, they must place their ignition tubes on their heat-resistant mats.

Sulphur (low hazard) – see CLEAPSS Hazcards and recipe book.

Iron filings (low hazard) – see CLEAPSS Hazcards and recipe book.

Sulphur dioxide (formed if the sulphur ignites) (toxic) – see CLEAPSS Hazcards and recipe book.

Equipment

For each group:

Ignition tubes one quarter filled with a ready prepared sample of iron and sulphur (7:4 ratio) with a plug of mineral wool

Test tube holders

Bunsen burner

Heat-resistant mat

For the teacher demonstration:

Magnet wrapped in cling film or paper (for teacher demonstration)

A4 sheet of paper

Sample of 4 g of sulphur and 7 g of iron in separate containers

5.7 The extraction of metals from their ores using carbon

Learning objectives

- To explore how carbon can be used to extract some metals from their ores.
- To explain why carbon can be used to extract some metals from their ores using an understanding of the reactivity series of metals.

Procedure

The reactivity series and the position of carbon within it can be used to predict whether carbon can be used to extract metals from their ores, for example iron from iron(III) oxide, lead from lead(II) oxide and copper from copper(II) oxide. Carbon in all these cases acts as a reducing agent. These combinations can then be tested in the laboratory as described below.

Iron(III) oxide and carbon

There are two methods recommended here: one from Earth Learning Ideas (i) and the other from the Royal Society of Chemistry (ii).

(i) Take a small wooden stick such as a coffee stirrer or a wooden splint and char it in a flame to produce charcoal at its tip. Dip the end with charcoal on it in iron(III) oxide. Heat this end in the hot inner blue part of a Bunsen flame until it glows orange. Extinguish the flame by stubbing it out on a heat-resistant mat and allow the ash to cool. Once cool, transfer to a mortar and pestle and grind. Empty the ground up ash on to a piece of paper and pass a magnet over the top; small pieces of iron metal should stick to the bar magnet.

(ii) A used match is charred and then moistened with a drop of water and some sodium carbonate crystals are rubbed on. The purpose of the sodium carbonate is to fuse the charcoal and iron(III) oxide reactants together. The charcoal point is dipped into iron(III) oxide and then heated again in the hot inner blue part of a Bunsen flame until the point glows strongly. The method thereafter is the same as in (i).

Copper(II) oxide and carbon

One spatula of copper(II) oxide is added to a small hard glass test tube (ignition tube) and then one spatula of charcoal is placed on top. The hard glass test tube is heated strongly in a Bunsen flame for five minutes. The tube is left to cool on a heat-resistant mat. Once cooled, a layer of copper should be observed where the charcoal and copper(II) oxide meet in the tube and the contents of the tube can be tipped on to a heat proof mat and examined and a red solid, copper metal, will be observed more directly.

Lead(II) oxide and carbon

Lead(II) oxide and charcoal can also be used and one spatula each of charcoal and lead(II) oxide are mixed and heated strongly for five minutes in a hard glass test tube (ignition tube). On cooling, the mixture can be tipped on to a heat-resistant mat and the lead will appear as small grey coloured globules.

Effectiveness matrix

	Domain of observables	Domain of ideas
What students do	Students can: • Set up the experiments as described above and identify the products in each case.	Students can: • Write correct word equations to show what is happening in each of the above reactions and explain the role of carbon in these reactions.
What students learn	Students can later: • Design similar experiments to test other metal ore/carbon systems. • Design a way to test for carbon dioxide gas.	Students can later: • Explain their predictions based on their knowledge of the reactivity series of metals and carbon's position within it. • Predict whether carbon will reduce other metal ores using the reactivity series of metals.

Keep in mind

The results for the lead(II) oxide and carbon are not as clear as the other two examples because the lead globules are difficult to observe. In addition, the use of lead(II) oxide presents some safety issues because of its toxicity, so teachers may prefer not to do this reaction.

Issues for discussion

Predict whether a range of metal ores can be reduced by carbon using the reactivity series of metals before beginning these experiments. Write word or chemical equations to show the products.

The reactions students predict will result in the ore being reduced by carbon and could also be used to discuss what students would then predict to observe as the reaction proceeds.

Students could research how these reactions are scaled up to an industrial scale, for example in the Blast Furnace and how previous civilizations have extracted metals from their ores, for example the extraction or iron from iron ore in Tanzania.

Students could also be asked to research how to extract metals from ores where carbon cannot be used, for example aluminium oxide (bauxite).

Health and safety

Laboratory goggles should be worn by all students.

Copper(II) oxide (harmful, dangerous for the environment) – see CLEAPSS Hazcards.

Lead(II) oxide (toxic, dangerous for the environment) – see CLEAPSS Hazcards.

Iron(III) oxide (low hazard) – see CLEAPSS Hazcards and recipe book.

Charcoal (low hazard) – see CLEAPSS Hazcards and recipe book.

Sodium carbonate (irritant) – see the CLEAPSS Hazcards and recipe book.

Danger of burns from hot ignition tubes.

Equipment

For each group:

2 small hard glass ignition tubes

Spatula

Test tube holder

Bunsen burner

Heat-resistant mat

If using bottle tops for copper(II) oxide and carbon

For each group:

Bottle top (with plastic interior removed)

Tongs

Chemicals

Burned matches, wooden splits

Charcoal

Lead(II) oxide

Copper(II) oxide

Iron(III) oxide

Sodium carbonate

5.8 Plants as indicators

Learning objectives

- To explore which parts of different plants make effective[1] acid/alkali indicators.

Procedure

This is a good practical to do after using common laboratory indicators, for example litmus and universal indicator. Red cabbage makes a good natural indicator.

A total of 50 cm^3 of water in a 250 cm^3 beaker is boiled on a tripod and gauze using a Bunsen burner. Students then add six pieces of red cabbage to the boiling water and simmer on a low heat for five minutes. The water turns blue. The Bunsen burner is turned off and the indicator solution is left to cool (the indicator could be prepared before it is used). The red cabbage can be removed by either filtering the solution or by using tongs to remove the red cabbage pieces.

The indicator can then be used to test for a range of acids, alkalis and neutral solutions in test tubes (see list 'For the testing of solutions'). A 2 cm height of the solution is put into the test tube and 2–3 drops of the red cabbage indicator is added using a plastic dropping pipette and the colour of the solution recorded in a table. Alternatively, these tests could also be done on a spotting tile where two drops of the solution under test is used with one drop of the indicator (see Figure 5.5).

Figure 5.5 Equipment set up

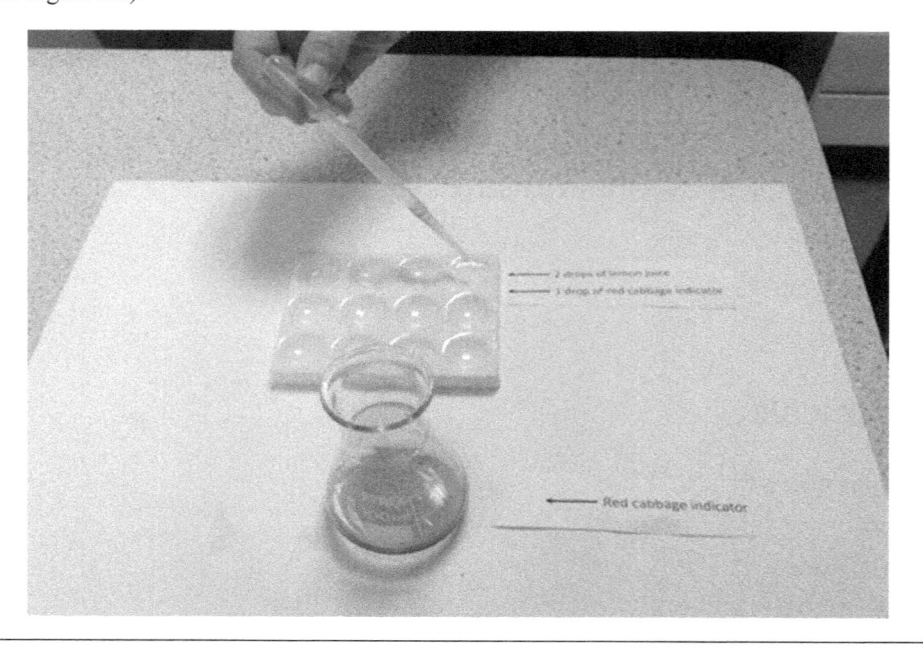

---

[1] The term 'effective' can be debated and decided on by the class to include criteria like: ease of preparation of indicator, its ability to distinguish between acid, alkaline and neutral solutions, how well it performs overall in comparison to commercial indicators like litmus and universal indicator.

Many other parts of plant which are coloured can act as an indicator, for example petals, beetroot, blackberries, raspberries, onion skins, hibiscus flowers (hibiscus tea bags work well here if hibiscus does not grow locally).

After making red cabbage indicator, students could be set a challenge to make other indicators from plants. Some coloured parts of plants do not dissolve in water so other solvents, for example ethanol, could be provided and other methods used such as crushing the plant matter in a mortar and pestle with the solvent.

Effectiveness matrix

	Domain of observables	Domain of ideas
What students do	Students can: • Extract the colour from red cabbage to make an indicator. • Use the red cabbage indicator to test a range of solutions.	Students can: • Use the results from using the red cabbage indicator to distinguish between acid, alkaline and neutral solutions.
What students learn	Students can later: • Repeat/adapt this practical to make another 'potential indicator' from other berries, leaves and petals.	Students can later: • Develop their own criteria about what makes a good indicator which might be. (i) Ease of preparation. (ii) Cost of preparation (commercial indicators are more expensive). (iii) Ability of the indicator to distinguish between acid, alkaline and neutral solutions. (iv) Ability to distinguish between weak acids and alkalis and between strong acids and alkalis.

Keep in mind

As well as making their own indicators, students could also be asked to bring in common substances from home such as toothpaste, washing up liquid, other soaps, vinegar for example to test, using their indicators. The substances students bring in would need to be risk-assessed before use. If other solvents are used to extract the colour from plant material, these must be risk-assessed.

Issues for discussion

Which indicators distinguish between acid, alkaline and neutral solutions? Did any indicators distinguish between weak and strong acids or between weak and strong alkalis?

Which indicators were water soluble and which needed another solvent and/or methods to extract the indicator from the plant material?

Why was water not suitable for the extraction of some indicators?

Which made the best indicator? Why?

Health and safety

Laboratory goggles should be worn by all students.

Risk assess any household chemicals students bring in not provided by the school.

Risk assess any other solvents used to extract the colour from plant material.

0.1 mol dm^{-3} solutions of:

Hydrochloric acid – see CLEAPSS Hazcards and recipe book.

Sodium hydroxide (irritant) – see the CLEAPSS Hazcards and recipe book.

Equipment for making the red cabbage indicator

For each group:

Beaker (250 cm^3)

Bunsen burner

Tripod

Gauze

Heat-resistant mat

Tongs (to remove red cabbage)

Filter funnel and filter paper (if filtering method is preferred)

Additional equipment and chemicals for other plant materials

Pestle and mortar

Ethanol

For the testing of solutions

Chemical solutions for testing (there are many others; these are just examples)

0.1 mol dm^{-3} of:

Hydrochloric acid

Sodium hydroxide

Others (please remember to risk assess):

Toothpaste

Milk

Water

Lemon juice

White vinegar

Equipment for testing solutions

For each group:

Test tube rack/test tubes *or* spotting tile

Plastic dropping pipettes

5.9 Diffusion of ions in solution – the case of lead(II) iodide

Learning objectives

- To explain the diffusion of ions in solution using the kinetic theory of matter.
- To explain why different ions diffuse in solution at different rates.

Procedure

A small amount of water is added to a Petri dish. A crystal of potassium iodide is placed on one side of the Petri dish using tweezers and a crystal of lead(II) nitrate is placed using tweezers on the opposite side (see Figure 5.6). When the experiment is set up, students can be asked to draw what they predict will happen after a period of time and then, as precipitation of the lead(II) iodide occurs, draw on what actually happens.

Figure 5.6 Experimental set up showing Petri dish with a small amount of water in the bottom with crystals placed where shown

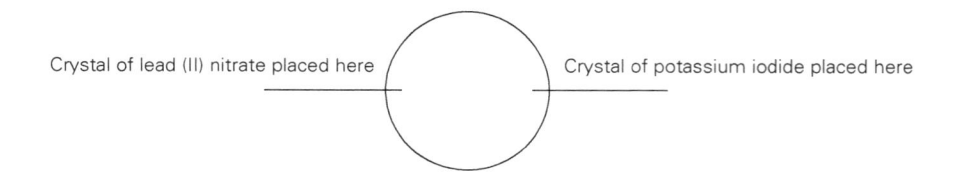

Effectiveness matrix

	Domain of observables	Domain of ideas
What students do	Students can: • Set up and carry out the experiment as described above.	Students can: • Explain and write a word equation for the formation of lead(II) iodide.
What students learn	Students can later: • Design experiments and predict where other precipitates will form in the Petri dish, for example silver nitrate with either potassium chloride, potassium bromide or potassium iodide.	Students can later talk about: • How the particle theory of matter can explain the formation of the lead(II) iodide precipitate. • Why the iodide ions diffuse faster than the lead(II) ions. • The precipitation of other systems and predict where they think the precipitate will form and why. • Why the precipitate forms in the Petri dish, using their understanding of diffusion.

Keep in mind

This experiment requires students to be able to:
Understand that the crystals first dissolve in the water so that the ions are mobile.

Apply their understanding of diffusion to explain how lead(II) ions and iodide ions eventually react to form lead(II) iodide.

Teachers might consider demonstrating and explaining the reaction of potassium iodide with lead(II) nitrate first. Some students may predict that the precipitate will form exactly half way between where the crystals are initially placed. The actual results can then be used to generate a discussion about the rates of diffusion of the different ions and then a follow-up investigation conducted with silver nitrate and potassium chloride, potassium bromide and potassium iodide. If the school does not have enough silver nitrate for students to do this in groups, it could be demonstrated and a visualizer used to show the whole class what happens.

Issues for discussion

What happens when potassium iodide and lead(II) nitrate crystals are first placed in the water?

Ask students to predict what will happen in the Petri dish after the crystals are added and dissolved in water.

Explore and discuss how the lead(II) ions and iodide ions have travelled from where they were placed and explore students' understanding of diffusion.

Discuss why the precipitate does not form half way between the crystals of potassium iodide and lead(II) nitrate.

Ask students to predict what they think would happen with other examples for example silver nitrate and potassium chloride, potassium bromide and potassium iodide. These could then be tried out as already described.

Health and safety

Laboratory goggles should be worn by all students.

Lead(II) nitrate (toxic, dangerous to the environment) – see CLEAPSS Hazcards and recipe book.

Potassium iodide (low hazard) – see CLEAPSS Hazcards and recipe book.

Equipment

For each group:

Tweezers
Petri dish

Chemicals

One crystal of lead(II) nitrate
One crystal of potassium iodide
Deionized or distilled water

5.10 Using universal indicator to illustrate the process of neutralisation

Learning objectives

- To be able to apply and use knowledge about pH scales to explain colour changes.
- To be able to apply knowledge about colour changes to solve a problem.

Procedure

Part one

Students are given a piece of filter paper and asked to draw on it in pencil two circles about 1 cm in diameter and about 2–3 cm apart, which they label 'acid' and 'alkali', respectively.

The filter paper is then placed on a white tile and students use dropping pipettes to place a few drops of the appropriate solution in each circle. The concentrations of the acid and alkali are not critical but they should be approximately the same. The solution will begin to spread out on the filter paper.

The students wait for a few minutes until the solutions have soaked through the filter paper towards each other and have met.

Students then place drops of universal indicator solution on the area of the filter paper where the acid and alkali have met and reacted. A 'rainbow' is produced showing the range of colours produced by universal indicator (see Figure 5.7).

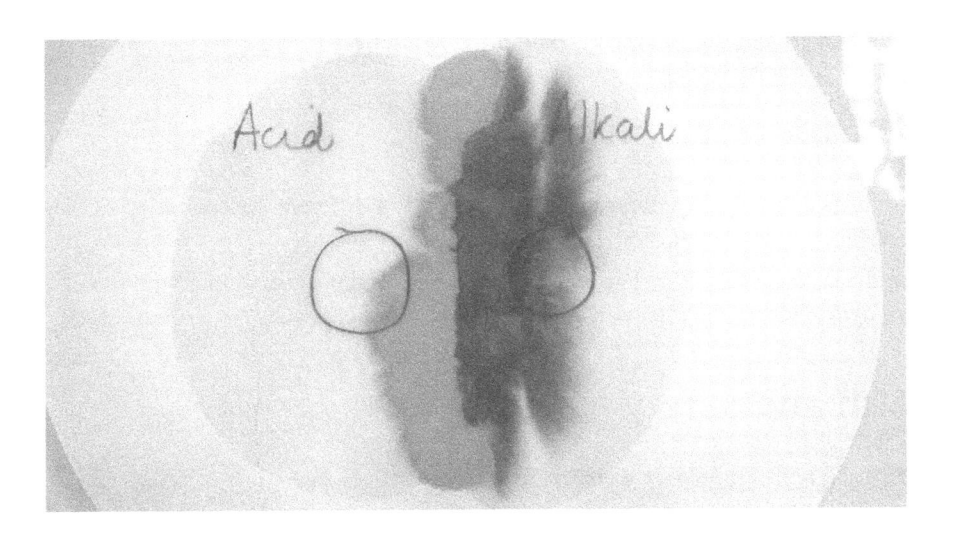

Figure 5.7
Experimental set up

Part two

Start with universal indicator solution, distilled water, hydrochloric acid and sodium hydroxide *only*.

Students should produce six different colours on the spotting tile provided: red, orange, yellow, green, blue and violet. Allow about 10 minutes for this. Ask students to share their results with each other.

Then ask each pair or group to produce and record a reliable 'recipe' for one colour. Allocate each pair a different colour. Orange is the most difficult to produce.

Each pair should then pass on their 'recipe' to be tested out by another group.

Effectiveness matrix

	Domain of observables	Domain of ideas
What students do	Students can: • Create neutralization circles.	Students can talk about: • The colour changes observed and explain this in terms of neutralization.
What students learn	Students can subsequently: • Produce six different colours on the well tile by applying their knowledge of neutralization to solve a colour change problem.	Students can explain: • The 'recipe' they have produced to produce a stable colour change.

Keep in mind

This practical activity is quicker, simpler and safer than the traditional method of illustrating neutralization by titrating acid with alkali using a burette.

Issues for discussion

Ask students to recall the colour changes produced in different concentration of acids in alkalis using universal indicator.

Ask students to explain what happened when the hydrochloric acid met with the alkaline sodium hydroxide on the filter paper. Explain the colour changes.

Health and safety

Laboratory goggles should be worn by all students.

Hydrochloric acid (Low hazard) – see the CLEAPPS Hazcards and recipe book.

Sodium hydroxide (Irritant) – see the CLEAPPS Hazcards and recipe book.

Universal indicator solution (Highly flammable).

Equipment

Each group of students will need:

Three dropping pipettes

A pencil

A white tile

A spotting tile

Chemicals

Access to sodium hydroxide solution, 0.1 mol dm^{-3} (irritant at this concentration)

Access to dilute hydrochloric acid, 0.1 mol dm^{-3} (low hazard at this concentration)

Universal indicator solution (low hazard at this concentration) (or alternative) in small dropper bottle

A sheet of filter paper, approximately 12.5 cm diameter (but the size is not critical). Whatman no. 1 works well; chromatography paper appears to be less successful.

5.11 Analysis of combustion products when a candle burns

Learning objectives

- To describe the reaction known as 'combustion'.
- To be able to explain the reaction which takes place when a candle burns.

Procedure

This demonstration practical allows students to identify some of the products of combustion, more specifically, incomplete combustion. Students can observe the colour change in the anhydrous cobalt chloride paper (from blue to pink) and identify that this indicates the presence of water. Additionally, they can observe the change in the limewater (from colourless to cloudy) and link this to the use of limewater as a test for the presence of carbon dioxide. Limewater is a saturated solution of calcium hydroxide which is filtered to produce a colourless liquid. This liquid will go cloudy if left in the laboratory in reagent bottles and should be freshly prepared from a stock saturated solution. Carbon dioxide reacts with the sparingly soluble calcium hydroxide to form solid calcium carbonate, which accounts for the milky appearance.

The black, sooty deposit on the funnel is a hint that the combustion is incomplete, and may be noticed by some students. This could form part of an extension activity or lead to a discussion about the differences between complete and incomplete combustion.

Assuming everything is already set up, this demonstration takes only a few minutes, although once set up, the apparatus can be left running for some time and students can file past in small groups to see it more closely. Alternatively, a camera linked to a projector can be used to show the whole class.

If students are not familiar with the cobalt chloride paper and limewater tests, either demonstrate these separately or allow students to try the tests themselves.

Set up the equipment as shown in Figure 5.8 (see advice later in health and safety section). Both boiling tubes and the funnel need to be clamped in place. Set up the delivery tube with the right-angle bend connected to the funnel with care because if this is made of flexible tubing, it can get hot and melt.

Figure 5.8
How to attach the funnel to the delivery tube

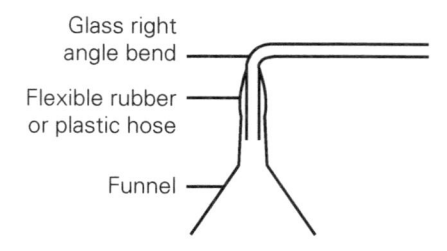

Glass right angle bend
Flexible rubber or plastic hose
Funnel

Ideally, the glass stem of the funnel should be bent into a right angle. Alternatively, join a standard funnel onto a right-angled piece of glass tubing using epoxy resin. A more temporary arrangement is to slide one arm of a right-angled piece of glass tubing inside the stem of the funnel and seal the joint on the outside with a piece of flexible tubing (see Figure 5.9).

Once the equipment is set up, the pump can be turned on and the tea light lit and placed under the funnel and its height adjusted so that it is not too close to the funnel, to risk being extinguished, or so far away that the gases given off will not be effectively collected.

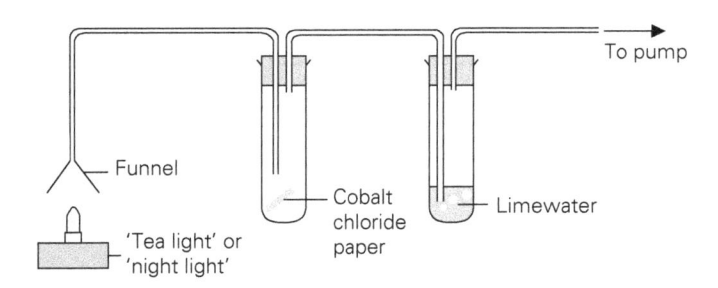

Figure 5.9 How to collect combustion products

Effectiveness matrix

	Domain of observables	Domain of ideas
What students do	This quadrant is intentionally blank in this task.	Students can: • Identify the products of combustion from the limewater test for carbon dioxide and the cobalt chloride paper test for water.
What students learn	This quadrant is intentionally blank in this task.	Students can later talk about: • What happens when a candle burns, using simple word equations.

Keep in mind

This is a good practical activity to set up argumentation and dialogue between teacher and students to structure the thinking and reasoning of students, particularly as they will not be able to 'see' the products of combustion given of by the candle and so need to be able to use the results from the limewater and cobalt chloride paper as evidence for the products carbon dioxide and water.

Issues for discussion

Candles give out light and heat energy from a chemical reaction known as combustion, in which the wax (made from carbon-based chemicals typically derived from petroleum) reacts with oxygen in the air to make a colourless gas called carbon dioxide. Water is also produced in the form of steam. Since the wax contains impurities, there is also a little smoke produced. The smoke is an aerosol (tiny particles of solid, unburned carbon from the wax mixed with the steam) and it often leaves a black, carbon, deposit on nearby walls or the ceiling above where it is burning. The steam is made in the blue part of a candle flame, where the wax burns cleanly with lots of oxygen; the smoke is made in the bright, yellow part of the flame, where there isn't enough oxygen for complete combustion to take place.

To find out more about how a candle works, visit http://www.explainthatstuff.com/candles.html.

For a follow up, ask the students to create a flick (flip) book to explain what happens when candles burn.

Health and safety

Laboratory goggles should be worn by all students.

Cobalt chloride/cobalt chloride paper (toxic, dangerous to the environment) – see CLEAPSS *Hazcards* and CLEAPSS *Recipe Book*.

Cobalt chloride paper can be stored in a desiccator.

Minimize handling of cobalt chloride paper (sensitizer) and wash hands after use (cobalt chloride is a category 2 carcinogen).

Calcium hydroxide solution, 'limewater', $Ca(OH)_2(aq)$, (treat as IRRITANT) – see CLEAPSS *Hazcards* and CLEAPSS *Recipe Book*. Ideally, the limewater should be made fresh on the day.

Special note on filter pumps

The use of traditional water-operated filter pumps for vacuum filtration and for drawing air through solutions is covered in section 10.6.4 of the *CLEAPSS Laboratory Handbook*.

It is strongly recommended that this is referred to before purchasing or using such pumps – it may not be possible or appropriate to use this type of equipment in your school or college.

Equipment

Apparatus:

Eye protection

Glass funnel, about 6 cm in diameter

2 boiling tubes

2 holed rubber bungs, to fit the boiling tubes, and fitted with one long and one short piece of glass tubing (see Figure 5.9)

White tile

Heating tongs

Access to balance

Chemicals

Candle

Piece of blue cobalt chloride paper (toxic)

Limewater (treat as irritant), about 20 cm^3

Pumping

Filter paper

Information about the type and use of various grades of filter papers can be found in section 9.11.4 of the *CLEAPSS Laboratory Handbook*.

Glass or plastic tubing for connections

5.12 The thermal decomposition of copper carbonate

Learning objectives

- To describe the effects of heating on copper carbonate.
- To be able to name the products of the decomposition of copper carbonate.

Procedure

Students weigh and record in the following table the mass of a large spatula of copper carbonate which has been placed in a clean dry test tube. They set up the equipment as shown in Figure 5.10. Copper carbonate is heated gently at first, then more strongly. It is crucial that students lift the delivery tube from the limewater *before, or as soon as*, the heating is stopped to avoid 'suck-back'. Students record their observations in the table. They might also be asked to notice what happens to the limewater and how long it takes to turn milky (if at all) and to notice any changes in the colour of the copper carbonate; this too can be recorded in the table at the top of p. 137. The apparatus is allowed to cool down and then students reweigh and record the mass of the test tube after heating.

Figure 5.10
Equipment set up

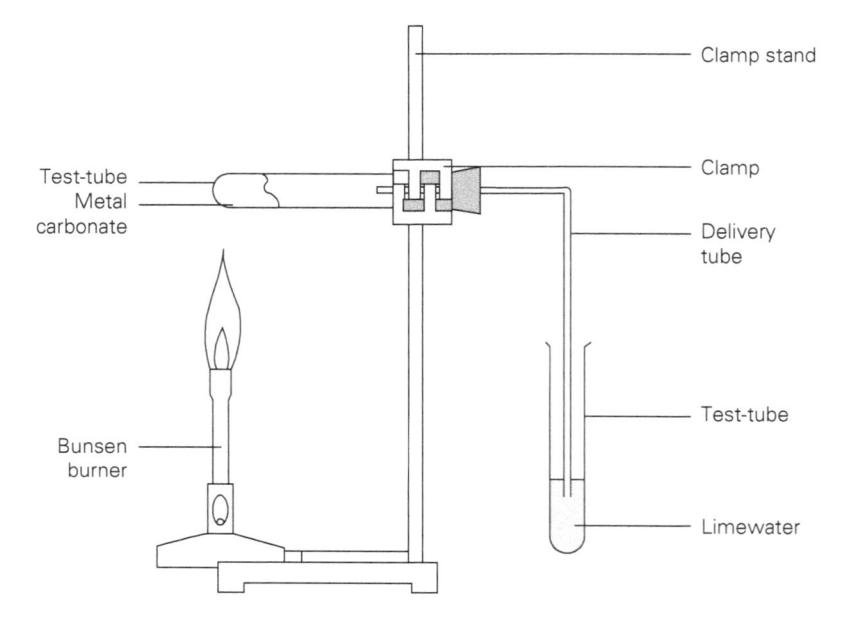

Group	Mass before heating	Mass after heating	Change in mass	Change in limewater and change in solid heated

Ask each pair or group of students to add their data to the whole class data set table.

Students can try our other metal carbonates, such as calcium carbonate, magnesium carbonate and sodium carbonate, for example.

Effectiveness matrix

	Domain of observables	Domain of ideas
What students do	Students can: • Weigh accurately the test tube before and after heating. • Set up the equipment as shown in Figure 5.10.	Students can talk about: • How the changes in appearance of the copper carbonate and the production of carbon dioxide provide evidence for its thermal decomposition. • How the change in the mass of copper carbonate also provides evidence for its decomposition.
What students learn	Students can subsequently: • Set up this experiment to find out if other metal carbonates decompose.	Students can later: • Write a word or chemical equation to show the decomposition of copper carbonate.

Keep in mind

The reaction illustrates the permanent change of green copper carbonate to black copper oxide. There will be a perceptible change in mass and carbon dioxide gas will be given off which reacts with the limewater. There is a lot of scope for erroneous results here, which will provide a good focus for subsequent discussion.

Display and present all the data for each pair working in the class as a class table. This could be done on a spread sheet which could show trends in the overall change in mass. Explain that sharing results will provide more evidence and will avoid the need for all pairs to have to replicate their findings.

Issues for discussion

What are the patterns observed in the data? Overall, the mass ought to decrease after heating and the limewater will become cloudy. Why might some of the data show an increase in mass?

What would students say in reply to the suggestion that the copper carbonate had been burned by the heating process and that the black layer was rather like the black layer left on toast when it is burned? What would be their evidence? The evidence that could be provided here is to take some carbon (from toast) and the products of this reaction and add each to a dilute solution of sulphuric acid. Nothing would happen with the carbon from toast but the addition of the copper oxide to dilute acid will produce a blue solution of copper ions, Cu^{2+}.

Use anthropomorphic modelling to try to explain and visualize what has actually happened. Designate five students to take on the role of each atom in the molecule $CuCO_3$ by producing five cards labelled Cu, C, O, O and O which are given one each to the five students. Then ask students to arrange themselves to show the products copper oxide (CuO) and carbon dioxide (CO_2). Write word equations with state symbols.

Health and safety

Laboratory goggles should be worn by all students.

It is important not to inhale dust of lead carbonate or the oxide formed. Wash hands after using lead compounds.

Limewater (calcium hydroxide solution), $Ca(OH)_2(aq)$, (treat as irritant) – see CLEAPSS *Hazcards* and *Recipe Book*.

Copper carbonate, $CuCO_3.Cu(OH)_2(s)$, (Harmful) – see CLEAPSS *Hazcards*.

Equipment

Apparatus

Test tube

Delivery tube (right angled)

Spatula

Bunsen burner

Clamp and stand

Chemicals

Limewater (calcium hydroxide solution)

About 2 g of copper carbonate

Chemistry: Session Guides 15–16

Ann Childs and Elaine Wilson

6

6.1 What ions are present in an unknown ionic solid? (p. 140)
6.2 Transition metal ions as catalysts – which works best? (p. 145)
6.3 Modelling the formation of igneous rocks (p. 148)
6.4 How does the concentration of a reactant affect the rate of reaction? (p. 152)
6.5 How does changing the temperature of a chemical reaction affect its reaction rate? (p. 155)
6.6 Electrolysis of ionic compounds in solution (p. 159)
6.7 Electricity from pairs of metals (p. 162)
6.8 Making an iodine clock or a Landolt Clock (p. 165)
6.9 Cracking hydrocarbons (p. 169)
6.10 Emulsifiers (p. 173)
6.11 Making nylon rope (p. 176)
6.12 Thermometric titration (p. 179)

6.1 What ions are present in an unknown ionic solid?

Learning objectives

- To identify the ions present in unknown ionic solids using common anion and cation tests.

Procedure

Stage 1: the tests for common cations and anions

Tests for cations	Tests for anions
Flame tests (adapted from Royal Society of Chemistry) • Soak wooden splints in distilled water the night before the experiment. • Have six boiling tubes half full with solutions of lithium chloride, sodium chloride, potassium chloride, calcium chloride and copper(II) chloride (0.5 mol dm^{-3}). • Immerse splints in each boiling tube (enough for one per group of students). • Students remove splint from stock solution and wave it through the blue flame of a Bunsen burner (emphasize that the splint should not be burnt). • Used splints can be put into a beaker of distilled water. *Results: flame colours* Orange = sodium (Na$^+$ ions) Carmine red = lithium (Li$^+$) ions Brick red = calcium (Ca^{2+}) ions Lilac = potassium (K$^+$) ions Blue/green = copper(II) (Cu^{2+}) ions	**Tests for halides (Cl$^-$, Br$^-$, I$^-$)** • Put solutions of Cl$^-$, Br$^-$, I$^-$ (0.5 mol dm^{-3}) ions to a height of 2 cm in three test tubes in a test tube rack. • Add a few drops of dilute nitric acid (0.4 mol dm^{-3}) to each test tube followed by a few drops of silver nitrate solution (0.1 mol dm^{-3}). *Results* White precipitate = chloride ions (Cl$^-$) Cream precipitate = bromide ions (Br$^-$) Yellow precipitate = iodide ions (I$^-$)

Tests for cations	Tests for anions
Tests for cations using sodium hydroxide solution • Put 2 cm height of solutions of Cu^{2+}, Fe^{2+}, Fe^{3+}, Al^{3+}, Mg^{2+}, Ca^{2+} (0.5 mol dm^{-3}) into separate test tubes and to each test tube add a few drops of dilute sodium hydroxide solution using a plastic pipette (0.4 mol dm^{-3}). • If a white precipitate forms, add an excess of sodium hydroxide solution (fill the test tube to the top with the sodium hydroxide solution). *Results:* • Blue precipitate = copper(II) ions (Cu^{2+}) • Green precipitate = iron(II) ions (Fe^{2+}) • Brown precipitate = iron(III) ions (Fe^{3+}) • White precipitate = aluminium ions (Al^{3+}), magnesium ions (Mg^{2+}) or calcium ions (Ca^{2+}). The white precipitate of aluminium hydroxide dissolves in excess sodium hydroxide solution.	**Tests for carbonates** (CO_3^{2-}) • Put a spatula of any metal carbonate, for example sodium carbonate, into a test tube. • Add about 2 cm height of hydrochloric acid (0.4 mol dm^{-3}). • Collect the gas and bubble through limewater (this can be done by connecting a delivery tube to the test tube and bubbling through limewater or removing the gas using a small plastic pipette and then bubbling it through a test tube of limewater). *Result:* • If the gas given off turns limewater milky, it is carbon dioxide, which confirms the solid contains the carbonate ion (CO_3^{2-}). **Tests for sulphates** (SO_4^{2-}) • Put about 2 cm height of a solution of a soluble metal sulphate into a test tube. • Add a few drops of barium chloride solution (0.1 mol dm^{-3}) using a plastic pipette. *Result:* • If a white precipitate is formed, sulphate ions (SO_4^{2-}) are present.

Stage 2: Identifying an unknown ionic compound

This can be done in a number of ways:

(i) Students in groups can be given unknown solids and asked to find out what ions are present using the tests in stage 1 and then to present their results to the rest of the class. Students could also be asked to design flow charts or keys to make their procedures more efficient so they do not have to try out all the tests at random.

(ii) To make it more interesting, this activity can be done in a more 'forensic science' context by perhaps providing the students with an imaginary map with a river and on the banks of the river are a number of chemical plants (making or using different ionic compounds). Students are given a sample of river water after a chemical spill is reported. The students have to identify the ions present in the river water and then identify the chemical plant responsible. Finally, students can be asked to write reports which can be presented as evidence in court. A real chemical spill of aluminium sulphate occurred from a water purification plant in Camelford (http://www.bbc.co.uk/news/uk-england-cornwall-24164253) that could be given as an example.

Effectiveness matrix

	Domain of observables	Domain of ideas
What students do	Students can: • Successfully carry out the chemical tests in stage 1.	Students can: • Use the results of the tests in stage 1 to identify the cations and anions in unknown ionic compounds.
What students learn	Students can later: • Use the chemical tests in stage 1 to identify an unknown ionic compound. • Design a flow chart to work out efficiently how to identify anions and cations.	Students can later: • Write chemical equations (where appropriate) to explain the reactions taking place. • Justify their design of a flow chart to systematically analyse an unknown sample.

Keep in mind

This experiment can take a number of lessons to teach the tests and then for students to plan their investigation. Other metal ions can be used in flame tests if they are available in school, such as those in caesium, rubidium and barium compounds but their toxicity must be checked first before use and they must be properly risk-assessed.

Issues for discussion

Students in groups could be asked to present:

Their results with chemical equations as appropriate.

Their flow charts or keys and the logic behind these.

If the river water simulation is tried out, a role play of a court could take place with a member of one group acting as an expert witness questioned by a prosecution lawyer.

Health and safety

Laboratory goggles should be worn by all students.

0.5 mol dm^{-3} solutions of:

Lithium chloride – see the CLEAPSS Hazcards and recipe book.

Sodium chloride, potassium chloride, potassium iodide, magnesium sulphate, potassium bromide (low hazard) – see the CLEAPSS Hazcards and recipe book.

Calcium chloride – see the CLEAPSS Hazcards and recipe book.

Copper(II) chloride – see the CLEAPSS Hazcards and recipe book.

Iron(II) sulphate (harmful) – see the CLEAPPS Hazcards and recipe book.

Iron(II) sulphate (irritant) – see the CLEAPSS Hazcards and recipe book. Aluminum sulphate (low hazard) - see the CLEAPPS Hazcards and recipe book.

0.4 mol dm^{-3} solutions of:

Hydrochloric acid (irritant) – see the CLEAPSS Hazcards and recipe book.

Sodium hydroxide and nitric acid (irritant) – see the CLEAPSS Hazcards and recipe book. Nitric acid (irritant) – see the CLEAPPS Hazcards and recipe book.

0.1 mol dm^{-3} solution of:

Silver nitrate, aluminium sulphate (low hazard) – see the CLEAPSS Hazcards and recipe book.

Barium chloride (harmful) – see the CLEAPSS Hazcards and recipe book.

0.02 mol dm^{-3} solution of:

Calcium hydroxide solution (limewater) – see the CLEAPSS Hazcards and recipe book.

Sodium carbonate solid (irritant).

Equipment

For each group:

Test tubes

Test tube racks

Splints

Beaker of distilled water

Bunsen burner

Heat-resistant mat

Two small plastic pipettes for sodium hydroxide solution (test for metal ions) and barium chloride solution (test for the sulphate ion)

Small plastic pipette or delivery tube with bung (to test for CO_2)

Small plastic pipettes for sodium hydroxide solution, barium chloride solution

One spatula

Chemicals

0.5 mol dm^{-3} solutions of lithium chloride; sodium chloride; potassium chloride; potassium bromide; potassium iodide; calcium chloride; copper(II) chloride; iron(II) sulphate; iron(III) sulphate; magnesium sulphate

0.4 mol dm^{-3} solutions of sodium hydroxide; hydrochloric acid; nitric acid

0.1 mol dm^{-3} solutions of silver nitrate; barium chloride; aluminium sulphate

Solution or solid of sodium carbonate (for carbonate test)

Limewater solution (0.02 mol dm^{-3})

Solutions or solids of unknown ionic compounds for stage 2 (choice for the teacher but Hazcards must be referred to in a risk assessment for the ionic compounds chosen)

6.2 Transition metal ions as catalysts – which works best?

Learning objectives

- To explore which transition metal ion is the most effective catalyst in the reaction between sodium thiosulphate and iron(III) nitrate solution.
- To explain how catalysts work.

Procedure

When iron(III) nitrate solution is added to sodium thiosulphate solution, a dark violet solution is initially formed which then goes colourless. This reaction can be catalysed by addition of small amounts of transition metal ions in solution.

50 cm^3 of sodium thiosulphate (0.1 mol dm^{-3}) is put into a 250 cm^3 conical flask. The flask is placed on a piece of card with a cross (X) drawn on it. 50 cm^3 of iron(III) nitrate solution (0.1 mol dm^{-3}) is added to the conical flask and, at the same time, the stop clock is started. An observer then looks down through the conical flask and the timer is stopped when the cross can first be seen. This method is repeated four times with one drop of each of the following solutions (catalysts) added to the reaction mixture:

- Cobalt(II) chloride solution
- Copper(II) sulphate solution
- Iron(II) sulphate solution
- Nickel(II) sulphate solution.

To add challenge to this experiment it could be left to the students to decide how exactly they will accurately and consistently determine when the solution goes colourless.

Effectiveness matrix

	Domain of observables	Domain of ideas
What students do	Students can: • Carry out the experiment using the instructions outlined above (using the cross on the card method).	Students can later: • Explain, from the results, which of the four transition metal ion catalysts speeds up reaction the most.
What students learn	Students can later: • Design their own way of determining the end point of the reaction and use this method as an alternative.	Students can talk about: • Why catalysts speed up chemical reactions, using their understanding of the activation energy for a chemical reaction.

Keep in mind

The concentration of the catalyst solutions must be kept at 0.1 mol dm^{-3}; if they are higher, the reaction will proceed too quickly. This is an example of homogenous catalysis and, as a result, it is hard to show that the catalyst itself is not used up and so other reactions involving catalysts, for example the decomposition of hydrogen peroxide with solid manganese (IV) oxide, could be done to demonstrate that catalysts do not get used up in the reaction.

Issues for discussion

Which was the best catalyst? Explain your answer.

How do catalysts speed up chemical reactions?

What other methods could be used to increase the rate of this reaction?

Give examples of the use of transition metals as catalysts in industrial processes.

Why do transition metal ions make good catalysts? This question could be a *challenge question* for students to research, particularly if they are going on to study chemistry in the future.

Health and safety

Laboratory goggles should be worn by all students.

0.1 mol dm^{-3} solutions of:

Cobalt(II) chloride (toxic) – see CLEAPSS Hazcards and recipe book

Copper(II) sulphate – see the CLEAPSS Hazcards and recipe book

Iron(II) sulphate (irritant) – see the CLEAPSS Hazcards and recipe book

Iron(III) nitrate – see CLEAPSS Hazcards and recipe book

Nickel(II) sulphate (toxic)

Sodium thiosulphate (low hazard) – see CLEAPSS Hazcards and recipe book

Equipment

For each group:

250 cm^3 conical flask

Plastic dropping pipettes (for the catalyst solutions which could be put into small 100 cm^3 beakers)

Two 100 cm^3 measuring cylinders to measure out iron(III) nitrate solution and sodium thiosulphate solution

Stop clock

Card with a cross marked on it in indelible black ink

Chemicals

0.1 mol dm^{-3} solutions of cobalt(II) chloride; copper(II) sulphate; iron(II) sulphate; nickel(II) sulphate; iron(III) nitrate; sodium thiosulphate

6.3 Modelling the formation of igneous rocks

Learning objectives

- To explain how intrusive and extrusive igneous rocks are formed.
- To explain why the crystal sizes in intrusive and extrude igneous rocks are different.

Procedure

Stage 1: Modelling the formation of crystal growth of salol at low and high temperatures

Molten salol is produced by putting two to three spatulas of salol (phenyl-2-hydroxybenzoate) into a test tube. The test tube is transferred to a water bath at 45 °C. Students should take four microscope slides and put two of them in a fridge and two on a radiator or in an oven (35–40 °C).[1] Students transfer their test tube containing the molten salol to a test tube rack using a test tube holder. A few drops of salol are transferred to one of the microscope slides from the fridge using a glass rod. The salol is covered with the second microscope slide from the fridge. This method is then repeated with the two microscope slides left on the radiator or in the oven.

Students can observe the rate and size of crystals formed on the microscope slides at the two temperatures using a microscope or a handheld magnifying lens. Students could be asked to draw the crystals formed at the different temperatures (fridge, radiator/oven).

Stage 1 is therefore designed to model the formation of crystals from a molten substance where there is fast and slow cooling of the molten substance. In this case, salol is the molten substance, but in igneous rocks, it is magma. Therefore, it is important that at some stage this point is discussed before considering samples of igneous rock in stage 2.

Stage 2

Students are given samples of igneous rock: extrusive, for example basalt; and intrusive, for example granite (see Figure 6.1). They are asked to use the findings from stage 1 to predict how they think the igneous rock was formed in terms of fast cooling of the magma (modelled by the slides in the fridge) or slower cooling of the magma (modelled by the slides left in the oven or radiator).

Stage 3

The final part of the modelling process is to link stages 1 and 2 to predict where students think extrusive and intrusive igneous rocks are formed as part of the rock cycle.

---

[1] If an oven or radiator is not available, room temperature would be an acceptable alternative.

Figure 6.1
Left: Basalt (small crystals). Right: Granite (large crystals).

Effectiveness matrix

	Domain of observables	Domain of ideas
What students do	Students can: • Carry out the experiments as described above. • Use a microscope/handheld magnifying lens to observe crystal formation. • Draw the crystals formed. • Identify igneous rock with small and large crystals with a handheld magnifying lens.	Students can: • Explain that smaller crystals are formed from fast cooling of the salol (e.g. on the slides taken from the fridge). • Explain that larger crystals are formed from slow cooling of the salol (e.g. microscope slides left on a radiator or in an oven). • Apply their understanding of crystal formation in stage 1 to the formation of crystals in samples of intrusive igneous rock, for example granite (large crystals) and extrusive igneous rock, for example basalt (small crystals).
What students learn	Students can later: • Take a wide range of igneous rock and classify them as extrusive or intrusive igneous rock.	Students can later: • Apply the results of this experiment to the rock cycle and predict where intrusive igneous and extrusive igneous rocks are formed and explain their prediction in terms of the size of the crystals.

Keep in mind

If students are using microscopes to draw the crystals, some may also draw air bubbles that can be trapped when the second slide is lowered onto the salol. Therefore, some preparation or discussion may need to take place before the experiment to focus students' observations.

Issues for discussion

This is an experiment which first models the formation of small and large crystals by fast and slow cooling using salol. It then uses this to explain where intrusive and extrusive igneous rock is formed and the discussion of each stage could take place as follows:

Stage 1 questions can be asked about:

Which crystals formed more quickly? Why?

Which crystals formed more slowly? Why?

What was the size of the crystals formed on fast cooling of the salol? Why?

What was the size of the crystals formed on slow cooling of the salol? Why?

Stage 2 then looks at samples of igneous rock such as basalt and granite. It may be that, depending on the nature of the group, these two clear examples are used first and then other samples provided as appropriate. Students can then be asked questions in their groups such as:

Which rock has the largest crystals? Using the results from the experiment, predict how you think the crystals were formed?

Which rock has the smallest crystals? Using the results from the experiment, predict how you think the crystals were formed?

Stage 3 would then be to show the rock cycle and identify two locations where intrusive and extrusive rocks are formed. Students then discuss what they think the speed of cooling will be like in these two locations and then they can be asked to predict which type of igneous rock would be formed at each location and why.

Health and safety

Laboratory goggles should be worn by all students.

Salol (irritant, dangerous to the environment) – see CLEAPSS Hazcards and recipe book.

Salol must be melted in warm water bath at 45 °C and not using a direct Bunsen burner flame.

Care must be taken when test tubes are removed from the water bath and so it is advisable for students to use test tube holders.

The oven should only be heated to 35–40 °C but students should take care when removing the hot slides.

Equipment

Water bath

For each group:

1 test tube

1 test tube holder

1 test tube rack

4 microscope slides

1 pair of tongs

Glass rod

Microscope and/or handheld magnifying lens

Chemicals

Salol

Examples of intrusive and extrusive igneous rock, for example granite and basalt (but also others)

6.4 How does the concentration of a reactant affect the rate of reaction?

Learning objectives

- To explore what happens to the rate of a chemical reaction when the concentration of reactants are increased.
- To explain why an increase in the concentration of reactants increases the rate of a chemical reaction using an understanding of collision theory.

Procedure

The reaction between sodium thiosulphate and hydrochloric acid produces a yellow precipitate of sulphur:

$$Na_2S_2O_{3(aq)} + 2HCl_{(aq)} \rightarrow S_{(s)} + 2NaCl_{(aq)} + SO_{2(aq)} + H_2O_{(l)}$$

The rate of this reaction can be measured by putting sodium thiosulphate solution into a 250 cm³ conical flask and then placing it on a piece of card with a cross (X) on it. Dilute hydrochloric acid is added and, at the same time, a stop clock is started (see Figure 6.2). An observer then looks through the solution and times how long it takes for the cross to disappear[2] as the cross is obscured by the formation of the sulphur precipitate. The following table shows how a range of different concentrations (A–E) of the sodium thiosulphate solution can be made up.

To add challenge to this experiment it could be left to the students to decide how exactly they will accurately and consistently determine when the cross on the card disappears.

	A	B	C	D	E
Volume of sodium thiosulphate (cm³)	10	20	30	40	50
Volume of water (cm³)	40	30	20	10	0
Volume of hydrochloric acid added (cm³)	5	5	5	5	5
Time taken for cross to disappear (seconds)					

---

[2] Teachers, in demonstrating this experiment, can use a light sensor to monitor the formation of the precipitate, which is then analysed using data logging software.

Effectiveness matrix

	Domain of observables	Domain of ideas
What students do	Students can: • Carry out the experiment using the instructions outlined above (using the cross on the card method.)	Students can: • Describe how the rate of reaction changes as the concentration of the sodium thiosulphate solution increases.
What students learn	Students can later: • Design their own way of determining the end point of the reaction and use this method as an alternative. • Suggest methods by which the reaction rates of other reactions can be measured, for example calcium carbonate and hydrochloric acid (including how to vary the concentration of hydrochloric acid).	Students can later: • Use ideas from collision theory to explain why the reaction rate increases as the concentration of the sodium thiosulphate increases. • Use the results from this experiment and collision theory and apply them to predict how increasing the pressure of a reacting mixture of gases would change the reaction rate.

Keep in mind

Good practice would be for students to do repeat measurements for each concentration in the table.

Issues for discussion

How do students know a chemical reaction is taking place? *Explore here the idea that the formation of the precipitate of sulphur is our way of knowing that the two colourless solutions have undergone a chemical reaction.*

Which of procedures A–E produces the most concentrated solution of sodium thiosulphate? Which is the most dilute? Students can be asked to explain their answers.

What happens to the rate of formation of sulphur as the concentration of the sodium thiosulphate solution increases?

How does reaction rate change as the concentration of the sodium thiosulphate solution increases? Why? *Use collision theory and the idea of activation energy to explain this.*

Consider a mixture of reacting gases, for example ammonia and hydrogen chloride, and discuss how increasing the pressure will affect the rate of reaction. *Discussion here can begin by considering particle density at low and high pressures and, in what ways and to what extent, this is analogous to high and low concentration in solution. Then move to discussing how an increase in pressure would affect the rate of reaction.*

What errors might occur in this experiment and how can students reduce error in this experiment?

Health and safety

Laboratory goggles should be worn by all students.

Hydrochloric acid, 2 mol dm^{-3} (irritant) – see CLEAPSS Hazcards and recipe book.

Sodium thiosulphate solution, 40 g dm^{-3} (low hazard) – see CLEAPSS Hazcards and recipe book.

The students must dispose of each reaction mixture down a sink as soon as they finish each reaction with large amounts of water. Be aware of asthma sufferers in the group as sulphur dioxide can adversely affect them.

Equipment

For each group:

250 cm^3 conical flask

Card with a cross marked on it in indelible black ink

Two 100 cm^3 measuring cylinders for measuring the distilled water and sodium thiosulphate solution

10 cm^3 measuring cylinder for measuring the hydrochloric acid

Stop clock

Chemicals

Sodium thiosulphate solution 40 g dm^{-3}

Hydrochloric acid 2 mol dm^{-3}

6.5 How does changing the temperature of a chemical reaction affect its reaction rate?

Learning objectives

- To explore what happens to the rate of a chemical reaction when the temperature of the reactants is increased.
- To be able to explain why an increase in temperature increases the rate of a chemical reaction using collision theory and the activation energy for chemical reactions.

Procedure

The reaction between sodium thiosulphate and hydrochloric acid produces a yellow precipitate of sulphur:

$$Na_2S_2O_{3(aq)} + 2HCl_{(aq)} \rightarrow S_{(s)} + 2NaCl_{(aq)} + SO_{2(aq)} + H_2O_{(l)}$$

10 cm³ of sodium thiosulphate solution (40 g dm⁻³) is put into a 250 cm³ conical flask and 40 cm³ of water is added to it. This solution is then placed on a piece of card with a cross drawn on it. 5 cm³ of dilute hydrochloric acid (2 mol dm⁻³) is added and the stop clock is started immediately. The mixture is swirled thoroughly to mix the reactants and the temperature taken. One student observer then looks through the solution (see Figure 6.2) and stops the clock as soon as s/he can no longer see the cross which is obscured by the formation of the precipitate of sulphur.[3] The time is recorded and the temperature of the

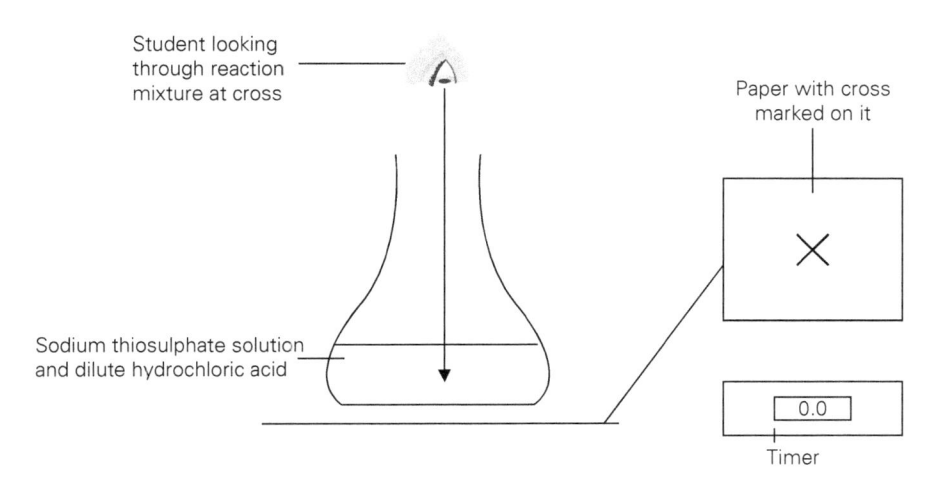

Figure 6.2 Apparatus for the reaction between sodium thiosulphate and hydrochloric acid

---

[3] Teachers, if demonstrating this experiment, can use a light sensor to monitor the formation of the precipitate and then analyse it using data logging software.

solution is taken again. An average temperature is then calculated from the start and end temperature. The following table can be used to record the results.

To add challenge to this experiment it could be left to the students to decide how exactly they will accurately and consistently determine when the cross on the card disappears.

Table X

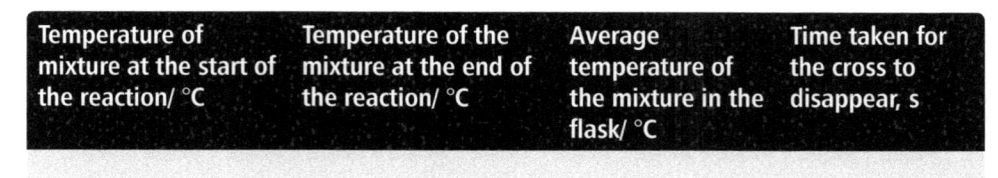

Temperature of mixture at the start of the reaction/ °C	Temperature of the mixture at the end of the reaction/ °C	Average temperature of the mixture in the flask/ °C	Time taken for the cross to disappear, s

A range of five different temperatures in the range 10–60 °C is desirable. The challenge of this experiment is getting a reasonable range of stable temperatures. A temperature of 10 °C or lower can be achieved by using water that has been in a fridge to add to the 10 cm^3 of sodium thiosulphate. Higher temperatures in the range 30–60 °C can be achieved by:

(i) Heating the solution of sodium thiosulphate (10 cm^3 sodium thiosulphate and 40 cm^3 water) on tripod and gauze over a Bunsen burner. The solution needs to be heated very gently and the temperature monitored. After heating, the conical flask needs to be removed carefully using a test tube holder or tongs to grip the neck of the conical flask and great care needs to be taken. Once removed from the tripod and placed on the cross, the temperature will still increase so it is advisable for students to allow the temperature to stabilize and then add the 5 cm^3 of dilute hydrochloric acid and take the initial temperature after the 5 cm^3 of hydrochloric acid has been added and then again at the end.

(ii) Providing the mixture of sodium thiosulphate (10 cm^3) with added water (40 cm^3) already made up as a stock solution in preset water baths for students for temperatures above room temperature. However, again care needs to be taken in removing the solutions of sodium thiosulphate from the hot water baths.

Effectiveness matrix

	Domain of observables	Domain of ideas
What students do	Students can: • Carry out all the procedures as described earlier, for example measuring the correct amount of each solution, measuring the time taken for the cross to disappear, achieving a good range of stable temperatures between 10 °C and 60 °C.	Students can: • Describe, using scientific terminology, how the rate of reaction changes as the temperature of the reaction mixture increases. • State that the higher the temperature of the reaction mixture, the faster the rate of reaction.

	Domain of observables	Domain of ideas
What students learn	Students can later: • Design their own way of determining the end point of the reaction and use this method as an alternative. • Suggest how other reactions, for example calcium carbonate and acid, can be adapted to measure how the reaction rate changes with increasing temperature.	Students can later: • Use ideas from collision theory and the activation energy of a chemical reaction to explain why the reaction rate increases as the temperature increases.

Keep in mind

When using a Bunsen burner the challenge is achieving and accurately measuring a staged temperature. In addition, if the temperature exceeds 70 °C, the reaction will be so fast that students will find it difficult to measure a stable temperature before the cross disappears.

Good practice would be for students to do repeat measurements for the same temperature. In practice, if using the Bunsen burner method, achieving exactly the same temperature range is very challenging. However, using the solutions left in a water bath where the temperature is stable is easier and students should be encouraged to repeat readings.

For students who are high attainers introducing the Maxwell–Boltzmann distribution of molecular energies may be useful in explaining why even small increases in temperature produce a large increase in reaction rate. This is taught at advanced level, but teachers may want to add this in to inject an element of challenge.

Sulphur dioxide is produced in this reaction and can affect asthma sufferers in particular (see health and safety below).

Issues for discussion

How do we know a chemical reaction is taking place? *Exploring here that the formation of the precipitate of sulphur is our way of knowing the two colourless solutions have undergone a chemical reaction.*

What happens to the rate of formation of sulphur as the temperature of the reacting solution increases? How has this been measured?

How does reaction rate change as the temperature of the reacting mixture increases? Why? *Use collision theory and the idea of activation energy to explain this. As already mentioned, depending on the students taught and the teacher's judgement, it may be appropriate to introduce the Maxwell–Boltzmann distribution of molecular energies.*

What errors might occur in this experiment and how can we reduce errors?

Health and safety

Laboratory goggles should be worn by all students.

Hydrochloric acid 2 mol dm^{-3} (irritant) – see CLEAPSS Hazcards and recipe book.

Sodium thiosulphate 40g dm^{-3} (low hazard) – see CLEAPSS Hazcards and recipe book.

Students must dispose of each reaction mixture down a sink as soon as they finish each reaction with large amounts of water. Be aware of asthma sufferers in the group as sulphur dioxide can adversely affect them.

Care should be taken with removing 'hot' solutions from the Bunsen burner or water bath.

Equipment

For each group:

250 cm^3 conical flask

Card with a cross marked on it in indelible black ink

100 cm^3 measuring cylinder

10 cm^3 measuring cylinder

Stop clock

Thermometer

Bunsen burner

Heat-resistant mat

Tripod and gauze

Test tube holder or tongs (to remove the conical flask from the water bath or from the tripod and gauze)

For the class if water bath method is preferred:
Water baths at temperatures between 30 and 60 °C with a stock solution of sodium thiosulphate (sodium thiosulphate (10 cm^3, 40 g dm^{-3}), water (40 cm^3))

Chemicals

Sodium thiosulphate solution 40 g dm^{-3}

Hydrochloric acid 2 mol dm^{-3}

6.6 Electrolysis of ionic compounds in solution

Learning objectives

- To state which products are formed at the cathode and anode when aqueous solutions of ionic compounds are electrolysed.
- To explain the products formed at the cathode using their understanding of the reactivity series of metals.
- To explain the products are formed at the anode using the rules for deposition for ionic compounds in solution.

Procedure

The equipment is set up as shown in Figure 6.3.

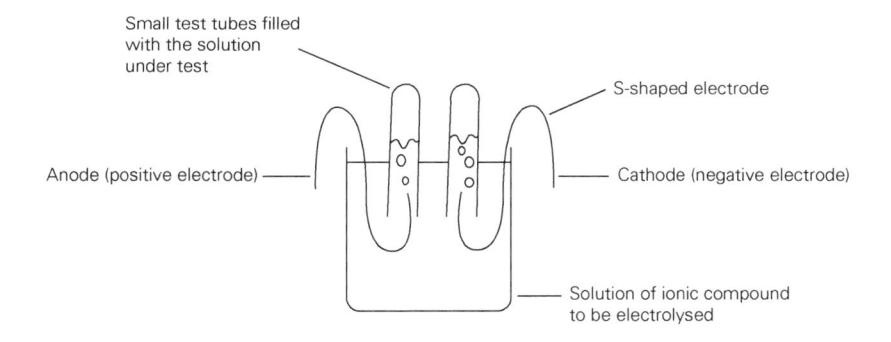

Figure 6.3 Electrolysis set up with S-shaped electrodes

0.5 mol dm^{-3} solutions of sodium chloride, copper(II) chloride, potassium iodide, sodium bromide and potassium sulphate can be tested in the equipment shown in Figure 6.3. Students will also need to know the tests for the gases hydrogen, oxygen, chlorine, bromine and iodine beforehand. The following table can be used to allow students to apply the rules for deposition at the anode and cathode and make a prediction before testing their prediction using the solutions listed above and the equipment in Figure 6.3.

Solution	Prediction		Results	
Sodium chloride	Cathode:	Anode:	Cathode:	Anode:
Copper(II) chloride	Cathode:	Anode:	Cathode:	Anode:
Potassium iodide	Cathode:	Anode:	Cathode:	Anode:
Sodium bromide	Cathode:	Anode:	Cathode:	Anode:
Potassium sulphate	Cathode:	Anode:	Cathode:	Anode:

Effectiveness matrix

	Domain of observables	Domain of ideas
What students do	Students can: • Set up the specified equipment and collect the gases evolved from the anode and cathode. • Use their predictions to test for any gases evolved.	Students can: • Identify and discuss, using scientific terminology, the products at the anode and cathode for each solution.
What students learn	Students can later: • Predict and carry out tests on gases for other solutions such as silver nitrate and lead(II) nitrate.	Students can later: • Explain, using scientific terminology, why these products were formed at the anode and cathode using the reactivity series of metals and the rules for deposition at the anode.

Keep in mind

Technically, the inversion of small test tubes over the electrodes in the figure is difficult for students. It is therefore advisable to use distilled water in the small test tubes to avoid getting solution on students' hands. Other solutions can be used, such as lead(II) nitrate or silver nitrate. Lead(II) nitrate is, however, toxic and silver nitrate is very expensive and so could be demonstrated after the students have predicted what will happen.

Issues for discussion

What substances were deposited at the anode and cathode after the electrolysis of each solution?

Discuss if students' predictions were correct. Where they were correct, get students to explain why the substance was deposited using their understanding of the reactivity series of metals and the rules for deposition at the anode for aqueous ionic solutions.

Students could be asked to explain the examples where their predictions were incorrect.

Discuss why reactive metals such as aluminium and sodium have to be extracted from their molten compounds and not from their compounds in solution.

Health and safety

Laboratory goggles should be worn by all students.

Bromine gas (very toxic, corrosive, dangerous for the environment) – see CLEAPSS Hazcards and recipe book.

Chlorine gas (toxic, dangerous for the environment) – see CLEAPSS Hazcards and recipe book.

Iodine (harmful, dangerous for the environment) – see CLEAPSS Hazcards and recipe book.

Hydrogen (extremely flammable) – see CLEAPSS Hazcards and recipe book.

Oxygen (oxidizing) – see CLEAPSS Hazcards and recipe book.

Because of the dangers that chlorine and bromine vapours cause, students should not produce these gases for very long and during the course of the experiment the laboratory needs to be well ventilated.

0.5 mol dm^{-3} solutions of:

Sodium chloride (low hazard) – see CLEAPSS Hazcards and recipe book

Copper(II) chloride – see CLEAPSS Hazcards and recipe book

Potassium iodide (low hazard) – see CLEAPSS Hazcards and recipe book

Sodium bromide (low hazard) – see CLEAPSS Hazcards and recipe book

Potassium sulphate (low hazard) – see CLEAPSS Hazcards and recipe book

Equipment

For Figure 6.3 for each group:

100 cm^3 beaker

2 small test tubes

S-shaped electrodes

2 leads with a crocodile clips attached to one end of each

Power pack (6–12 V)

Splints (to do lighted splint test for hydrogen and glowing splint test for oxygen)

Chemicals

0.5 mol dm^{-3} solutions of:

Sodium chloride

Copper(II) chloride

Potassium iodide

Sodium bromide

Potassium sulphate

Universal indicator paper (test for chlorine gas – damp universal indicator is bleached by chlorine gas)

6.7 Electricity from pairs of metals

Learning objectives

- To explain why a pair of metals placed in an electrolyte produces a potential difference.
- To predict the size of the potential difference a pair of metals will produce using the reactivity series of metals.

Procedure

Students set up the apparatus as in Figure 6.4 for the zinc and copper combination. They are asked to try combinations of other pairs of metals and to predict, using their understanding of the reactivity series of metals, whether a pair of metals will have a bigger or smaller potential difference than the zinc–copper combination. For example, a combination of magnesium and copper would be predicted to give a larger potential difference because the metals are further apart in the reactivity series than zinc and copper, whereas a combination of zinc and iron would have a smaller potential difference because they are closer together in the reactivity series than zinc and copper.

Figure 6.4
How to set up equipment to illustrate electrode potential

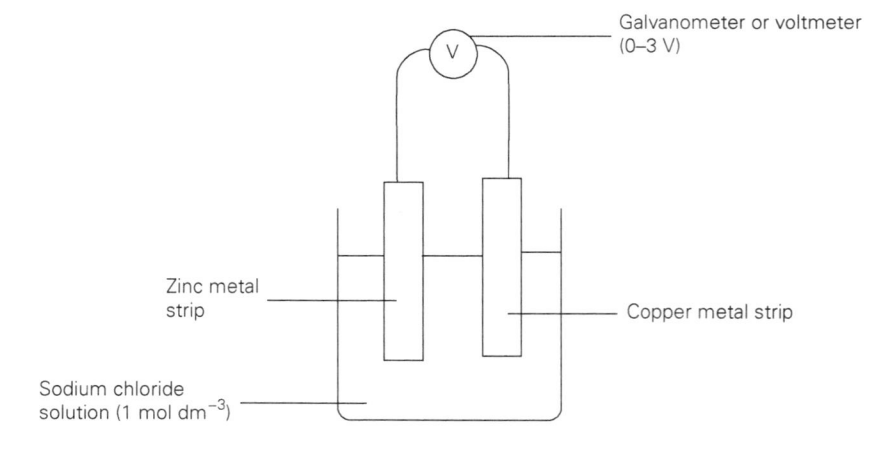

The following table could be used to record the students' results (three examples given – many more can be tried)

Pair of metals	Prediction of voltage – higher or lower than the zinc–copper combination. Explain your prediction	Actual voltage
1. Zinc and magnesium		
2. Zinc and iron		
3. Magnesium and copper		

Effectiveness matrix

	Domain of observables	Domain of ideas
What students do	Students can: • Set up a specified arrangement of zinc and copper metal electrodes in the cell arrangement shown in Figure 6.4. • Accurately record the reading from the voltmeter/galvanometer.	Students can talk about: • Why a potential difference is produced for a pair of metals using their understanding of the reactivity series of metals. • Identify the positive and negative electrodes for zinc and copper.
What students learn	Students can later: • Repeat this practical for other combinations of metal electrodes and accurately record the readings for the new pairings.	Students can later: • Predict and explain which metal electrode systems will produce potential differences larger or smaller than the zinc–copper cell using their understanding of the reactivity series of metals. • Identify the positive and negative electrodes for all other pairs of metals using their understanding of the reactivity series of metals.

Keep in mind

Although a 100 cm^3 beaker could be used for this practical to save on use of chemicals, it is more challenging for the students to keep the two metal electrodes from touching in this smaller beaker.

All chemicals from this practical can be re-used so teachers should have efficient systems of collecting the electrodes and the sodium chloride solution at the end of the practical.

Lead is toxic and it may be that this metal can be left out as there are plenty of other examples that can be used.

Issues for discussion

What are the positive and negative electrodes in the zinc–copper cell? Ask students to explain their answers.

Ask students to explain their predictions for other metal pairs and how they used the reactivity series of metals to inform their predictions.

Ask students to identify the positive and negative electrodes in all the metal electrode pairings and explain their reasoning.

What would happen with cells where both metal electrodes were made of the same metal?

Discuss the uses metal electrode systems can be put to.

Health and safety

Laboratory goggles should be worn by all students

Lead (toxic) – see CLEAPSS Hazcards and recipe book (wash hands after handling lead metal strips)

Magnesium ribbon (low hazard) – see CLEAPSS Hazcards and recipe book

Iron metal (low hazard) – see CLEAPSS Hazcards and recipe book

Zinc metal (low hazard) – see CLEAPSS Hazcards and recipe book

Copper metal (low hazard) – see CLEAPSS Hazcards and recipe book

Sodium chloride solution 1 mol dm^{-3} (low hazard) – see CLEAPSS Hazcards and recipe book

Equipment

For each group:

Beaker (250 cm^3)

Two wires and two crocodile clips

Galvanometer or voltmeter (0–3 V)

Chemicals

Magnesium ribbon

Strips of zinc

Iron nails (or strips of iron metal)

Strips of lead

Strips of copper

Sodium chloride solution (1 mol dm^{-3})

6.8 Making an iodine clock or a Landolt Clock[4]

Learning objectives

- To discuss how concentration affects the rate of reaction.
- To establish the rate order of reactants involved in rate determining steps.

Effectiveness matrix

	Domain of observables	Domain of ideas
What students do	Students can: • Carry out the complex multistage practical so that the clock reaction takes place.	Students can talk about: • Factors which affect the rate of the reaction.
What students learn	Students can subsequently: • Carry out controlled timed reactions at 15-, 30-, 45- and 60- minute intervals.	Students can later talk about: • How collision theory can explain why changing the concentration of reactants A and B changes the rate of reaction for the iodine clock.

Procedure

50 cm^3 of solution A (2.3 g of potassium iodate (V), KIO$_3$ in 450 cm^3 distilled water) is placed in a 250 cm^3 conical flask. To this is added 50 cm^3 of solution B (7 g of sodium metabisulphite, NaS$_2$O$_5$ in 450 cm^3 distilled water with 20 cm^3 of 1 per cent starch solution added), giving the flask a good swirl. A stop clock is started as soon as solution B is added to the conical flask. When the mixture has gone black, stop the clock and the time can be recorded in the following table. The contents of the flask can be disposed of by pouring them into the waste bucket or beaker provided (this contains sodium thiosulphate to stop the reaction mixture causing problems when it is poured down the sink). Students can try this again with 10 cm^3 solution B and 40 cm^3 distilled water in measuring cylinder B, recording the results in the following table.

Does diluting solution A and keeping solution B the same concentration have the same effect on the clock period? If, after four minutes, no reaction has taken place – record 'NO RESULT'.

---

[4] This reaction is called the Landolt Clock Reaction because it was discovered by Hans Heinrich Landolt in 1886.

Mixture	Time taken/s
50 cm³ solution A + 50 cm³ solution B	
50 cm³ solution A + (25 cm³ solution B and 25 cm³ distilled water)	
50 cm³ solution A + (10 cm³ solution B and 40 cm³ distilled water)	
(25 cm³ solution A and 25 cm³ distilled water) + 50 cm³ solution B	

1 Start the stop clock as you pour solution B into the conical flask. Give the flask a good swirl.

2 Investigate the effect of changing the concentration of solution B on the clock period by pouring 25 cm³ solution B and 25 cm³ distilled water into measuring cylinder B. Add 50 cm³ of solution A to measuring cylinder A, just as before. Mix the two solutions and time the clock period with the stop clock.

Extension/challenge

Students can be asked to make a chemical clock which 'ticks' at 15 seconds, 30 seconds, 45 seconds and 60 seconds. They will need to develop solutions of A and B, which have the right concentrations to do this and smaller scale experiments using the 100 cm³ beakers and 50 cm³ measuring cylinders.

Once students have their reactions 'tuned', they can be asked to set up the kitchen clock on the bench with a clean 100 cm³ beaker at each of the 12 o'clock, 3 o'clock, 6 o'clock and 9 o'clock positions. By putting the correct amount of solution A in each of the beakers and having solution B ready to add in four measuring cylinders as the second hand gets to '12 o'clock', all four portions of solution B can be added to the beakers. Students could be judged on how close each of the colour changes in the beakers is to the second hand on the clock when the solutions change colour.

Keep in mind

This practical will take an extended period of time to carry out.

Issues for discussion

Students can be asked to try to suggest an explanation for how the Landolt Clock works using what they know about reaction rates and collision theory.

It may help understanding if the students are already familiar with the reactions of starch and iodine, and of iodine and sodium thiosulphate; so it may be worth demonstrating these beforehand.

The basic reaction is:

$$H_2O_2(aq) + 2I^-(aq) + 2H^+(aq) \rightarrow I_2(aq) + 2H_2O(l)$$

[For more advanced discussions or investigations – this reaction is the rate determining step and is first order with respect to both H_2O_2 and I^-.]

As soon as the iodine is formed, it reacts with the thiosulphate to form tetrathionate ions and recycles the iodide ions by the fast reaction:

$$2S_2O_3^{2-}(aq) + I_2(aq) \rightarrow S_4O_6^{2-}(aq) + 2I^-(aq)$$

As soon as all the thiosulphate is used up, free iodine (or, strictly, I_3^- ions) remains in solution and reacts with the starch to form the familiar blue-black complex.

The time for the blue colour to appear can be adjusted by varying the amount of thiosulphate in solution A, so a 'clock' of any desired time interval can be produced.

Per pair of students

You will need

Chemicals

Solution A: 2.3 g of potassium iodate(V), KIO_3, in 450 cm^3 distilled water

Solution B: 7 g of sodium metabisulphite, $Na_2S_2O_5$, in 450 cm^3 distilled water with 20 cm^3 of 1 per cent starch solution added

Equipment

Conical flask, 250 cm^3

Stop clock

Two measuring cylinders, 100 cm^3

Access to a kitchen clock with a second hand

Access to an OHP permanent marker pen

Additional equipment for the extension/challenge activity

One measuring cylinder, 10 cm^3

Two measuring cylinders, 100 cm^3

Two measuring cylinders, 50 cm^3

Two beakers, 500 cm^3

Four beakers, 100 cm^3

Four beakers, 50 cm^3

Health and Safety

Laboratory goggles should be worn by all students; Potassium iodate(V), KIO_3, is a strong oxidizing agent. Avoid contact with skin.

Sodium metabisulphite, $Na_2S_2O_5$, is irritating to the skin and mucous membranes. When mixed with acid, sulphur dioxide gas is released, which can irritate the gaseous exchange system.

Some people are hypersensitive to sulphites and should avoid doing this experiment.

Do not mix solid potassium iodate(V) with solid sodium metabisulphite.

6.9 Cracking hydrocarbons

Learning objectives

- To be able to explain the process of cracking and the products that arise from cracking.
- To be able to distinguish between a saturated and an unsaturated hydrocarbon using common tests.
- To be able to explain the difference between the reactions and reactivity of saturated and unsaturated hydrocarbons, drawing on knowledge of the structures of saturated and unsaturated hydrocarbons.

Procedure

Students set the equipment up as show in Figure 6.5. They strongly heat the catalyst in the middle of the tube for a few minutes, until the glass is up to a dull red heat, avoiding heating the tube too close to the rubber bung. While keeping the catalyst hot, the flame can be flicked from time to time to the end of the tube for a few seconds to vaporize some of the liquid paraffin to produce a steady stream of bubbles from the delivery tube. Students should collect four tubes full of gas by holding them over the Bunsen valve and placing a rubber bung in the tube once full with gas, while the tube is inverted in the water trough before moving it to the test tube rack.

Note: Danger of suck-back (this is where water from the water bath sucks back into the hot tube and causes it to shatter).

To avoid this:

(i) *During the experiment* students must be careful not to heat the liquid paraffin too strongly or let the catalyst cool down. If suck-back looks as if it is about to occur, students should lift the whole apparatus by lifting the clamp stand and avoid at all costs touching the hot tube.

(ii) *When gas collection is complete* students should first remove the delivery tube from the water by tilting or lifting the clamp stand and only then stop heating.

Figure 6.5
Equipment set to carry out cracking of hydrocarbon oil

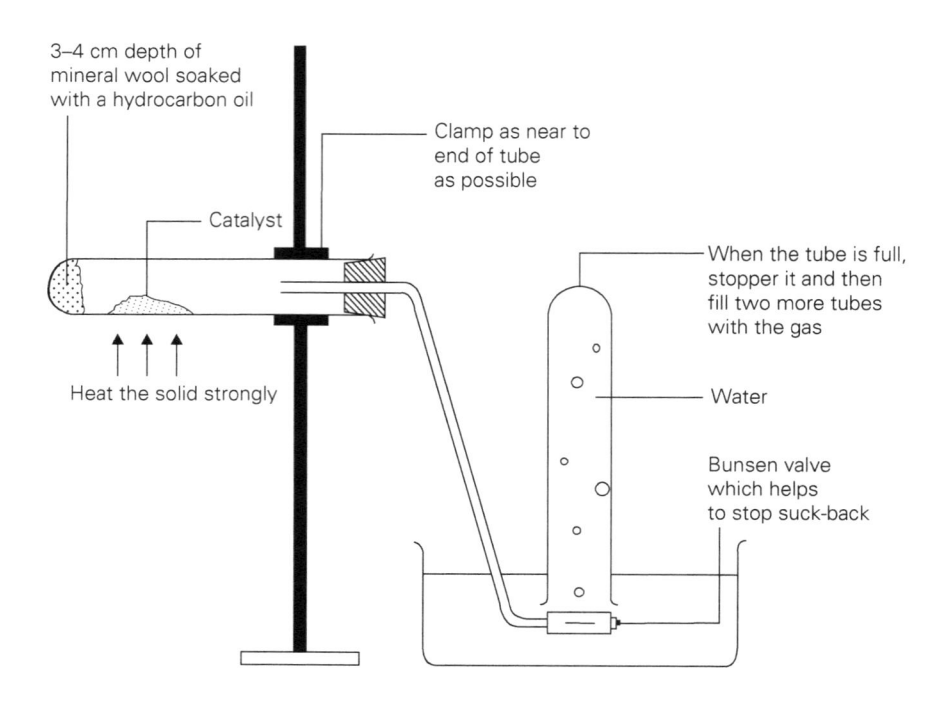

Labels on diagram:
- 3–4 cm depth of mineral wool soaked with a hydrocarbon oil
- Catalyst
- Heat the solid strongly
- Clamp as near to end of tube as possible
- When the tube is full, stopper it and then fill two more tubes with the gas
- Water
- Bunsen valve which helps to stop suck-back

The four test tubes of gas can be tested with the original hydrocarbon as described in the following table.

Test	Results with the gas formed during the experiment	Results with the hydrocarbon oil
Describe what the samples look like.		
Do the samples of gas and oil smell?		
Try to light the gas. Will a few drops of oil on a crucible lid catch fire?		
Add one or two drops of dilute, acidified potassium manganate(VII), then shake.		
Add one or two drops of aqueous bromine and then shake.		

Effectiveness matrix

	Domain of observables	Domain of ideas
What students do	Students can: • Set up the experiment as shown in Figure 6.5. • Collect products of combustion. • Carry out the tests on the four tubes of gas as described.	Students can describe: • The differences in the reactions of saturated and unsaturated hydrocarbons using the results of common tests (appearance, smell, combustion, addition of bromine water and acidified potassium manganate (VII)).
What students learn	This quadrant is intentionally blank in this task.	Students can later explain why: • Saturated and unsaturated hydrocarbons give different results for the tests (combustion, addition of bromine water and acidified potassium manganate (VII)), using their knowledge that saturated hydrocarbons are made up of carbon-to-carbon single bonds and unsaturated hydrocarbons have a carbon-to-carbon double bond.

Keep in mind

This experiment models the industrial cracking process, more information on which can be found at http://www.essentialchemicalindustry.org/processes/cracking-isomerisation-and-reforming.html.

Which is the more reactive: the oil or the product of the reaction? Explain why, drawing on the results of the tests to explain your answer.

What evidence is there to show that cracking has occurred in the reaction, for example larger molecules have been turned into smaller ones?

What is the evidence that the oil is a saturated compound while the product is unsaturated?

Health and Safety

Medicinal paraffin (liquid paraffin – *not* the fuel), about 2 cm^3

Porous pot or pumice stone fragments

Bromine water, 0.01 M – diluted to a pale yellow-orange colour (Harmful), about 2 cm^3

Acidified potassium manganate(VII) solution, about 0.002 M, about 2 cm^3

Mineral wool (preferably 'superwool')

The boiling tube should be a hard glass (borosilicate) 150 mm × 25 mm test tube.

It is important to ensure that the bung and the boiling tube fit well. Bunsen valves (see diagram below) can be made by attaching a 3 cm long piece of clean, unused, soft rubber tubing to the delivery tube, and then attaching a short length (1–2 cm) of glass rod, as shown in Figure 6.6. The rubber tubing should be slit on one side along about 1 cm of its length in the direction of the tubing. The use of a Bunsen valve should stop 'suck-back' occurring. See CLEAPSS *Laboratory Handbook* 13.2.1.

Porous pot chips can be made by crushing broken crucibles into pea-sized fragments.

Figure 6.6

Detail of the equipment used to prevent 'suck-back'

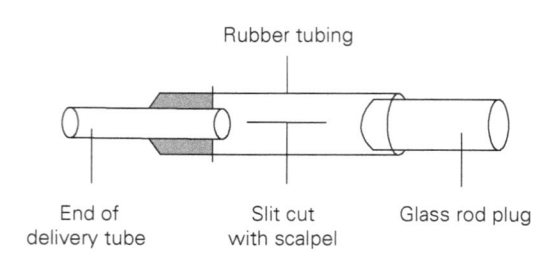

Rubber tubing

End of delivery tube — Slit cut with scalpel — Glass rod plug

Equipment

Laboratory goggles should be worn by all students
Safety screens (for demonstration)

Each working group requires:
Test tubes, 4
Bungs, to fit test tubes, 4
Test tube rack
Boiling tube (Note 1 above)
Bung, one-holed, to fit boiling tube
Delivery tube fitted with a Bunsen valve (Note 2 above)
Small glass trough or plastic basin, for gas collection over water
Bunsen burner
Heat-resistant mat
Stand and clamp
Dropping pipette
Wooden spill
'Oily liquid' sample; a solution of cyclohexene in tap water (harmful and irritant)

Note: Illustrations taken from http://www.nuffieldfoundation.org/practical-chemistry/cracking-hydrocarbons.

6.10 Emulsifiers

Learning objectives

- To identify which household substance is the most effective emulsifier.
- To define what an emulsifier is and how it stabilizes a colloid.

Procedure

1. Six clean test tubes are taken and into each one students carefully measure 5 cm^3 of water and then add 1 cm^3 of vegetable oil.
2. A bung is placed into one of these test tubes (test tube 1) and it is shaken vigorously for about 10 seconds. Students time how long it takes for the oil (the dispersed phase) and water (the continuous phase) to separate into two distinct layers.

To the further five test tubes, add one drop of detergent (emulsifier) and a small quantity of sugar (test tube 2), flour (test tube 3), mustard powder (test tube 4), egg white (test tube 5), egg yolk (test tube 6).

Step 2, shaking the tubes vigorously, is repeated for each of the other test tubes and students again time how long it takes for the oil and water to separate. If the substance added acts as an emulsifier, then the oil and water will not separate.

Note: Test tubes must be very clean and must not be contaminated with detergent. If fresh eggs are used, ensure no yolk contaminates the white – the other way round is less important. Due to the risk of salmonella, handling raw eggs should be kept to a minimum, so provide disposable pipettes with the egg for students to transfer it to the test tubes.

Effectiveness matrix

	Domain of observables	Domain of ideas
What students do	Students can: • Test various emulsifiers and record stabilizing times.	Students can: • Identify the most effective emulsifier and explain why it is this one.
What students learn	Students can subsequently: • Recommend suitable emulsifiers in new contexts.	Students can later talk about: • How emulsifiers stabilize colloids, and use technical vocabulary, such as continuous and dispersed phases, micelle formation and emulsifiers.

Keep in mind

Colloids are formed when particles of one substance are mixed and dispersed with particles of another substance. A mixture of oil and water is not a colloid because it usually separates out quickly. However, substances which act as emulsifiers can be added to the oil and water mixture which prevent separation, and so a colloid called an emulsion (immiscible liquids where one liquid is dispersed in another) is formed. In this activity, students test a range of things commonly found in the kitchen to see which stabilizes an oil and water mixture to form an emulsion. An example of a colloid that students could make at home is salad dressing using oil and vinegar and they can use various emulsifiers like mustard to stabilize it.

Issues for discussion

An emulsifier is a substance that stabilizes an emulsion. Detergent, egg yolk and mustard are examples of emulsifiers.

Deeper level chemistry

Water (H_2O) is a polar molecule, meaning it has positively and negatively charged ends. This polarity is created because the electrons are attracted to the oxygen (O) atom of the molecule more than to the hydrogen (H) atom. The distribution of electrons therefore makes the oxygen end of the molecule slightly negative while the hydrogen end is slightly positive.

When salt (sodium chloride) is put into water, it breaks down to form charged ions: a positively charged sodium ion (Na^+) and a negatively charge chloride ion (Cl^-). The water is attracted to the ions and surrounds them so the ions are mixed evenly throughout the water. We call this dissolving. So, ions or molecules with a slight or strong charge can dissolve in water.

Oil does not have a polarity so it is not attracted to water. Oil molecules clump together. They are known as hydrophobic molecules from the Greek *hydro*, meaning water and *phobos*, meaning fear. Sugar does dissolve in water because it has an unequal distribution of charge in its molecule, which although slight, means the molecule is polar and therefore attracted to the water. Sugar is known as a hydrophilic molecule from the Greek *hydro*, meaning water and *philia*, meaning love.

Health and Safety

Students should be warned against tasting anything – for example sugar – in the laboratory. Eggs have a salmonella risk and should be marked with the lion symbol. Raw egg should be handled as little as possible, and a disposable pipette should be used to transfer it to the boiling tubes.

Equipment

Apparatus

Test tubes and bungs

Small measuring cylinder (to measure water)

Stop clock

Disposable teat pipettes (to measure oil)

Spatulas or small spoons

Chemicals

Cooking oil

Detergent

Sugar

Flour

Mustard powder

Egg white

Egg yolk

6.11 Making nylon rope

Learning objectives

- To identify and be able to explain the nylon polymerization reaction.

Procedure

Before the demonstration

A solution of 2.2 g of 1,6-diaminohexane (Corrosive) in 50 cm^3 of deionized water is made up. This solution is approximately 0.4 mol dm^{-3}. A solution of 1.5 g of decanedioyl dichloride (corrosive) in 50 cm^3 of cyclohexane is made up (highly flammable and harmful). This solution is approximately 0.15 mol dm^{-3}.

The demonstration

5 cm^3 of the aqueous diamine solution is poured into a 25 cm^3 beaker and then 5 cm^3 of the cyclohexane solution of the acid chloride is carefully poured on top of the first solution so that mixing is minimized. This can be done by pouring the second solution down the wall of the beaker or by pouring it down a glass rod. The cyclohexane will float on top of the water without mixing. The beaker is placed below a stand and clamp as shown (see Figure 6.7).

A greyish film of nylon will form at the interface. Wearing a pair of nitrile gloves this can be picked up with a pair of tweezers and lifted slowly and gently from the beaker; it should draw up behind it a thread of nylon. Pull this over the rod of the clamp so that this acts as a pulley and continue pulling the nylon thread at a rate of about half a metre per second. It should be possible to pull out several metres. Care should be taken as the thread may be coated with unreacted monomer and may in fact be a narrow, hollow tube filled with monomer solution.

Figure 6.7
How to extract and store 'nylon rope'

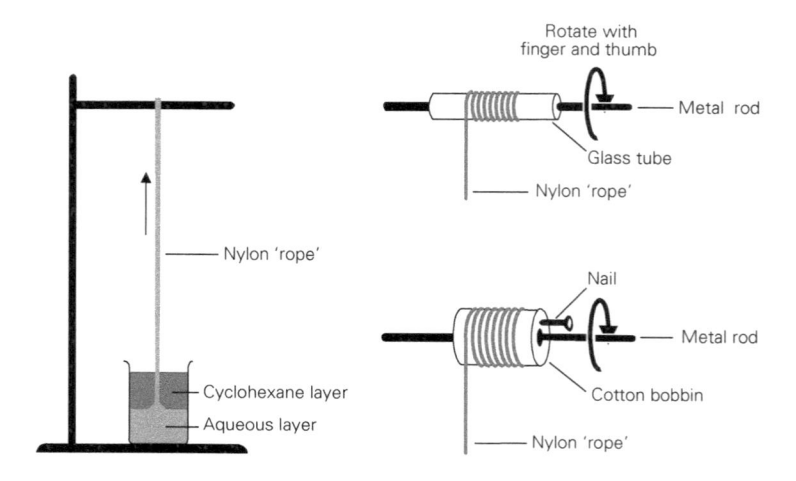

Effectiveness matrix

	Domain of observables	Domain of ideas
What students do	Students can: • Produce a sample of nylon rope.	Students can talk about: • Nylon rope polymer, using scientific terminology such as monomer, polymer and polymerization.
What students learn	This quadrant is intentionally blank in this task.	Students can later explain: • How nylon is produced, using technical language.

Keep in mind

This practical is usually done as a demonstration. However, if the volumes used are less than 5 cm³ and the students wear gloves and the task is closely supervised, then Key Stage 4 students are able to carry this out competently.

Issues for discussion

Although students may understand the theory behind polymer synthesis, it is unlikely they will be prepared for the alien nature of the thread being drawn from the aqueous layer in the beaker. If this demonstration is used at the beginning of a series on polymer chemistry, it may serve as a good way to stimulate questions about the nature of polymers and how they interact. Equally, if used during or near the end of a series of lessons, this demonstration is a useful opportunity to consolidate and challenge theory.

Point out that this demonstration is different from the industrial method of making nylon which takes place at a higher temperature. Molten nylon is then forced through multi-holed 'spinnerets' to form the fibres.

The reaction is a condensation polymerization:

$$nH_2N(CH_2)_6NH_2 + nClOC(CH_2)_8COCl \rightarrow H_2N[(CH_2)_6NHCO(CH_2)_8]_nCOCl + nHCl$$

The nylon formed is nylon 6–10, so called because of the lengths of the carbon chains of the monomers. Nylon 6–6 can be made using hexanedioyl dichloride (adipoyl chloride). The diamine is present in excess to react with the hydrogen chloride that is eliminated. An alternative procedure is to use the stoichiometric quantity of diamine dissolved in excess sodium hydroxide solution.

Health and Safety

Hexane-1,6-diamine (hexamethylene diamine, 1,6-diaminohexane, $H_2N(CH_2)_6NH_2$ (Corrosive) – refer to CLEAPSS® Hazcard 3B and CLEAPSS® Recipe Card 45

Decanedioyl dichloride (sebacoyl chloride, ClOC(CH$_2$)$_8$COCl) (Corrosive) – refer to CLEAPSS® Hazcard 41 and CLEAPSS® Recipe Card 45

Cyclohexane (highly flammable and harmful) – refer to CLEAPSS® Hazcards 45B

Laboratory goggles should be worn by all students.

Nitrile gloves should be worn at all times when handling the chemicals.

The room should be well ventilated and there must be no sources of ignition.

Details for waste disposal can be found in the CLEAPSS *Handbook* section 7.5.

This demonstration has been described in many sources using chlorinated solvents for the acid chloride. These are no longer considered safe and will soon become unavailable. Cyclohexane is less dense than water, whereas chlorinated solvents are denser. The layers are therefore inverted compared to the old method.

Cyclohexane is preferred to hexane as it is less harmful.

Dispose of the mixture as follows: First, shake the reaction to mix the two layers. A lump of nylon will be produced which can be removed with tweezers, rinsed well with water and disposed as solid waste. Failure to do this may result in the polymerization taking place in the sink, leading to a blockage. The remaining liquids can be mixed with detergent and washed down the sink.

Equipment

(The chemical quantities given are for one demonstration.)

Apparatus

One 25 cm³ beaker

A pair of tweezers

Retort stand with boss and clamp

Chemicals

2.2 g of 1,6-diaminohexane (hexamethylene diamine, hexane-1,6-diamine, H$_2$N(CH$_2$)$_6$(NH$_2$) (corrosive)

1.5 g of decanedioyl dichloride (sebacoyl chloride, ClOC(CH$_2$)$_8$COCl) (corrosive)

50 cm³ of cyclohexane (highly flammable and harmful)

50 cm³ of deionized water

Note: Figure taken from http://www.rsc.org/learn-chemistry/resource/res00000755/making-nylon-the-nylon-rope-trick?cmpid=CMP00000834

6.12 Thermometric titration

Learning objectives

- To calculate the end point of a neutralization reaction based on the observed maximum temperature change.
- To calculate the maximum temperature reached in a chemical reaction through extrapolation using a cooling curve.

Procedure

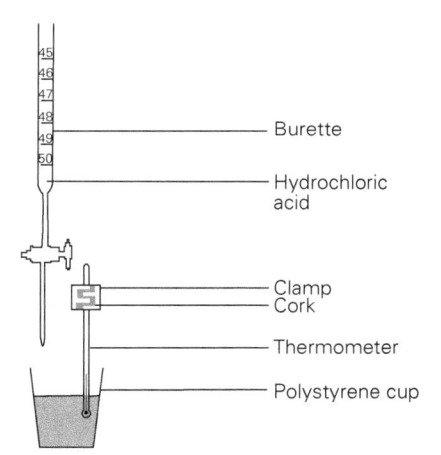

Figure 6.8 Equipment set up for acid–base titration

See Figure 6.8. An insulated cup is placed in a beaker for support to which 20 cm^3 (or 25 cm^3) of sodium hydroxide is transferred using a pipette and safety filler. The temperature is then measured. Using the burette, a small portion (3–5 cm^3) of dilute hydrochloric acid is added to the solution in the cup, noting the actual volume. The solution is then swirled and the highest temperature reached is measured. Immediately, a second small portion of the dilute hydrochloric acid is added and stirred, and again the highest temperature and the volume are noted. This procedure is continued until there are enough readings to determine the maximum temperature reached. Students are then asked to plot a graph of temperature against volume of acid added, and use extrapolation to deduce the maximum temperature reached (assuming no heat loss) and to use their results to calculate the concentration of the hydrochloric acid.

Alternatively, a temperature sensor attached to a computer can be used in place of a thermometer. Data logging software could then be used to provide a detailed plot of the readings. To reinforce the theory involved here, an indicator could also be used to show that the end point really did occur at the highest temperature.

The main concern in this practical is the heat loss. If possible, a lid should be used. More reliable results can be achieved using two polystyrene cups (one placed inside the other).

Effectiveness matrix

	Domain of observables	Domain of ideas
What students do	Students can: • Use a pipette to accurately measure 20–25 cm^3 of sodium hydroxide. • Use a burette to an accuracy of 0.1 cm^3. • Use a thermometer to an accuracy of 0.5 °C.	Students can talk about: • How neutralization has occurred at the point when the maximum temperature of the reaction mixture was reached.
What students learn	Students can subsequently: • Plot graphs so that they can use the data to calculate the end point of a titration.	Students can later: • Calculate the concentration of hydrochloric acid from the results of the experiment. • Explain the reaction taking place using appropriate scientific terminology and outline limitations to the data collected.

Keep in mind

With higher attaining or older students, it is possible to discuss the extrapolation of the cooling curve to estimate the maximum temperature reached without heat loss.

Issues for discussion

To reinforce the theory involved here, an indicator could also be used to show that the end point really did occur at the highest temperature. This could lead to a discussion about these two different titration methods: thermometric titration and titrations which use indicators. For example, students could be asked to discuss the scientific principles of why each one can be used to determine the concentration of hydrochloric acid and the advantages and disadvantages of each.

Health and Safety

Laboratory goggles should be worn by all students.

Hydrochloric acid, HCl(aq), (Irritant at concentration used) – see CLEAPSS *Hazcard* and CLEAPSS *Recipe Book*. This concentration is necessary to achieve a reasonable change in temperature. The concentration of the hydrochloric acid should not be indicated on bottle available to the students.

Sodium hydroxide solution, NaOH(aq), (Corrosive at concentration used) – see CLEAPSS *Hazcard* and CLEAPSS *Recipe Book*. This concentration is necessary to achieve a reasonable change in temperature. The concentration of the sodium hydroxide should be indicated on bottle available to the students.

Equipment

Each group will need:
Apparatus
Thermometer (0–100 °C)
Two insulated (polystyrene) cups
Beaker (250 cm^3)
Burette (50 cm^3)
Burette stand
Clamp and stand (optional)
Cork, one-holed (optional – to fit thermometer)
Pipette (20 or 25 cm^3)
Pipette safety filler

Chemicals
Hydrochloric acid, 2.00 M (irritant), about 75 cm^3
Sodium hydroxide solution, 1.50 M (Corrosive), about 30 cm^3

Note: Illustration taken from http://www.rsc.org/learn-chemistry/resource/res00000429/a-thermometric-titration?cmpid=CMP00003294

Physics: Session Guides 11–14

James de Winter and Michael Inglis

7

7.1	Measuring the speed of moving objects (p. 184)	
7.2	Motion graphs (p. 187)	
7.3	Relationship between force and extension for a helical spring (p. 190)	
7.4	Observing the appearance of the Moon over time (p. 193)	
7.5	Thermal conduction (p. 196)	
7.6	Thermal insulation (p. 199)	
7.7	Comparing the energy content of fuels (p. 201)	
7.8	The law of reflection (p. 203)	
7.9	The law of refraction (p. 205)	
7.10	Filters and colours (p. 207)	
7.11	Investigating the magnetic field around a bar magnet (p. 209)	
7.12	Factors that affect the strength of a simple electromagnet (p. 212)	

7.1 Measuring the speed of moving objects

Learning objectives

- To be able to understand the term 'average speed'.
- To know what measurements are needed to be able to calculate the average speed of a moving object.

Procedure

Students will drop a cupcake case from a known height and measure the time it takes to fall to the floor and then use the values for distance travelled and time taken to calculate an average speed. They should be encouraged to repeat each result to increase the level of accuracy of their value for the speed. They can then vary the height from which the cupcake case is dropped and investigate if the average speed changes.

Effectiveness matrix

	Domain of observables	Domain of ideas
What students do	Students can: • Measure, to an acceptable accuracy, the distance an object travels. • Measure, to an acceptable accuracy, the time it takes to travel that distance. • Divide the distance by the time.	Students can talk about: • Speed as a quantity (a compound variable) that depends upon both distance and time and is determined by dividing the distance by the time. • How a *faster* object will travel a given distance in less time than a *slower* one.
What students learn	Students can later: • Measure distances that objects travel and then measure the time it takes them to do this in order to calculate an average speed.	Students can later talk about: • The idea that the calculated speed of their object may not be constant over the whole journey and so the speed they measured is an *average* speed. • The relationship between speed, distance travelled and time taken and how changes in one of these variables will affect the others. • How the value of an average speed can provide a description of the motion over a whole journey but may not tell the actual speed at any one point in time.

Keep in mind

The single falling cupcake case is a good choice for introductory calculations of speed because it falls relatively slowly over a distance of 1–2 m and so measurements are easy while also providing opportunities to discuss accuracy and evaluate the method.

When dropped, a single cupcake case quickly reaches a constant falling speed, known as terminal velocity, where the air resistance up is the same as the weight down so it does not accelerate. You do not need to explain or make reference to terminal velocity if you do not wish to; the idea of a constant speed (not increasing or decreasing) suffices and also avoids having to introduce the difference between speed and velocity. It is not recommended that you vary the number of cupcake cases dropped from a fixed height to investigate the speed as the pattern can be confusing for some students with the speed initially increasing with the number of cupcake cases and then levelling off to an approximately constant value, apparently independent of mass at around four or five cases.

Issues for discussion

You may wish to ask the students some of the following questions to help develop their thinking:

If it took longer to travel the same distance, would the speed go up or down? *This helps them explore the inverse relationship between speed and time for a given distance (e.g. time up, speed down for a given distance) in a qualitative manner.*

If we drop the cupcake case from twice as high and it falls as the same speed what will happen to the time it will take to fall? *This question can allow students to make predictions based on their results without having actually to calculate speed. These could be of the form bigger/smaller/the same or actual numerical values.*

Health and safety

In order to drop cupcake cases from over 1 m students are likely to have to stand on stools or tables and so care is needed to make sure that this is done safely.

Equipment

Cupcake cases, ideally two different sizes. Other objects that move at a roughly steady speed that could be measured can be used instead. For example, spinning paper helicopters or toys cars powered by a wound spring. *A time period of a few seconds and distance of 1–2 m are most likely to yield practical and useful results for a class at this age range.*

Stopclocks

Metre rulers

Calculators

7.2 Motion graphs

Learning objectives

- To investigate the motion of a moving object to collect quantitative data to produce a distance/time graph.
- To be able to describe the motion of an object based on a distance/time graph.

Prior knowledge: It is assumed that students will be familiar with the term 'speed', able to calculate it from a given distance and time.

Procedure

Students use a stopclock and appropriate measuring equipment (tape measure/metre rule) to collect data for distance travelled and time taken for an object moving at constant speed and then draw a graph of this data. This could be collected for almost any object that can move at a constant speed.

One example might be a student walking. Along a field or running track, place markers at 10 m intervals and tell one student, when instructed to walk/run along the track at as close to a constant speed as they can. Students are provided with a stop clock and asked to record the time it takes from when the runner/walker starts to when they have travelled a certain distances. This can be done as an individual exercise where students record the time for each distance or could be done as a collaborative data collection exercise where students collect only one time and then all data is shared. This can be repeated with different students asked to travel at different constant speeds – for example, one student runs and another walks slowly.

Effectiveness matrix

	Domain of observables	Domain of ideas
What students do	Students can: • Collect data for distance travelled and time for a object moving with constant speed. • Plot a line graph of their distance travelled and time data and draw a best fit line through or near to the data points.	Students can talk about: • How the motion of the moving object can be represented by a distance/time graph. • How the steepness of the line on the graph can indicate speed, with a steeper line meaning a greater speed.

Effectiveness matrix (continued)

	Domain of observables	Domain of ideas
What students learn	Students can later: • Plot a distance/time graph for an object moving at a speed that is not constant and draw a best fit line through or near to the data points.	Students can later talk about: • How to compare the relative speeds of objects from distance time graphs by comparing the gradients of the lines. • How the gradient of a distance time graph can be used to calculate speed of an object.

Keep in mind

This activity is designed to be one of the first occasions that students connect the motion of an object and its distance and time data to a graphical representation and so trying to provide them with data that shows a pretty constant speed is important. It is known that for some students, drawing graphs can cause some challenges and so time and support may be required with respect to this part of the activity, for example, you may wish to have some pre-drawn axis or select times and speeds that make the selection of axis scales easier.

This activity helps students explore the relationship between speed, distance and time. It does not consider the ideas around direction and velocity which will be addressed at a later date.

Issues for discussion

You may wish to ask the students some of the following questions to help develop their thinking:

(Before they plot their graph) What do you think a graph of distance against time might look like? *This is designed to help them consider how numerical data may be represented in a graph. You may wish to add extra prompts such as 'does the distance go up by roughly the same time each time?'*

(From their graph) What do you think the graph would look like if the object was travelling slower/faster? *The idea here is to encourage them to relate the gradient of the graph to the speed of the object. This may be in the range from something as simple as steeper=faster to a more sophisticated look at how the value of the gradient will equal the speed assuming that they know how to calculate gradients.*

(From their graph, selecting a time greater than they have data for) How long you think it would take to go x metres? *This question is designed to help students explore the predictive power of the graph by using data that they have to estimate data that they do not have. If the object were travelling at constant speed the time for x should be double the time it took to travel half of x.*

Health and safety

If students are running outside, care needs to be taken to ensure that footwear is appropriate.

Equipment

Metre ruler/measuring tape
Stopclock(s)
Graph paper

7.3 Relationship between force and extension for a helical spring

Learning objectives

- To be able to describe the relationship between force and extension on a helical spring.
- To be able to describe the way in which force/extension relationships for other objects could be investigated.

Prior knowledge: It is assumed that students will be familiar with the difference between mass and weight, will know that on the surface of the Earth 1 kg can be considered to have a weight of 10 N (and 100 g a weight of 1 N) and will be able to convert from mass to weight and vice versa.

Procedure

Students affix the spring to a clamp and stand in a secure way and then measure the extension of the spring as increasing force is added (see Figure 7.1). They record the force applied to the spring via the hanging of masses on the end and the extension of the spring, each time calculating the extension *compared to the original length when no force was applied*.

Figure 7.1 Measuring the extension of a helical spring

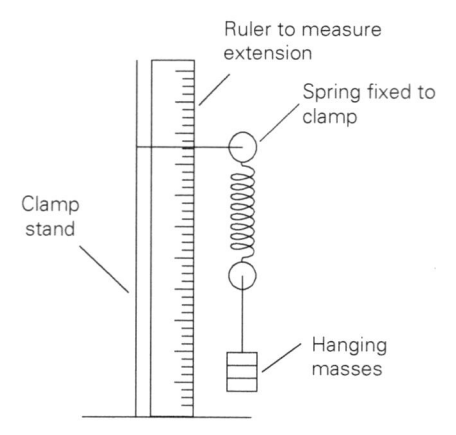

Effectiveness matrix

	Domain of observables	**Domain of ideas**
What students do	Students can: • Set up the apparatus as required and take measurements of mass on the spring and length. • Calculate the extension of the spring from the original length and the extended length.	Students can talk about: • The idea that when a force is added to the spring, it will change the length of the spring. • The idea that if you increase the force on the spring, then the length will increase.
What students learn	Students can later: • Set up the apparatus required to measure lengths of other springs or similar objects, measuring them accurately, minimizing errors such as parallax.	Students can later talk about: • That for a helical spring force and extension are directly proportional. • The relationship, directly proportional or otherwise, between force and extension for other objects based on experimental data.

Keep in mind

This practical is designed to explore the directly proportional elastic behaviour of the spring, in that it extends in a way that the extension is proportional to the force applied but also that the spring will return to its total length when the force is removed. The linear relationship between force and extension is known as Hooke's law. It is common for some students to measure mass rather than force and the length of the spring rather than the extension. In both cases this will yield a relationship and a straight line graph but the correct, directly proportional relationship is that between force and extension. Students may investigate the behaviour of different springs or materials, such as stretchy toys or fruit lace sweets to see if they display the same relationships.

Issues for discussion

You may wish to ask the students some of the following questions to help develop their thinking:

If you kept adding more force to the spring, what might happen? *This will allow students to make a prediction as to what might happen as well as consider that while there may be a relationship between two variables it may not continue indefinitely and so the idea of a 'limit' could be introduced.*

Looking at your data, can you predict what a graph of force and extension might look like? *This can help reinforce the value of graphing data as well as encouraging them to articulate the relationship between force and extension.*

What might the extension be if I used a force of x N? (Select x as a value between two data points they have or above their maximum force.) *This will encourage them to consider the predictive power of the data that they have.*

Health and safety

It is possible that the springs may fail and/or fly off the stand or the stand may fall over and so students should wear safety goggles at all times. If the masses fall to the ground they could hurt students' feet and so it is recommended that you warn them of this possibility and do not provide them with total mass over 500 g. This will also prevent permanent damage for most springs commonly used for this experiment.

Equipment

Helical spring. There is no specific requirement here but it is suggested that they are chosen such that the maximum mass used, suggested at 500 g, will result in an extension that can be measured with a 30 cm ruler.

30 cm ruler.

Masses with hook to be attached to spring. The amount will depend upon the spring used but it is suggested that a total mass of under 500 g is used and that students will be able to take at least six results.

Clamp boss and stand.

7.4 Observing the appearance of the Moon over time

Learning objectives

- To understand that the position and appearance of the Moon changes over time and be able to describe some of these changes.
- To understand that the position and appearance of the Moon depends on the relative positions of the Sun, Earth and Moon.
- To be able to explain that that the changes that are observed in the position and apparent shape of the Moon over time are caused by the relative motions of the Sun, Earth and Moon.

Procedure

Students keep a Moon diary over at least one month. They should record the apparent shape of the Moon for as many nights as it is visible (by sketching or photograph). They should also record the position of the Moon in the sky over at least one evening by recording time against compass coordinate.

Effectiveness matrix

	Domain of observables	Domain of ideas
What students do	Students can: • Record the position of the Moon (height and location) in the sky over time. • Record the apparent shape of the Moon over time.	Students can talk about: • The Moon appears in different positions in the sky on different evenings. • How the apparent shape of the Moon changes over time. • How the Moon appears in different positions in the sky over the course of one evening. • The apparent shape of the Moon remains the same over one evening.

Effectiveness matrix (continued)

	Domain of observables	Domain of ideas
What students learn	Students can later: • Generate observational data such as position for any observable astronomical object such as a planet, star or constellation. This can be at the same time each day over a sequence of days or over the course of one evening.	Students can later talk about: • How the changes in apparent shape of the Moon are caused by the positions of the Sun and Moon relative to the Earth. • How, over the course of one evening, the Moon appears to move across the sky and that this is caused by the rotation of the Earth. • How the changes in the position and shape of the Moon over time are caused by the relative motion of the Earth and Moon and the position of the Sun relative to them.

Keep in mind

This activity provides an opportunity to carry out an observation over a much longer period of time compared to 'usual' classroom experiments.

The terms used to describe the shape of the Moon and its changes such as *waxing, waning, new, crescent, gibbous* and *full* can be introduced but are not necessary.

It is worth noting that while it can be relatively straightforward for students to collate and present a selection of images that show how the apparent shape of the Moon changes over time, appreciating the causes for this are quite challenging conceptually as it requires a three-dimensional model with three objects (Sun, Earth and Moon) all behaving in a different way, a considerable feat for anyone, especially when considering the distances involved.

It is common for students to think different phases of the Moon are seen in different parts of the world on the same day. This is not true; the apparent shape is the same for everyone, fixed by the relative positions of the Sun, Earth and Moon at any one time. However, the orientation of the Moon will be different depending upon location. For example, in the Southern Hemisphere, the Moon will appear 'upside down' compared to how it is seen in the Northern Hemisphere, but the shape will be the same

Issues for discussion

You may wish to ask the students some of the following questions to help develop their thinking:

Does the Moon really change shape and if not, why does it look different? *It may seem an obvious question to ask but it is important to get students to articulate the difference between what we see and what is actually the case.*

If the Moon were to orbit round the Earth twice as quickly, what would happen to the patterns of position and apparent shape you observed? *This question is to try and help students explore their understating of the causes of the changes in shape and position. If the Moon was moving twice as fast around the Earth it would cycle through the same pattern of phases from full to new and back again but roughly twice as quickly.*

Health and safety

It is worth telling students that their eyes will adapt to a darkened situation after a while (5/10 minutes) and they should be cautious when working in the dark.

Equipment

Compass (Navigation)

Pen and paper – although students could take photographs if wished

7.5 Thermal conduction

Learning objectives

- To establish that some materials are better conductors of 'heat' than others.
- To consider critically how the thermal conductivity of different materials can be compared in a way that is scientifically valid.

Procedure

A series of metal rods or strips of equal length but of different metals should be set up so that they are suspended horizontally, perhaps by resting on top of a tripod stand. They should be arranged so that one end of all the rods can be simultaneously heated in a Bunsen burner flame. Some schools will have an item of kit consisting of four strips of metal arranged in a cross specifically for this activity (see Figure 7.2). At the other end of each rod, a drawing pin should be stuck using a blob of wax so that when the rods are heated the wax will eventually melt and the drawing pins will fall off. Students will need a stopclock to record the time taken from the start of heating for the far end of each rod to become hot enough to melt the wax and allow the pin to fall.

Figure 7.2 Metal rods set up for heating

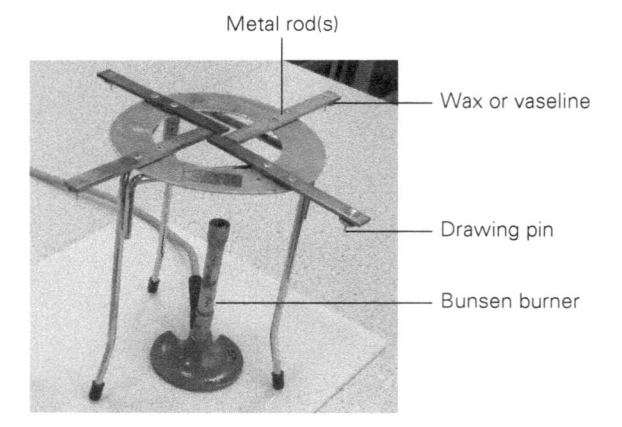

Effectiveness matrix

	Domain of observables	Domain of ideas
What students do	Students can: • Use a stopclock to measure the time taken for each object to be released.	Students can talk about: • Thermal conduction in terms of stationary but vibrating particles 'passing on' vibrations to their neighbours. • A period of time needed for particles to 'pass on' vibrations and that this time period depends on the material.
What students learn	This quadrant is intentionally blank in this task.	Students can later talk about: • The need to take into account the dimensions of the test materials, especially cross-sectional area, when comparing conduction. • How heat loss to the surrounding air might influence the apparent conductivity of a material.

Keep in mind

The actual reasons why different materials have different conductivities are complex and not intuitive. It will be sufficient to ensure that students recognize that time is required for a vibrating particle to initiate vibration of its neighbours and this time is a property of a material.

Issues for discussion

You may wish to ask the students some of the following questions to help develop their thinking:

How/why does the shape of the test material affect its conductivity?

How is it useful to know how well a substance conducts heat? In what circumstances might it be important to have materials of high/low thermal conductivity?

If you wanted to quantify thermal conductivity, what units could you use? *This could form the basis for a homework/research task, as a variety of different units are used depending on context.*

How might the initial temperature of a substance affect how well it conducts heat? *For some materials, the thermal conductivity depends on temperature.*

Health and safety

Consortium of Local Education Authorities for the Provision of Science Services (CLEAPSS) advice should always be followed. The usual warnings will be needed about use of Bunsen burners, care with hot materials, etc.

Equipment

Bunsen burner.
Tripod
Selection of rods of different metals
Lengths and diameters
Wax
Drawing pins
Stopclock

7.6 Thermal insulation

Learning objectives

- To establish the features of materials that are effective insulators.
- To identify how these materials function as insulators in terms of the scientific ideas of conduction, convection and radiation.
- To consider critically how the insulating properties of different materials could be compared in a way that is scientifically valid.

Procedure

Students are tasked with using a selection of materials to minimize the temperature loss/gain of hot/cold water in a soft drinks can (e.g. coke can). Materials to include sponge, bubble wrap, tissue paper, packing beads and tin foil. Containers of fixed volume should be supplied which are large enough to contain a drinks can with plenty of space around which to pack material. A control can should be set up with no insulation around it. Record the initial temperatures of the water in the insulated and control cans, and that of the ambient air. Then the temperature of the water in the insulated and control cans should be measured after a fixed period of time (or record the time taken for a fixed temp change). This practical would be particularly suitable for use of datalogging kit as it will require most or all of a lesson to complete, and a logger could capture continuous temperature data to enable the additional examination of rate of change, generation and use of graphs, etc.

Effectiveness matrix

	Domain of observables	**Domain of ideas**
What students do	Students can: • Use a thermometer correctly to measure temperature of the water over time.	Students can talk about: • Thermal insulation in terms of minimizing 'heat transfer' through conduction, convection and radiation. • Why a control is needed in terms of the scientific idea of a fair comparison.
What students learn	Students can later: • Independently design and set up an equivalent activity using a different range of materials and water containers.	Students can later talk about: • How the physical structure of any material relates to its insulating properties in terms of factors that affect conduction, convection and radiation.

Keep in mind

The reasons why different materials have different thermal insulation properties are not always evident at a macroscopic scale, that is, different samples of apparently structurally similar solids can have very different thermal conductivities.

Issues for discussion

You may wish to ask the students some of the following questions to help develop their thinking:

Does the thickness/weight/density of a material relate to how good an insulator it is?

Can a material that is good at reducing radiative heat transfer also be good at reducing transfer through conduction/convection?

How could you use or arrange foil (which is good at reducing radiative heat transfer) to also increase its effectiveness at reducing transfer through conduction/convection?

How could you maximize the insulation of the can, but minimize the amount of material used?

For a valid comparison, should all of the cans in the room contain water with the same initial temperature?

If you wanted to quantify how good an insulator a material is, how could you do this? What units would you use?

Health and safety

Usual warnings needed here about use of hot water.

Equipment

Selection of packing materials (e.g. foam, different types of paper, bubble wrap, aluminium foil, fabric, packing beads), large containers of identical volume and shape which can contain a drinks can surrounded by packing material, empty drinks cans, supply of hot water, thermometers, stopclocks.

7.7 Comparing the energy content of fuels

Learning objectives

- To compare the energy content of a selection of fuels.
- To consider critically how the energy content of fuels can be compared in a way that is scientifically valid.

Procedure

Students place samples of fuels (e.g. meths, camping stove tablet, candle) of fixed mass under a beaker on a tripod stand (see Figure 7.3). The beaker should be filled with a fixed volume of water and the initial temperature of the water should be recorded. A lid should be fitted to the beaker with a hole to allow insertion of a thermometer (liquid-in-glass type or a probe attached to a datalogger) into the water. The fuel is lit and then the temperature rise over a fixed period of time is recorded. Repeat for a selection of fuels, ensuring that the initial temperature of the water is the same in each case.

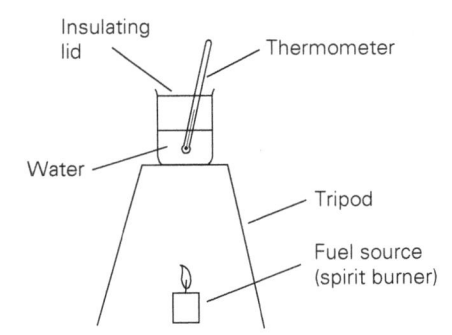

Figure 7.3 Heating a fixed volume of water with different fuel sources

Keep in mind

The volume of water used should be large enough so that the water does not boil while the fuel is burned (the temperature of boiling water stays constant while the input energy goes into the water changing state from liquid to gas). As the water becomes hotter, more energy is transferred to the surroundings. The need to use the same starting temperature of the water each time will require the beakers to be rinsed before filling, or have a supply of unused beakers to hand.

Issues for discussion

You may wish to ask the students some of the following questions to help develop their thinking:

Does the shape of a fuel sample change the results?

Why does the same volume of water have to be used each time? What would happen if more/less water was used for one of the fuels?

What happens if the water boils? How might this affect the conclusions?

For a fair test, how can the energy loss to the surroundings be minimized?

Health and safety

CLEAPSS advice should always be followed. The usual warnings will be needed about burning materials, the need for safety goggles, use of hot water and handling of hot objects.

Equipment

Selection of samples of fuel, beakers, tripod stands, stopclocks, thermometers, lids for beakers, supply of water of constant initial temperature.

Effectiveness matrix

	Domain of observables	Domain of ideas
What students do	Students can: • Use a thermometer correctly to measure temperature of the water to an appropriate level of accuracy.	Students can talk about: • Substances that burn are 'stores' of energy; particularly 'concentrated' stores are fuels; burning results in the 'transfer' of energy associated with the fuel to the water; energy is conserved so all of the transferred energy ends up with the water *and* the environment. • Why fixed masses of fuel, volumes of water and initial water temperatures are needed to make a valid comparison.
What students learn	Students can later: • Given different possible masses of fuel, select appropriate volumes of water to enable measurement of a reasonable temperature change without the water boiling.	Students can later talk about: • Possible mechanisms for the 'transfer' of 'heat' (e.g. convection of the air between fuel and beaker). • The limitations of the practical set-up and how they can be addressed to minimize or take account of energy 'lost' to the environment.

7.8 The law of reflection

Learning objectives

- To explore the behaviour of light as it reflects off a plane surface.
- To practise the use of a normal line to determine angles of incidence and reflection.
- To understand the need for a range of repeated measurements to identify an underlying relationship.

Procedure

Students should place a straight mirror on a piece of paper and draw a line along the front edge of the mirror. Using a ray box, a ray should be aimed at the mirror. The path of the ray should be marked on the paper for the incident and reflected rays, along with the point of incidence. The mirror can then be removed and a normal line (a line perpendicular to the mirror) drawn. The angles of incidence and reflection should then be measured by using a protractor to measure the angles between the rays and the normal line. The reflected angles for a variety of incident angles should be measured.

Effectiveness matrix

	Domain of observables	Domain of ideas
What students do	Students can: • Set up a specified arrangement of a ray box and plane mirror to visualize behaviour of a ray of light. • Draw a normal line at the point of incidence with the mirror and measure angles of reflection for a range of incident angles.	Students can talk about: • A normal line and angles of incidence and reflection. • A pattern of the angle of reflection always appearing to be approximately the same as the angle of incidence.
What students learn	Students can later: • Draw independently appropriate normals at points of incidence for mirrors of *any shape* and measure accurately angles of reflection for a range of incident angles.	Students can later talk about: • A general Law of Reflection that applies to all wave phenomena. • The need for multiple measurements and use of a graph to determine a relationship from results with a degree of measurement uncertainty.

Keep in mind

When straight mirrors are used, drawing and using normal lines appears to add an unnecessary step to a simple procedure (incident and reflected angles could simply be measured with respect to the mirror). You will need to explain the use of normal lines to enable reliable measurement of angles when incident surfaces are curved. Be aware of the difficulty many children experience if expected to 'discover' scientific relationships independently. Several measurements of reflected angles for a range of incident angles will be needed, possibly followed by use of a graph, to facilitate the identification of the relationship *incident angle = reflected angle*. For example, measurement errors will lead some children to interpret a measured reflected angle that is greater than the incident angle to mean that the reflected angle should always be greater than the incident angle.

Issues for discussion

You may wish to ask the students some of the following questions to help develop their thinking:

How does the width, or spreading out, of the rays affect the accuracy of the angles you measure? How could you allow for this? *Students could be encouraged to consider using one edge of the ray.*

How could you test the law of reflection for other wave phenomena, such as sound or water waves?

Health and safety

CLEAPSS advice should be followed at all times. Some designs of ray box (especially those that use incandescent bulbs rather than newer boxes that use LEDs) can become quite hot after a few minutes of use. There should also be the usual precautions taken about electrical safety, such as ensuring power supplies are switched off until the ray boxes are connected, etc.

Equipment

Ray boxes with appropriate power supplies and slits for forming rays, plane mirrors, plain paper, protractors.

7.9 The law of refraction

Learning objectives

- To explore the phenomenon of light changing direction as it travels from one substance into another.
- To understand the use of a normal line to determine angles of incidence and refraction.

Procedure

Students use a ray box to send a ray of white light into a rectangular glass/perspex block. The ray box and block should be placed on plain paper so students can draw round the block and mark the paths of all rays. Students should mark on the paper the point of incidence of the ray with the edge of the block and the point of exit of the ray at it leaves the opposite face of the block. The paths of the ray as it enters, travels through and then leaves the block can then be drawn. The students should then draw normal lines at the edges of the block where the ray enters and leaves it. They can then measure and record the incident and refracted angles for a range of incident angles.

Effectiveness matrix

	Domain of observables	Domain of ideas
What students do	Students can: • Set up a specified arrangement of a ray box and rectangular glass block to visualize behaviour of a ray of light. • Draw a normal line at the point of incidence and measure angles of refraction for a range of incident angles.	Students can talk about: • Light changing direction as it travels from air into glass and from glass into air. • A normal line and angles of incidence and refraction. • A pattern of light always changing direction towards a normal line as it travels from air into glass and away from a normal line as it travels from glass into air.
What students learn	Students can later: • Draw independently appropriate normals at points of incidence for a glass block of *any shape* and measure accurately angles of refraction for a range of incident angles.	Students can later talk about: • Light changing direction as it crosses a boundary between materials due to changes in speed. • A general Law of Refraction in terms of light changing direction towards/away from a normal line as it travels across a boundary between materials of different densities.

Keep in mind

The need for sufficient blackout conditions to make the rays easy to observe and to remind the students about why we use normal lines (to enable reliable measurement of angles when incident surfaces are curved). In particular you will need to draw attention to the dispersion of the white light produced by the ray boxes during refraction (i.e. the white light can be observed to separate into the colours of the visible spectrum) and how this might be noticed and commented upon by students. During Key Stage 4 Mathematics, students will be introduced to trigonometry, so it may be appropriate to introduce Snell's Law to students to enable them to apply their new mathematics knowledge to quantifying the relationship between the incident and refracted angles they make during this practical activity.

Issues for discussion

You may wish to ask the students some of the following questions to help develop their thinking:

Why do you see colours in the refracted beams? *White light is a mixture of colours. Different colours are refracted by different amounts so the colours in the white ray start to separate out and become noticeable.*

How does the width, or spreading out, of the rays affect the accuracy of the angles you measure? How could you allow for this? *Students could be encouraged to consider using one edge of the ray.*

How could you test to see if refraction happens for water waves or sound waves? *The intention with this question is to draw students' attention to refraction as a property of all wave phenomena.*

Health and safety

CLEAPSS advice should be followed at all times. Some designs of ray box (especially those that use incandescent bulbs rather than newer boxes that use LEDs) can become quite hot after a few minutes of use. There should also be the usual precautions taken about electrical safety, such as ensuring power supplies are switched off until the ray boxes are connected.

Equipment

Ray boxes with appropriate power supplies and slits for forming rays, rectangular glass or perspex blocks, plain paper, protractors.

7.10 Filters and colours

Learning objectives

- To investigate the effects of combining primary-coloured light sources to produce white light and the secondary colours.
- To explain the effect of filters in terms of transmission and absorption of light.
- To predict the apparent colour of an object when illuminated by a range of different coloured light sources, in terms of absorption and reflection of different colours.

Procedure

Some schools will have kit specifically for this activity, consisting of red, blue and green lights mounted on a frame and the ability to switch on and off, or continuously vary the brightness of, each light independently. If you do not have this equipment, then a common alternative is to use three ray boxes and a selection of coloured filters to create independent sources of red, blue and green light. Students should shine all three coloured lights onto a white screen so that the separate spots of light overlap. It should be possible to observe the secondary colours (magenta, cyan and yellow) where each pair of spots overlap, and white light where all three spots overlap. Students can then shine the lights, separately and in combinations, onto a selection of coloured objects and observe the apparent colours of the illuminated objects.

Effectiveness matrix

	Domain of observables	Domain of ideas
What students do	Students can: • Set up the supplied coloured light sources so as to produce white light and the three secondary colours.	Students can talk about: • White light as a mixture of primary colours and secondary colours arising from the addition of primary colours. • A filter as a material that transmits certain colours of light and absorbs the others. • Blue objects (for example) appearing blue because they reflect blue light and absorb other colours.
What students learn	This quadrant is intentionally blank in this task.	Students can later talk about: • How to predict the apparent colour of an object when it will be illuminated by a range of coloured light sources.

Keep in mind

Depending on the quality and hue of coloured filters you have to go with your ray boxes, it might not be possible for the students to produce pure white light when they combine all three primary colours. This can be turned to your advantage by leading into a discussion about how a wide range of different colours can be produced, beyond the three primary and three secondary colours portrayed in textbooks. Be aware that some students might have less than perfect colour vision, with male students more likely to be affected (difficulty in discriminating between some shades of red, green and brown is thought to affect around 8 per cent of the male population).

Issues for discussion

You may wish to ask the students some of the following questions to help develop their thinking:

What happens to white light when it passes through a red (for example) filter?

What happens to the light that is absorbed by a filter? *The filter material will warm up and radiate heat.*

What happens when you shine white light through a red filter and a green filter together? *In theory no light will be transmitted. The red filter will only transmit red light, which will then be absorbed by the green filter.*

What colour will you see if you shine a blue light onto a red car? What if you shined it onto a yellow car? *The car would look black in blue light as the paint will only reflect red light. Yellow light is a mixture of red and green light, so the car's paint will reflect the red light, that is, the car will look red.*

Health and safety

Some care might be needed if the ray boxes become hot and students should be warned not to stare into bright light sources.

Equipment

Ray boxes, power supplies and coloured filters. A selection of coloured objects will be useful, such as soft drinks cans.

7.11 Investigating the magnetic field around a bar magnet

Learning objectives

- To know that if a magnetic object is brought near a magnet it will experience a force.
- To understand that the space around a magnet where magnetic objects experience a force is called a magnetic field.
- To know that magnetic fields have characteristic shapes and what that shape is for a bar magnet.

Prior knowledge: It is assumed that students will know the difference between a magnet and a magnetic object.

Procedure

Students move a plotting compass around a bar magnet, moving it to different positions, paying particular attention to the areas close to the ends of the magnet. Then they pick a point at the end of one of the magnet, mark that (with an x or dot). They then place the plotting compass at that point and plot another mark at the other end of the plotting compass needle pointing away from the end of the magnet. They then move the plotting compass so that the needle is next to the mark and plot a new mark at the other end of the needle. Repeat this procedure until the plotting compass is back next to the magnet. Remove the plotting compass and then join up all the marks to draw a single field line including an arrow or arrows showing the direction the needle on the plotting compass was pointing. Repeat this several times from a different starting points until multiple field lines are drawn.

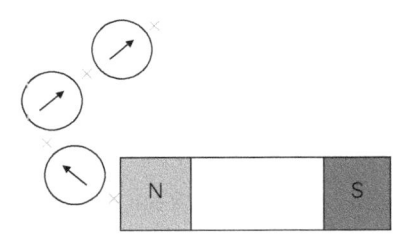

Figure 7.4 Plotting the magnetic field of a bar magnet

Effectiveness matrix

	Domain of observables	Domain of ideas
What students do	Students can: • Arrange plotting compasses near a permanent magnet and use them and their orientation to sketch the field pattern around a bar magnet.	Students can talk about: • That a magnetic object near a magnet will experience a force in a particular direction. • That the plotting compass changes orientation because it is effected by magnetic field of the bar magnet. • That the force exerted on a magnetic object near a magnet may change depending on the magnet and the position of the object and/or magnet.
What students learn	Students can later: • Use plotting compasses to show and draw the field around other magnetic objects such a electromagnet or two bar magnets (attracting or repelling).	Students can later talk about: • The idea that magnetic fields that exist around all magnetic objects. • That these magnetic fields have characteristic shapes and to be able to describe the one for a bar magnet. • That the field lines drawn can show the direction of the force a magnetic object would experience if it were near the magnet.

Keep in mind

While it is comparatively straightforward to find and draw the magnetic field lines with the process described above, the concept of a magnetic field and a field line are quite challenging for students and so care is needed is supporting them to understand what the lines that they draw actually mean. As they are drawn here, the field lines show the direction the north pole of a compass would point if it were placed there. A more accurate description relates to the lines showing at any point the direction of the force that a north pole of a magnet would experience when placed at that point. A north pole will be repelled by another north pole which is why field lines always go from north to south.

Another convention is to show stronger magnetic fields by drawing more field lines closer together although this is only of use in showing a comparison between magnets and not an absolute or quantifiable measurement. In many schools, larger magnets will have a stronger magnetic field around them but this is not always the case and so the terms *stronger* and *weaker* should be used to compare magnets. The terms *bigger* and *smaller used to describe magnets* **should not be used**. It may be worth clarifying for some students that the needle inside a plotting compass is a magnet as they may not know this.

Issues for discussion

You may wish to ask the students some of the following questions to help develop their thinking:

How can the magnet make the compass move without actually touching it? *The aim of this question is to promote discussion about the magnetic field force being a non contact force, able to pass through empty space.*

If you were to repeat the experiment with a stronger magnet, would your results be different and if so how? *You cannot measure the strength of a magnetic field with a plotting compass and so the results would be unchanged. This experiment can only show the direction of the field lines but not the strength.*

Health and safety

Previously, iron filings had been used in this experiment however they present a safely risk, particularly if they get into students' eyes where they can cause damage to the cornea and so **should not** be used.

Equipment

Bar magnet

Plotting compass

A4 plain paper

7.12 Factors that affect the strength of a simple electromagnet

Learning objectives

- To understand that when a current flows through a wire or coil of wire that this creates a magnetic field and this object is called an electromagnet.
- To be able to describe the ways in which the strength of the field created by an electromagnet can be altered.

Procedure

Students wind part of the insulated wire round an iron nail to make a set of coils close to each other, leaving enough free wire at the ends to connect to the power supply. They then connect the ends of the wire to a low-voltage DC power supply such that a large enough current passes through the coil to generate a magnetic effect, such as picking up steel paperclips (see Figure 7.5). With a fixed number of coils, students increase and decrease the current (by varying the voltage on the power supply) and explore the effect this has on the strength of the electromagnet, assessed by the number of paperclips it can pick up. Using the same total length of wire and a fixed current, students can then vary the number of coils of wire and explore the effect this has on the strength of the electromagnet. *It is suggested that they begin with 20 coils and work in multiples of 10 or 20 in the second part of the experiment but this may vary depending upon the equipment.*

Figure 7.5
An electromagnet made with a coil of insulated wire and an iron nail

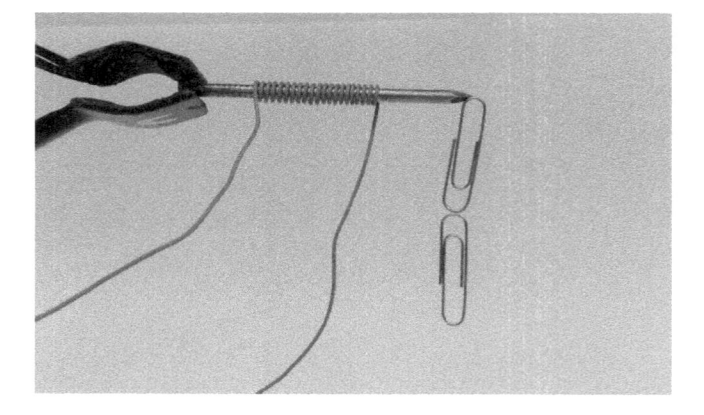

Effectiveness matrix

	Domain of observables	Domain of ideas
What students do	Students can: • Follow instructions to set up the correct circuit with coil of wire around an iron nail and power supply to create an electromagnet. • Take simple measurements (such as paperclips picked up) to identify if the strength of the electromagnet has increased or decreased when varying number of coils or current.	Students can talk about: • How the current in the wire is generating a magnetic field that is only present when the current is flowing and that this is called an electromagnet. • The fact that the strength of the electromagnet can be changed by the current in the coil or number of turns of wire.
What students learn	Students can later: • Independently make an electromagnet and be able to vary its strength in at least one way (current/coils).	Students can later talk about: • The relationship between the current in a wire and the strength of the magnetic field it creates.

Keep in mind

The strength of the electromagnet created by a coil of wire can be quite small and so the iron nail is used as a core, which itself becomes magnetized and thus increases the strength of the wire and nail electromagnet overall. Depending upon the equipment used, it is possible that when the current is turned off both the iron nail and the steel paperclips may remain slightly magnetic. This can be hard to avoid and can cause some contradiction with the teaching idea that electromagnets can be easily turned on and off. However, the strength when the current is turned on should be significantly higher and so this relationship can be explored and the small, residual magnetism acknowledged if needed.

The nature of this experiment makes it difficult to collect reliable numerical results that yield linear relationships. It is suggested that students focus on whether increasing the number of coils or current increases, decreases or has no effect on the strength of the electromagnet qualitatively, not quantitatively.

Issues for discussion

You may wish to ask the students some of the following questions to help develop their thinking:

If I increase the number of coils of wire/current, what do you think will happen to the strength of the electromagnetic and why? *There is a predictive element to this question, hoping to encourage students to make the connection between the number of coils or size of the current and magnetic field strengths.*

What happens to the electromagnet when the current is not flowing? *This is designed to help the students consider the idea that the magnetic effect is caused by the current flowing in the wire and not the wire itself and so when there is no current, there is no magnetic field.*

Health and safety

Without a load in the circuit, the currents involved might cause a heating effect, you may wish to introduce a load to a circuit to reduce this or exercise caution.

Equipment

Coated wire, ideally a length of 1–2 m with bare ends

Iron nail

Steel paperclips or drawing pins (brass drawing pins will not work).

Note: these need to be checked that they are not magnetized

Low-voltage DC power supply

Leads with crocodile clip connectors

Physics: Session Guides 15–16

James de Winter and Michael Inglis

8

- **8.1** Circular motion (p. 216)
- **8.2** Efficiency and energy transfer (p. 219)
- **8.3** Personal power (p. 222)
- **8.4** Specific heat capacity (p. 224)
- **8.5** The pressure law (p. 227)
- **8.6** Estimating absolute zero/Charles' law (p. 230)
- **8.7** Critical angle and total internal reflection (p. 233)
- **8.8** Finding the focal length of a lens and making a telescope (p. 236)
- **8.9** Potential difference and current characteristics for an Ohmic resistor (p. 240)
- **8.10** Resistance of a wire (p. 243)
- **8.11** Electromagnetic induction (p. 246)
- **8.12** Electrolysis (p. 249)

8.1 Circular motion

Learning objectives

- To be able to describe that for an object moving in a circular path the direction of motion is changing, meaning it must be accelerating.
- To know that the force causing this acceleration is acting towards the centre of the circle.

Prior knowledge: It is assumed that students will be familiar with the terms speed and velocity and understand that if the size and/or direction of a velocity changes, then an object is accelerating.

Procedure

Students take a rubber bung and attach it firmly to a string, passing through a plastic tube with a mass hanging from the end. They mark the string at a known distance from the rubber bung (between 1 m and 2 m is suggested) and then start swinging the bung around in a horizontal circle until the mark is just at the top of the tube, meaning that the radius of the circular path is the distance from the bung to the mark. Using as little force from their hand as possible and keeping the bung rotating at a constant speed, they measure the time for 10 or 20 revolutions (see Figure 8.1). Using this time and a calculation for the circumference of the circle from the radius, they calculate, T, the time for one revolution. This experiment can be repeated for different masses hanging down.

Figure 8.1 Equipment to observe and explore circular motion

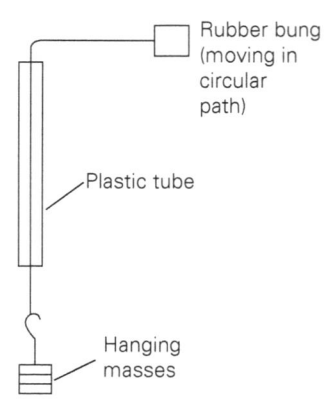

Effectiveness matrix

	Domain of observables	Domain of ideas
What students do	Students can: • Whirl a rubber bung in a circular path of fixed radius at a roughly constant speed. • Measure the time for multiple (ten) rotations, the radius of the circular path and calculate the speed of the object.	Students can talk about: • That the circular motion of an object can be described in terms of the speed and the radius of the path. • The fact that there is a force making the object move in a circular path. • That this force is coming from the tension in the string.
What students learn	This quadrant is intentionally blank in this task.	Students can later talk about: • An object moving in a circular path needing a force acting upon it because it is changing direction and thus accelerating. • This force acts towards the centre of the circular path. • If an object of the same mass were to move in a circular path with a different force then it would have to have a different radius or speed or both.

Keep in mind

It is quite tricky for students to keep the bung rotating at a perfectly constant speed; however, the average across ten or twenty rotations is designed to help generate a better value for T and this experiment provides an opportunity to talk to and with students about precision and accuracy.

The experiment as described here does not require the mass of the bung or hanging mass in any calculation. However, it is possible, and for higher levels of understanding of value, to equate the force causing the mass in circular motion ($F = mv^2/r$) with the force causing the tension in the string ($F = mg$). As such, knowing these masses is of value. It is worth noting that the two values of m in the above quantities are different, the first is the mass of the rotating bung and the second the mass of the hanging mass.

The idea that an object travelling at a constant speed is accelerating is known to be a challenge for many students. They are often introduced to the idea of acceleration as simply *speeding up* or *slowing down* and so the relevance of a changing direction indicating acceleration may be unfamiliar to them.

Issues for discussion

You may wish to ask the students some of the following questions to help develop their thinking:

Which direction is the force acting upon the bung and does it change or stay the same during one rotation? *This question is designed to get the students to consider both the size and the direction of the force that causes the circular motion and how one or both of these may change during the motion.*

When the bung is moving in a circular path at constant speed, is it accelerating? *This is to prompt a discussion about the nature of acceleration being a change in the size and/or direction of a velocity and that the bung must be accelerating as it is changing direction.*

Health and safety

As the radius of the path of the bung can be quite large and it can move quite quickly, there is a risk that students are hit by the bung; it is recommended this is done in a large space, perhaps outside. It is suggested that eye protection is worn by all students, not just those swinging the bung.

Equipment

A thin plastic tube. It is important for the friction between the string and the tube to be kept at a minimum, a plastic ballpoint pen casing with the ink/nib removed can be used.

A strong thread. Nylon kite string is particularly suitable as it also reduces the friction.

Hook or some kind of fixing to attach to the thread with known masses. This can be either 10/20/50 g masses or metal washers.

A rubber bung. One with a pre-drilled hole makes attaching the thread much easier.

Figure 8.1 Mass moving in a circle

8.2 Efficiency and energy transfer

Learning objectives

- To investigate quantitatively the efficiency of the bounce of a ball.
- To analyse the behaviour of a dropped ball in terms of the scientific concepts of energy transfer, gravitational potential energy (GPE), energy conservation and efficiency.
- To apply, and develop use of, mathematical language to describe the quantitative relationship between the initial GPE of a dropped ball and the GPE at the top of its first bounce, for a range of drop heights or ball masses.

Procedure

Students use scales to determine the mass of a ball. The ball is then dropped from a measured height and the height of the first bounce is recorded. The height could be measured by eye, against metre sticks held vertically in the background (see Figure 8.2), or by video recording the drop and playing back in slow motion. Repeat to obtain at least three results and then calculate a mean bounce height. The students first calculate the gravitational potential energy (GPE) of the ball at its release height and the averaged first bounce height, and then calculate the efficiency of the bounce (using the GPE at the top of the bounce as the useful energy out). This procedure can be repeated for a range of different ball masses, drop heights or surfaces the ball is dropped onto depending on the level of challenge required.

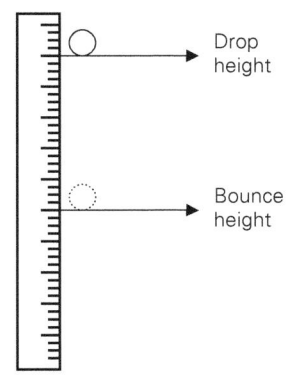

Figure 8.2 Using a ruler to measure bounce height

Effectiveness matrix

	Domain of observables	Domain of ideas
What students do	Students can: • Measure the bounce height using an appropriate method and to an appropriate accuracy.	Students can talk about: • Energy stores and transfers throughout the motion of the ball that might account for the apparent 'loss' of energy during the bounce. • The effect on the calculated efficiency of uncertainty in the bounce height measurement and how it could be reduced.
What students learn	Students can later: • Select and use appropriate ICT kit (such as video recording or data logging) to improve the accuracy and precision of the measured bounce heights.	Students can later talk about: • The quantitative relationship between the release height, or the mass of the ball, and the calculated efficiency of the bounce using appropriate mathematical language and ideas about energy transfer mechanisms.

Keep in mind

There are various factors that affect the bounce height of a ball, such as the material properties and construction of the ball; the temperature of the ball; and the nature of the material the ball is dropped onto.

Issues for discussion

You may wish to ask the students some of the following questions to help develop their thinking:

Why is there an energy transfer during a bounce? If you could film the bounce in close-up and play it back in slow motion, what would you see? What is happening to the ball? *The aim here is to get the students to consider the deformation of the ball* and the surface it bounces off, *and the vibrations produced in both.*

How could you change the mass of the ball but keep the GPE at release constant? *Using GPE = mgh, doubling the mass and halving the release height will give the same value of initial GPE, that is GPE is directly proportional to height and mass.*

How can you describe the relationship between the $GPE_{release\ height}$ and $GPE_{bounce\ height}$? Does this relationship stay the same if you change the release height/mass of the ball?

What properties are needed for the material used in the ball/bounce surface to increase the efficiency of the bounce?

What happens to the energy 'lost' during the bounce? Why might somebody say that it is not correct to describe it as 'lost'? *You are looking here for students to apply the law of conservation of energy and identify transfer mechanisms for the 'lost' energy. 'Lost' might be appropriate if you are referring to energy transferred into forms that are not* useful, *such as the sound created by the bounce.*

How might air resistance affect your results? How might your results be affected by the temperature of the air/ball? *The idea here is to encourage students to consider possible factors that might affect their results and to use scientific ideas to justify them. The actual effects are not straightforward! It is encouraging the scientific thinking that matters here rather than the answers.*

Health and safety

Some care might be needed to ensure students do not let the bouncing balls hit them in the eyes!

Equipment

Selection of balls (such as tennis balls, table tennis balls, squash balls, etc.), metre sticks, selection of materials the balls could be dropped onto, kit for video recording and play back of the drop (e.g. iPads would be ideal here but any camcorder or smartphone camera would do)

8.3 Personal power

Learning objectives

- To calculate their personal power during an activity involving a change in gravitational potential energy (GPE).
- To compare their calculated personal power to power values associated with everyday objects or activities.
- To identify that their calculated personal power does not account for all of the transferred energy, that is some is 'lost' as heat.

Procedure

Students determine their own mass using scales. They then run or walk up a flight of stairs and use a stop clock to measure the time taken to do this in t seconds. The height gained should be measured using metre sticks or a tape measure. The students then calculate the change in their gravitational potential energy (GPE) using $GPE = mgh$ (where 'h' is the change in height) and then go on to calculate their power (P) using $P = GPE/t$. This procedure can be repeated for a range of different heights or walking/running speeds.

Effectiveness matrix

	Domain of observables	Domain of ideas
What students do	Students can: • Measure the height gained using an appropriate method and to an appropriate accuracy.	Students can talk about: • Their personal power as a measure of the *rate* at which they change their GPE. • How their calculated personal power values compare to everyday objects or phenomena, such as the power rating for light bulbs.
What students learn	This quadrant is intentionally blank in this task.	Students can later talk about: • Some of the energy they transferred from chemical stores in their body appearing as heat and some resulting in a gain of GPE, using the term *efficiency*.

Keep in mind

The terms *energy* and *power* are often used interchangeably by students (and in everyday life). The scientific distinction between them should be reinforced. Some students struggle to understand that a small energy transfer can result in a large power if the transfer time is small.

Issues for discussion

You may wish to ask the students some of the following questions to help develop their thinking: Why do you have to transfer energy when you gain height?
The aim here is to encourage students to recognize that they have to move upwards against a force acting in the opposite direction (gravity).

Does the horizontal distance travelled during the climb affect your personal power values? Are you transferring energy when you run/walk horizontally? *The aim here is to encourage the students to recognize that a change of GPE depends only on a change in height and not on total distance travelled.*

Are all of the energy they transfer during their climb the same as the amount of GPE they gain? How might the amount of energy 'lost' during the climb depend on the speed of the climb? *The aim here is to get the students to recognize that some of the energy they transfer is 'lost' as heat and to consider the relationship between the personal power and amount of energy wasted, that is the gain in GPE is fixed, but the amount of energy wasted might depend on the rate of transfer (power).*

Health and safety

Appropriate warnings should be given about the risks of running up or down stairs.

Equipment

Weighing scales (e.g. bathroom scales), metre sticks or measuring tape, stop clocks.

8.4 Specific heat capacity

Learning objectives

- To apply the scientific concepts of *specific heat capacity, energy* and *power* to determine the power output of a Bunsen burner.
- To develop scientific skills of manipulating equipment, selecting variables, recording accurate measurements and calculating quantities through carrying out an experimental procedure to determine the power output of a Bunsen burner.
- To evaluate the accuracy of the calculated value of output power and the possible limiting factors of the experimental procedure.

Procedure

This activity can be used to encourage an investigative approach. The idea of specific heat capacity should have been covered. Students heat a beaker of water using a Bunsen burner and measure the time taken for a particular rise in temperature (see Figure 8.3). Using the specific heat capacity of water (4,200 J kg^{-1} °C^{-1}), the energy transferred to the water can be calculated from *energy transferred (J) = mass of water (kg) × specific heat capacity (J kg^{-1} °C^{-1}) × temperature change (°C)*. The power output of the Bunsen burner can then be calculated using *power (W) = energy (J)/time (s)*. The students should choose an appropriate mass of water and temperature rise (or time interval) to aim for, and be encouraged to think critically about the strengths and limitations of their choices.

Figure 8.3
The measurement of specific heat capacity

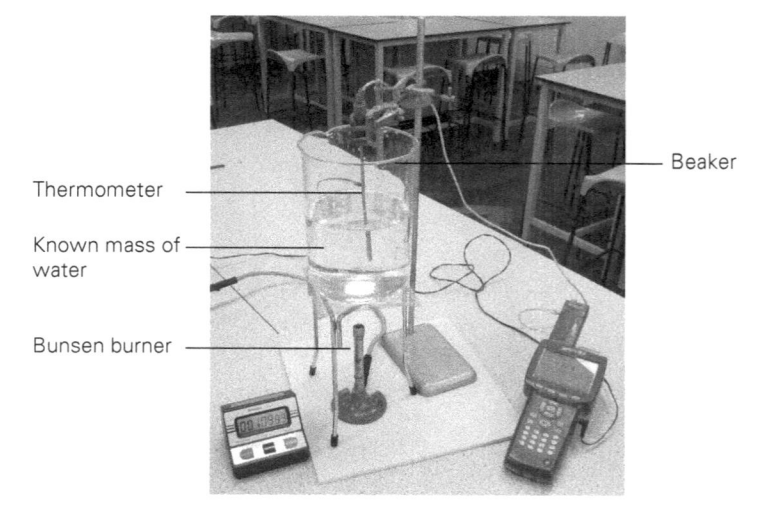

Effectiveness matrix

	Domain of observables	Domain of ideas
What students do	Students can: • Make appropriate and justified choices for mass of water, time interval and/or temperature rise. • Measure quantities to appropriate and justified levels of accuracy and precision.	Students can talk about: • *Specific heat capacity* as a property of a material that links temperature change with a corresponding quantity of energy. • The reasons for their choices of mass of water, time interval or temperature rise using scientific ideas.
What students learn	Students can later: • Make appropriate and justified adjustments to their practical set-up to improve the accuracy or precision of their results.	Students can later talk about: • The limitations of their calculated value of Bunsen burner power using appropriate scientific ideas and language.

Keep in mind

The water must not be allowed to boil, otherwise the idea of *specific latent heat* would need to be introduced and taken account of.

Issues for discussion

You may wish to ask the students some of the following questions to help develop their thinking:

Is all of the output energy from the Bunsen burner transferred to the water? If not, what happens to it? *Students should observe that some of the heat from the Bunsen flame is transferred into the surrounding air: into heating the tripod stand, is radiated away by the hot water and hot beaker and so on.*

If the water boiled, how might that affect your results? What could you do to avoid this from happening? *If the water boiled then the energy transferred from the Bunsen flame is changing the state of the water from liquid to gas instead of changing the temperature. If the students are trying to achieve a certain temperature rise that exceeds 100 °C (!), then the time interval they record would become very large!*

How might changing the mass of water and/or time interval and/or temperature rise affect your result? *The aim here is to encourage the students to consider critically how these variables might influence their calculated results. For example, using a smaller mass of water would result in a greater temperature rise in a fixed time interval. What are the pros and cons of this?*

How could you improve the experimental set-up to improve the accuracy of your results? What additional equipment or materials would you want and why? How could this procedure be adapted to use a gas or a solid as the material to be heated? *The aim is to encourage the students to evaluate the procedure and think creatively, but critically, about how to improve it.*

Health and safety

CLEAPSS advice should always be followed. The usual precautions should be taken for practical work involving use of Bunsen burners, hot water and hot objects.

Equipment

Bunsen burners, tripod stands, beakers, supply of water, thermometers, stop clocks, digital balances.

8.5 The pressure law

Learning objectives

- To investigate quantitatively the relationship between the pressure (P) and temperature (T) of a gas of fixed volume (V) and mass (m), and to describe that relationship using mathematical language.
- To apply the apparent relationship between P and T to predict the temperature of the gas where the pressure would fall to zero.
- To explain the relationship between pressure and temperature in terms of the scientific ideas of energy and collisions between particles.
- To explain how an absolute temperature scale can be defined based on the temperature where the pressure of a gas would be expected to be zero.

Procedure

Attach a pressure gauge to the opening of a conical or round bottom flask which is filled with air at atmospheric pressure (see Figure 8.4). The gauge should be attached so that the flask is sealed and a constant mass of trapped air is maintained throughout the practical activity. Students immerse the flask in a large beaker filled with water at ambient temperature. After waiting for a few minutes to allow the temperature of the water and the air in the flask to equalize, students should record the temperature of the water using a thermometer and the pressure of the air in the flask. The beaker should then be heated using a Bunsen burner by approximately 20 °C and the new temperature maintained for several minutes (requiring careful and controlled use of the Bunsen burner) to allow the air in the flask to reach the temperature of the water. A water bath could be used instead. Students then record the new temperature and pressure readings. This procedure should be repeated at several temperatures. The results should be plotted on a graph of *pressure* against *temperature (in °C)*.

Figure 8.4
Equipment for measuring the pressure of a fixed volume of air as it is heated

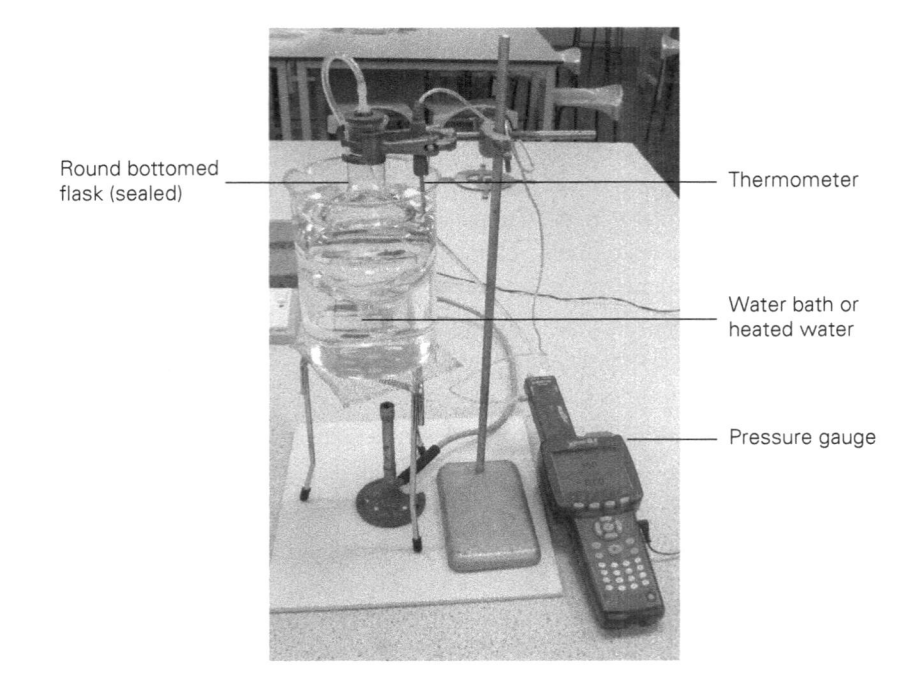

- Round bottomed flask (sealed)
- Thermometer
- Water bath or heated water
- Pressure gauge

Effectiveness matrix

	Domain of observables	**Domain of ideas**
What students do	Students can: • Set up the apparatus so that the mass of air in the flask will remain constant. • Judge appropriate periods of waiting time for the temperature of the air in the flask to reach equilibrium with the surrounding water.	Students can talk about: • The pressure of the air in the flask in terms of collisions between particles. • An increase in temperature means that the particles have gained kinetic energy and therefore collide more frequently, which is experienced as an increase in pressure. • The general relationship between the pressure and temperature of the air using appropriate mathematical language.
What students learn	Students can later: • Select and use appropriate data logging kit to improve the accuracy and precision of the measured temperature and/or pressure.	Students can later talk about: • What will happen to the pressure of the air, in terms of collisions between particles, if the temperature is *decreased* below the starting temperature in this activity (including below 0 °C). • How an absolute temperature scale can be created based on the point on the *P vs. T* graph derived during this practical where the pressure is predicted to drop to zero.

Keep in mind

A complete explanation of the pressure law, and how it relates to the other gas laws (Boyle's and Charles' laws), is not introduced to students until kinetic theory is explored during A-level physics. The students will need to understand the distinction between *temperature* and *heat*, and should understand how the Celsius scale is defined in terms of the properties of water.

Issues for discussion

You may wish to ask the students some of the following questions to help develop their thinking:

What happens to the molecules of a gas when it cools or is heated? *It might be necessary to check students' understanding of the terms 'molecules' and 'particles'.*

Why is it important to keep the volume and amount (i.e. mass) of gas constant during this practical activity? How would your results have been affected if air had been free to enter or leave the flask, or the flask was free to expand, when you heated it?

If the volume or mass of air were not held constant, then the pressure of the trapped air would have remained fixed throughout the activity (i.e. the pressure would have been at atmospheric pressure throughout).

How was the Celsius temperature scale created? What is significant about 0 °C and 100 °C?

This could form an interesting starting point for a discussion about how temperature scales are defined and that there have been many different temperature scales in use in the past, depending on which fixed points were used as references.

At what temperature on your graph will the pressure of the air in the flask be zero? At this temperature, how would you describe the behaviour of the air particles?

According to the classical kinetic theory model that the gas laws are derived from, the particles would be stationary. However, the classical model breaks down at such low temperatures due to quantum effects, so that the prediction of zero pressure at absolute zero cannot be achieved and is not valid.

Health and safety

CLEAPSS advice should always be followed. Some care might be needed about working with hot water as the temperature increases, especially if the water is allowed to boil.

Equipment

Conical or round bottom flask, water bath, thermometer, pressure gauge that can be attached so the opening of flask remains sealed throughout the activity.

8.6 Estimating absolute zero/Charles' law

Learning objectives

- To investigate quantitatively the relationship between the temperature (T) and volume (V) of a fixed mass (M) of gas at constant pressure (P).
- To explain the relationship in qualitative terms with respect to kinetic (particle) theory.
- To use the relationship identified to predict the temperature of the gas at the point where the pressure would be zero.

Prior knowledge: It is assumed that students will be familiar with the basic idea around kinetic (particle) theory and the motion and behaviour of particles in a gas.

Procedure

Students take a plastic syringe with a known volume of air in it and seal the end with a cap (suggested to be about half full, see Figure 8.5). They record the ambient temperature and the volume. As best they can, they then fully immerse the syringe in a water bath at a known temperature, leaving it for a few minutes for the syringe and gas inside to reach the same temperature as the water. They remove the syringe and record the new volume, and temperate. They repeat this number of times for different temperatures, each time recording the volume. These results can be plotted on a line graph of volume against temperature and students can describe the relationship as well as extrapolate the line to estimate absolute zero as the temperature when the volume would be zero.

Figure 8.5
Using a sealed syringe to investigate Charles' Law

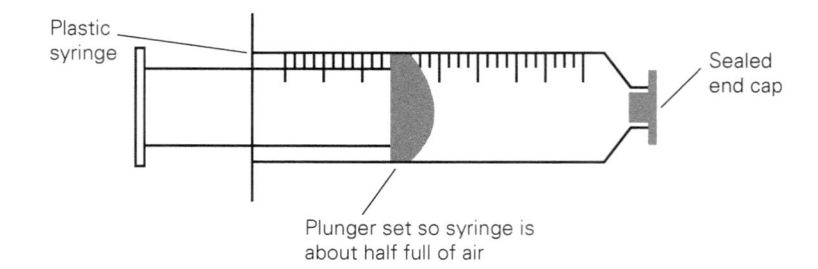

Effectiveness matrix

	Domain of observables	Domain of ideas
What students do	Students can: • Measure the volume of gas in the syringe at different temperatures. • Draw a graph of their results for volume against temperature.	Students can talk about: • How the change in temperature causes the gas to expand or contract. • That there is a relationship between the temperature and volume of a fixed mass of gas at constant pressure. • How they can estimate a value for absolute zero from their data.
What students learn	This quadrant is intentionally blank in this task.	Students can later talk about: • How the relationship between temperature and volume of a fixed mass of gas at constant pressure can be explained in terms of kinetic (particle) theory. • How absolute zero can be estimated from this relationship by using kinetic (particle) theory.

Keep in mind

It is possible that the syringe plunger may not move freely when the gas expands or contracts and so students may need to tap or nudge it gently to get it to move. The variation in the volume readings may only be of a fraction of 1 ml and so care is needed for students to try and be as accurate as possible.

It is worth noting that this experiment provides a simple way to estimate absolute zero using readily available materials rather than being a secure scientific measurement, but this allows students to discuss the strengths and limitations of the experiment on a practical and theoretical level.

This practical aims to both explore a key relationship in thermodynamics as well as develop students' understanding of how a limited data set can be used to predict/estimate an unknown value. The full detail of classical kinetic theory is not addressed until higher levels of study but the idea that most of the volume of a gas is the space between particles can be explored to suggest why it might be assumed that when the particles are not moving at all, at absolute zero, the volume is very close to zero. In reality, at very low temperatures, quantum effects cause the classical model to break down; however, the values that students calculate from this experiment are often near to known value of $-273\ °C$ within a reasonable margin of error.

Issues for discussion

You may wish to ask the students some of the following questions to help develop their thinking:

How is the pressure kept constant in this experiment? *The ability for the syringe plunger to move freely allows the pressure inside to be kept the same as that outside.*

(when they have their data) When you increase the temperature, the volume increases, can you explain this in terms of kinetic (particle) theory? *This is to encourage stents to make a connection between the temperate and the motion and collisions made by the particles.*

If absolute zero is the point when the particles stop moving, how can you predict its value from your data? *It is assumed that the actual space taken up by the particles is so small compared to the spaces between them that at absolute zero, when the particles are not moving, the volume can be assumed to effectively be zero.*

Health and safety

The syringes are sealed but the temperate involved should not result in anything more than the expansion of the gas within the syringe. When working with the hot water baths, students should be aware of and consider the possibility of scalding.

Equipment

Thermometer

Three water baths, set at approximately 40 °C, 60 °C and 80 °C

Plastic syringes with caps to seal the ends (60 ml syringes have been found to work well)

Graph paper.

8.7 Critical angle and total internal reflection

Learning objectives

- To explore the phenomenon of total internal reflection.

Procedure

Students use a ray box to send a ray of white light into a semi-circular glass/perspex block. The ray box and block should be placed on plain paper so students can draw round the block and mark the paths of all rays. The ray box should be placed so that the incident ray strikes the block on the curved edge and is aimed at the centre of the straight edge (i.e. the incidence ray travels along a radius so that it does not change direction as it enters the block). Students should mark on the paper the point of incidence of the ray with the straight edge of the block and the paths of the rays on either side of this boundary. They should then draw a normal line at this point of incidence and measure the incident and refracted angles at the straight boundary for a range of incident angles. Students should note the incident angle where the refracted angle tends to 90° (i.e. the refracted ray appears to travel along the straight boundary of the block) (see Figure 8.6).

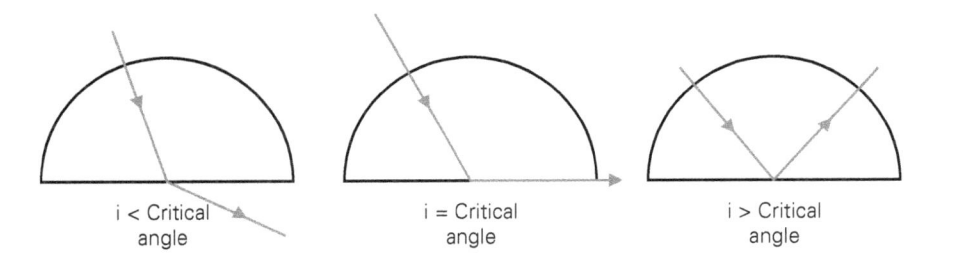

Figure 8.6 Incident and refracted/reflected rays for three different incident angles

Effectiveness matrix

	Domain of observables	Domain of ideas
What students do	Students can: • Set up a specified arrangement of a raybox and semi-circular glass block to visualize behaviour of a ray of light. • Draw a normal line at the point of incidence with the straight boundary and measure the angle of incidence when total internal reflection commences.	Students can talk about: • *Total internal reflection* as where a ray reflects off the internal surface of a material, instead of refracting through it, above a certain incident angle called the *critical angle*. • The fact that the internally reflected ray obeys the law of reflection.
What students learn	Students can later: • Repeat this practical using a glass block of *any shape* and measure accurately the critical angle of incidence within the block. • Notice that some light is internally reflected before the critical angle is reached.	Students can later talk about: • The transition between refraction and internal reflection is not sudden, but happens progressively as the incident angle approaches the critical angle. • The usefulness of this phenomenon for transmitting light long distances within optical fibres.

Keep in mind

The need for sufficient blackout conditions to make the rays easy to observe and to remind the students about why we use normal lines (to enable reliable measurement of angles when incident surfaces are curved). In particular, you will need to draw attention to the dispersion of the white light produced by the ray boxes during refraction (i.e. the white light can be observed to separate into the colours of the visible spectrum) and how this might be noticed and commented upon by students. Internal reflection becomes noticeable *before* the critical angle is reached and only becomes *total* above the critical angle, that is it is not a phenomenon that is suddenly 'switched on' at a precise angle, but happens progressively as the critical angle is approached.

Issues for discussion

You may wish to ask the students some of the following questions to help develop their thinking:

Why do you see colours in the refracted beams? *White light is a mixture of colours. Different colours are refracted by different amounts so the colours in the white ray start to separate out and become noticeable.*

How does the width or spreading out of the rays affect the accuracy of the angles you measure? How could you allow for this? *Students could be encouraged to consider using one edge of the ray.*

How could you test to see if total internal reflection happens for water waves?

How is total internal reflection used to keep light within an optical fibre?

Health and safety

CLEAPSS advice should be followed at all times. Some designs of ray box (especially those that use incandescent bulbs rather than newer boxes that use LEDs) can become quite hot after a few minutes of use. Usual precautions about electrical safety should also be taken, such as ensuring power supplies are switched off until the ray boxes are connected.

Equipment

Rayboxes with appropriate power supplies and slits for forming rays, semi-circular glass or perspex blocks, plain paper, protractors.

8.8 Finding the focal length of a lens and making a telescope

Learning objectives

- To know how to find and measure the focal length of a converging lens.
- To know how to use two converging lenses of different focal lengths to make a telescope.
- To understand how a converging lens forms images in terms of the refraction of light.

Procedure

Students should stand with their backs to the window and hold the sheet of paper (as a screen) at arm's length. They hold the lens between their eyes and the paper and move the lens towards and away from the paper until they see a clear image of the window. They measure the distance between the lens and the paper to find the focal length (see Figure 8.7).

To make a telescope, students should fix with blu-tack (or alterative fixings) two lenses on a metre ruler. The eyepiece lens (nearest the eye) should be the one with the shorter focal length and the one that is further away is the objective lens. The distance between the lenses should be the sum of their focal lengths.

Effectiveness matrix

	Domain of observables	Domain of ideas
What students do	Students can: • Move a converging lens so a clear image of a distant object forms on a screen in order to see that the image formed is smaller than the object and is upside down. • Use two lenses to create a telescope.	Students can talk about: • The image on the screen being formed from light that has come from the object, through the lens and onto the screen. • The focal length as the distance between a lens and a clear image on a screen. • Any two lenses will make a magnified image only if they are a fixed distance apart, that this distance depends upon the focal lengths of the lenses and is their sum.

	Domain of observables	Domain of ideas
What students learn	Students can later: • Find and measure the focal length of any converging lens. • Set up and make a telescope using two converging lenses of previously unknown focal lengths.	Students can later talk about: • The lens is creating an image by refracting the light from the object. • Different lenses refract light by different amounts, which is why they have different focal lengths. • Why the image from a single lens is inverted in terms of the path of the light from the object.

Keep in mind

To get a clear sharp image that students can see easily, it can really help to make the classroom as dark as possible. If you wish to explore different lens combinations and introduce the idea of magnification, a sheet with reversed text printed in different sizes can be placed on the far side of the classroom wall. In order to describe the path of the light in more detail, it is likely that ray diagrams will be needed.

A single converging lens will form a *real* image (can be projected on a screen). A *virtual* image such as the one created by the telescope cannot be projected on a screen. You can use these descriptive terms but they are not required.

Issues for discussion

You may wish to ask the students some of the following questions to help develop their thinking:

Single lens

What would happen to the image if you turned the screen upside down? *No change. This is to help students appreciate that the lens generates the image; the screen allows us to see it.*

What would happen to the image if I covered half the lens? *Students might suggest that some (half) of the image may disappear (a misconception) rather than get dimmer.*

Telescope

Why do we need two lenses for a telescope? *The first lens (objective) captures the light and the second lens (eyepiece) magnifies it. Students should have noted that the image from one lens was smaller (diminished), and so not useful for a telescope on its own.*

How could I make this a better telescope? *'Better' could mean at least two things: the size and brightness of the image. A larger objective lens will collect more light for a brighter image and changes to the eyepiece lens can provide greater magnification.*

Health and safety

Glass lenses can break or splinter if dropped.

Under absolutely no circumstances allow students to look at the Sun through a telescope or single lens as this can cause permanent damage to the eyes.

Equipment

Converging lenses of various focal lengths (10 and 50 cm work particularly well) *Note:* Some lenses may be labelled with their power, measured in dioptres. This is equal to the reciprocal of the focal length measured in metres (focal lengths of 10 and 50 cm will be 10D and 2D, respectively).

White paper A4.

Wooden metre ruler (plastic ones can be used but they tend to bend making it more difficult)

Blu Tack.

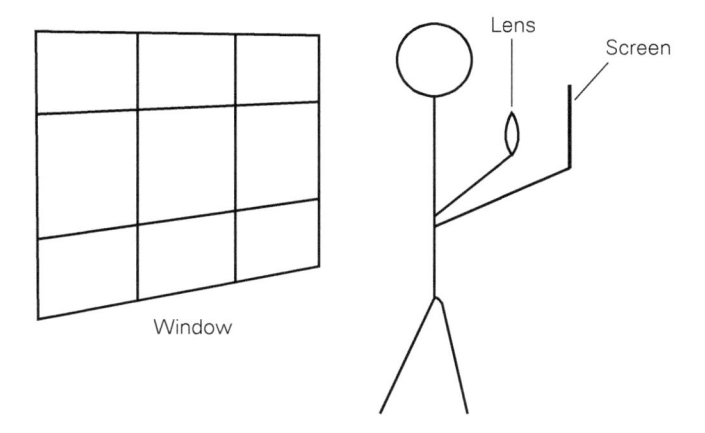

Figure 8.7
Measuring the focal length of a converging lens and using two converging lenses to make a telescope

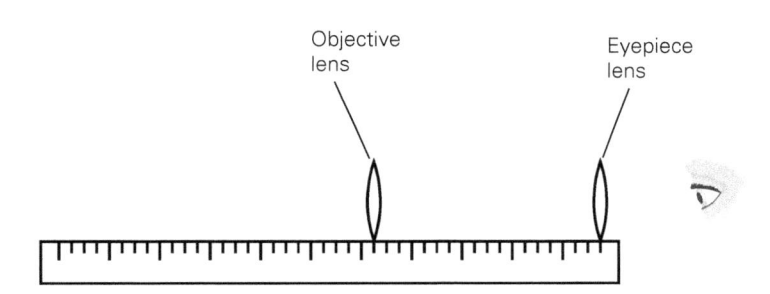

8.9 Potential difference and current characteristics for an Ohmic resistor

Learning objectives

- To be able to set up a circuit with a voltmeter, ammeter and a resistor.
- To be able to correctly measure potential difference and current in a circuit.
- To explore the relationship between current and voltage for an Ohmic resistor.

Prior knowledge: It is assumed that students will be familiar with the terms current and potential difference.

Procedure

Students set up the circuit as shown in the circuit diagram, measuring the potential difference across one or more resistors in a circuit, in series with an ammeter (see Figure 8.8). They vary the potential difference and collect a set of corresponding values for the current flowing through the resistor. By dividing the potential difference by the current they can calculate resistance in each case. This experiment can be repeated with different resistors to collect multiple data sets. Students can plot their potential difference/current data on a graph to investigate if the resistance changes over a range of potential differences.

Figure 8.8 Measuring the potential difference across an Ohmic resistor

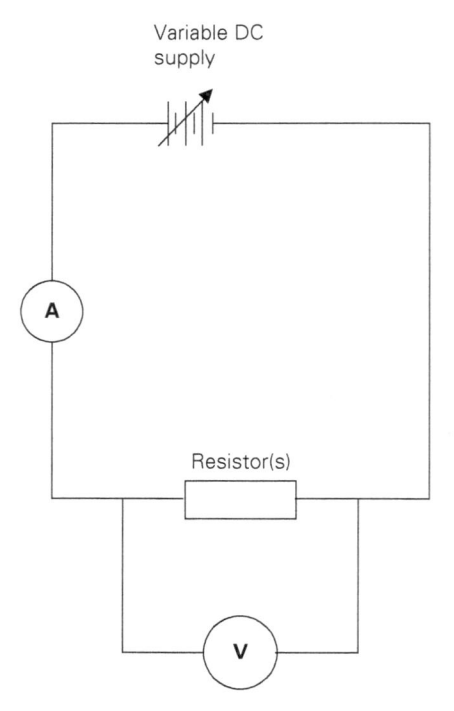

Effectiveness matrix

	Domain of observables	Domain of ideas
What students do	Students can: • Set up the correct circuit with the voltmeter in parallel to and the ammeter in series with the resistor. • Use the voltmeter and ammeter to correctly record a set of potential difference and current readings for a particular resistor. • Plot a line graph of their current and potential difference data and draw a best fit line through or near to the data points.	Students can talk about: • The idea that potential difference, current and resistance are related to each other. • The resistor being a component that restricts or resists the current for a given potential difference and that this resistance causes changes in stores of energy (such as the increase in the thermal energy of the resistor). • How the graph they have drawn provides a visual representation of the relationship between potential difference and current.
What students learn	Students can later: • Set up circuits with voltmeter and ammeters and one or more components (such as a filament light bulb) to collect data for potential difference and current. • Draw a graph of different experimental data sets, choosing appropriate scales and drawing lines of best fit where appropriate.	Students can later talk about: • The fact that potential difference across an Ohmic resistor is directly proportional to current. • Whether or not a component is Ohmic based on potential difference and current data (e.g. a filament light bulb). • How a graph can be used to help identify, or not, a relationship between two variables.

Keep in mind

Students should calculate the resistance from potential difference and current readings and not from the gradient of a graph of potential difference against current. For an Ohmic resistor this graph should be a straight line through the origin, indicating a constant resistance. The value of the gradient is numerically equal to the resistance but as resistance is a value not a rate of change, the gradient method is misleading. Using a filament light bulb instead of a resistor will produce a curved graph as resistance increases with temperature. To identify if resistance is changing, students should compare values calculated from individual potential difference and current readings.

Issues for discussion

You may wish to ask the students some of the following questions to help develop their thinking:

Why is the voltmeter connected across the resistor (in parallel) but the ammeter in-line with it (series). *The intention here is to help them show their understanding of the nature of and difference between potential difference and current.*

If I increase the potential difference across the same resistor, what do you think will happen to the current? *This will give students an opportunity to make a prediction about the relationship between the variables, making sure that they consider all three of them, the fact that the resistance remains constant being an important part of the relationship.*

What might you expect a graph of potential difference against current to look like? *This provides an opportunity to enter into a discussion about how the graph can represent the data and what the shape of the graphs may, or may not, be able to tell you about the relationships between the variables.*

Health and safety

The currents involved mean that the resistors may get very hot and could burn students, so they should be warned of this and if possible the resistors contained within electrical trunking or in component boxes.

Equipment

Variable DC power supply (0–12 V)

Connecting leads

Voltmeter (analogue or digital 0–12 V)

Ammeter (analogue or digital, range will depend upon resistor chosen but 0–5 A will suffice in most circumstances)

Resistor(s) – suggested values between 20 and 100 Ohms will give sufficiently large current readings, making it easy to measure in class. Wirewound ceramic encased resistors of this magnitude are readily available from electrical component suppliers.

8.10 Resistance of a wire

Learning objectives

- To be able to set up a circuit to measure the current and voltage for wires of different lengths.
- To explore the relationship between the resistance of a wire and its length.

Prior knowledge: It is assumed that students will be familiar with the terms current, potential difference, resistance and how to calculate resistance from current and potential difference.

Procedure

Students connect a circuit with the piece of wire in series with an ammeter in series and parallel with a voltmeter. They collect potential difference and current readings for lengths of wire. For each piece of wire they should collect a number of pairs of potential difference and current readings. In each case, by the dividing potential difference by the current they can calculate a value for the resistance of the wire and from these values an average resistance can be calculated. They try to identify the qualitative effect (increase, decrease, no effect) that the length of a wire has on its resistance. The length can be varied by using a crocodile clip attached to one end of the wire to allow you to move it along the wire, changing its effective length easily (see Figure 8.9). They can also explore these relationships for different materials and a mathematical pattern relating resistance to length if they wish.

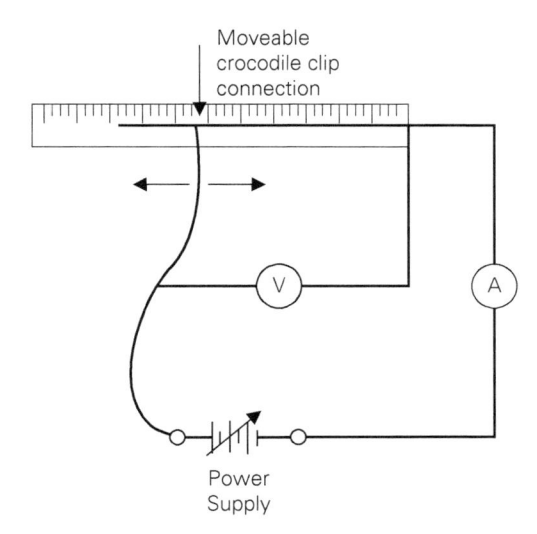

Figure 8.9 Measuring the resistance of a wire

Effectiveness matrix

	Domain of observables	Domain of ideas
What students do	Students can: • Set up the correct circuit and measure current and potential difference for different lengths of wire.	Students can talk about: • The idea that the length of a wire has an effect on its resistance. • How the data that they have collected describes the effect that the length of a wire has on its resistance.
What students learn	This quadrant is intentionally blank in this task.	Students can later talk about: • The effect that the length of the wire will have on its resistance. • Why the length of a wire will have an effect on its resistance.

Keep in mind

There is scope here to spend some time exploring issues around accuracy and precision when working with students. For example, the thickness of the wire is likely to be given on packaging but they could measure this with an apparatus such as a vernier callipers, which may give measurements to ±0.05 mm, and then compare this with the readings that they can take from using a metre rule to measure the length, which are often ±0.5 mm, depending upon the scale.

Issues for discussion

You may wish to ask the students some of the following questions to help develop their thinking:

(before collecting data) What effect do you think making the wire longer will have on the resistance of the wire. *These questions are designed to get the students to consider the effect that the length of the wire will have on its resistance. For some students, the relationship seems intuitive, but encourage them to try and explain their answer.*

(once they have analysed the data) What do you think the resistance of a wire that is x metres long will be? *This question is designed to help students explore the predictive power of the pattern that they have found is to estimate data that they do not have. If the wire has a length of x metres, then its resistance should be double that of a wire whose length was half of x.*

Health and safety

The large currents, particularly when the length of the wire is short, mean that the wires can become very hot, enough to burn skin and melt or scorch the surface they are resting on. It is suggested to carry out preliminary experiments in order to identify limits of a maximum voltage for the power supply and minimum lengths for each wire used. If using mains power supplies rather than cells, it is also possible that the high current will melt the wire or trigger the inbuilt safety mechanisms and the supply will shut off and so appropriate readings need to be suggested. Students should be encouraged to set the circuit up, then connect the power supply, take readings quickly and then disconnect the power supply.

Equipment

Variable DC power supply (0–12 V) or multiple cells

Connecting leads and crocodile clips

Voltmeter (analogue or digital 0–12 V)

Ammeter (analogue or digital, range will depend upon resistor chosen but 0–5 A will suffice in most circumstances)

Various wires – it is suggested that constantan (also known as Eureka) wire is used. Different diameters between 0.20 mm and 0.75 mm (e.g. 34/30/26/22 SWG) as well as other wires of the same diameter but different materials, such as copper should all be suitable

Metre ruler

8.11 Electromagnetic induction

Learning objectives

- To investigate how the movement of a magnet near a coil of wire can induce a potential difference and thus a current in that wire.
- To investigate the factors that affect the size of the induced potential difference and this current.

Prior knowledge: It is assumed that students will be familiar with the idea that a magnet has a magnetic field around it as well as with the terms current and potential difference.

Procedure

Students take a piece of wire and wind it into a coil of twenty to thirty turns. The coil needs to be large enough to move a bar magnet in and out of it easily. Connect the ends of the wire to a sensitive ammeter/galvanometer (see Figure 8.10). Students move the magnet in and out of the coil of wire and note the size and direction of the induced current. Students explore the effect that changing the number of coils, the orientation of the magnet and the speed of motion each have on this induced current.

Figure 8.10 Measuring electromagnetic induction

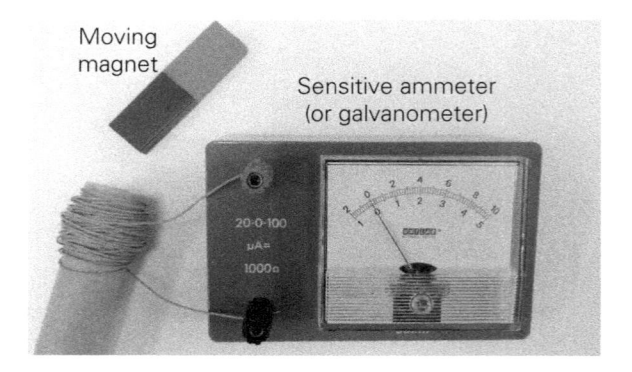

Effectiveness matrix

	Domain of observables	Domain of ideas
What students do	Students can: • Connect the circuit up correctly and move the magnet so that it can produce a reading on the ammeter.	Students can talk about: • That the interaction between the magnet and coil of wire generates current. • That the speed of motion and number of coils effect the size of the induced current. • That the direction of movement and orientation of the magnet effect the direction of the induced current.
What students learn	This quadrant is intentionally blank in this task.	Students can later talk about: • How the field around the bar magnet interacts with the electrons in the wire and how this causes the induced current. • How the rate and direction of movement between the magnetic field and the electrons will affect the size and direction of the induced current. • How the number of coils of wire will affect the size and direction of the induced current in terms of the number of electrons interacting with the changing magnetic field.

Keep in mind

You may wish to get students to wind the coil of wire around a small cardboard tube to allow them to get a good tight coil. Leaving the tube in place will have minimal effect upon the experiment and may make it easier. Instigating the effect of the speed of movement can be very tricky for students. It is suggested that this is done after the other two variables and may need to be demonstrated.

The current generated are quite small and flow very briefly, so if possible very sensitive ammeters should be used. Analogue metres are preferable here as a small deflection can be seen easily, even if a direct reading cannot be taken. This experiment is designed to explore qualitative relationships (bigger, smaller, the same) and so directly numerical readings are not needed, the students need to make comparative judgements. You will need to experiment with your equipment to ensure that students are able to observe readings. Some ammeters may not be sensitive enough to record the effects of varying the speed of movement. Using a pre-wound transformer coil will give larger readings and make it easier to observe the effect of changing the speed of movement.

The students will be measuring the current induced, but strictly speaking, the movement between the coil and the magnet induces a potential difference in the wire, which causes a current to flow. From previous work in this topic, they should know that a potential difference is required for a current to flow.

Issues for discussion

You may wish to ask the students some of the following questions to help develop their thinking:

Does it matter if you move the magnet or the coil? *This is designed to help them appreciate that a current will flow only when there is relative movement between the magnet and the coil although it does not matter which one is moving.*

What happens when the magnet and coil are stationary, even when the magnet is inside the coil? *There is no current unless there is movement.*

What happens when you move the magnet (or coil) faster? *The faster the relative movement, the greater the current.*

What happens if you keep everything the same but change the number of coils of wire? *If you increase the number of coils but keep everything else the same, the current will be greater.*

What happens when you change the direction of movement or turn the magnet around? *The direction of current depends upon the direction of movement or the orientation of the magnet and will reverse if one of these is reversed.*

Health and safety

Equipment

Coated wire, ideally a length of 1–2 m with bare ends

Leads with crocodile clip connectors

Permanent bar magnet

Ammeter. An analogue ammeter with a high sensitivity is preferred here; if available a galvanometer can be used

8.12 Electrolysis

Learning objectives

- To establish a mathematical relationship between mass of deposited metal during electrolysis and applied current or time for which current is applied.
- To explain these two relationships in terms of the idea of *electric charge* and Faraday's Laws of Electrolysis.
- To develop scientific skills of manipulating equipment, recording accurate measurements and interpreting results.

Procedure

A low-voltage variable DC supply is connected to two copper electrodes suspended in a beaker filled with copper sulphate solution (see Figure 8.11). An ammeter and a switch should be included in the circuit. The students should record the mass of each electrode before the activity starts. Faraday's Laws of Electrolysis state that the mass of metal deposited at an electrode is proportional to the current and to the time for which the current flows (i.e. is proportional to the total charge, from the relationship *charge (coulombs) = current (amperes) × time (seconds)*). The students can measure either the mass of each electrode after each interval of time (for several intervals at a fixed current) or the mass of each electrode after each value of current (for several different values of current applied for fixed intervals of time).

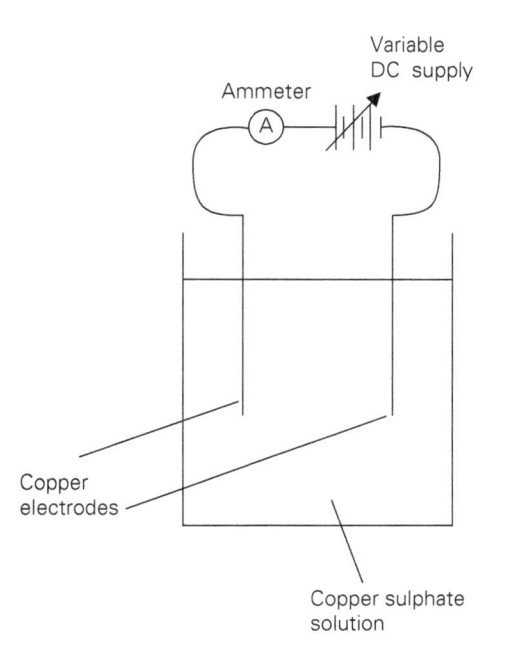

Figure 8.11 Equipment arrangement for electrolysis

Effectiveness matrix

	Domain of observables	Domain of ideas
What students do	Students can: • Measure and record values of electrode mass, current and time to appropriate levels of accuracy and precision.	Students can talk about: • What they observe happening at the electrodes in terms of the scientific ideas of *molecules, ions, electric charges, attraction* and *repulsion*. • The relationship between the mass of deposited copper and the current/time of application of current using mathematical language.
What students learn	Students can later: • Make appropriate adjustments to the planned time intervals or current values based on initial results.	Students can later talk about: • The mass of deposited copper in terms of a calculated value of *total electric charge*.

Keep in mind

The student will also observe bubbles of hydrogen forming at the cathode.

Issues for discussion

You may wish to ask the students some of the following questions to help develop their thinking:

Which electrode will positive/negative ions be attracted to when the switch is closed?

Why is a DC supply used? What would happen if you used an AC supply? *Copper ions would be liberated from one electrode (when it is temporarily an anode) and then immediately attracted back to the same electrode (which has now become a cathode) as the polarity of the AC supply is reversed.*

What is happening at each electrode when the current is increased? *The aim is to encourage students to think about current as a flow of electric charge and the relationship between the charge delivered by the power supply and the charge transferred to/from ions at the electrodes.*

What happens to the total mass of copper in the beaker plus the electrodes? *The total mass is constant as no copper is added or removed from the beaker + electrodes system during the activity.*

Health and safety

CLEAPSS advice should be followed about handling copper sulphate solution. The DC supply should be limited to prevent the application of large voltages.

Equipment

Beakers, DC power supplies, ammeters, stop clocks, copper sulphate solution, digital balances, copper electrodes, wires and crocodile clips, safety goggles

Additional Effective Practical Work

Ian Abrahams and Michael J. Reiss

9

Chapters 3–8 contain a total of seventy-two practicals but, of course, there are far more practicals in secondary school science (across the 11–16 age range) that might benefit from the approach we have been advocating in this book. In particular, we are well aware that by sticking to the conventional division of school science into biology, chemistry and physics (in which we have included astronomy), we have included little that falls within other branches of the natural sciences, such as earth science and psychology. Such subjects might themselves benefit from extended treatments based on the domain of observables and the domain of ideas.

We would be delighted, therefore, to see in such journals as *Education in Chemistry*, *Journal of Biological Education*, *Physics Education* and *School Science Review* suggestions as to how existing, familiar practicals could be adapted so as to maximize the conceptual learning that students derive from them. Such adaptations might entail producing effectiveness matrices and/or ideas for discussion.

In addition, of course, there are always new practicals being developed, including by such charities as Science and Plants for Schools (funded by the Gatsby Charitable Foundation), the Wellcome Trust and the Salters' Company.

We are also mindful that we have mostly stuck in this book to student-centred practicals that can be undertaken within fifty minutes. Yet there are other types of science practical. Demonstrations, for example, have a long history within school science and remain of importance, particularly when there is an element of risk where the practical to be undertaken by students or where the equipment is expensive or large so that class sets are not available. There is only one demonstration included in here yet it is clear that other demonstrations might benefit from the use of effectiveness matrices and explicit issues for discussion. Indeed, these seem particularly likely to be important for demonstrations, otherwise there is surely a danger that many students won't even remember what has been done let alone understand the science behind the phenomena they may or may not have observed.

Similarly, fieldwork has received little treatment in here yet all fieldwork would benefit from students thinking and talking about the science behind their observations. It is one thing to spend half a day producing a map of the distribution of organisms up a rocky shore, enjoyable as it can be to find crabs, splash one's friends and have one's lunchbox carried away by the tide. It is another thing to understand the changes in the distribution of organisms as one moves up a rocky shore by relating these validly to changes in the abiotic and biotic environments.

More generally, students undertaking independent projects at any stage of their science education should be encouraged to relate what they observe to causal explanations for such observations. We rather doubt that there is any need for students themselves to become familiar with the language of domains of observables and of ideas. However, just as we would hope that the approach we have advocated here becomes internalized by teachers, so that it becomes second nature to them to ensure that students engage with the key ideas of science as well as develop their manipulative proficiency or other scientific skills, so we would hope that students too, in due course, would develop the ability to realize that science is all about producing testable models intended to explain observable features of the natural world. That really would suggest that student practical work is worth undertaking.

Conclusions
Ian Abrahams and Michael J. Reiss

At the end of a book that has as its focus the effective use of practical work in school science, it is worth pausing to note that some science educators have raised serious doubts as to the value of practical work within the context of science education. Indeed, Hodson (1991) claims that 'as practised in many countries, it is ill-conceived, confused and unproductive' (p. 176) and similarly Osborne (1998) has suggested that it 'only has a strictly limited role to play in learning science and that much of it is of little educational value' (p. 156). Neither of these claims is, we would suggest, necessarily anti-practical work per se but rather should be seen as an indictment of the way in which much practical work is carried out in our schools. Certainly, we would hope that most science teachers, especially after having used some of the practical tasks within this book, would concur with our view that practical work *can* play a very important role in the teaching and learning of science, but that in order to do so, it is essential that we make its use more effective than is all too often the case.

It was to contribute towards such an improvement in the effectiveness of practical work, through initiating changes from teachers' predominantly 'hands-on' approach to one that demonstrates a more equitable balance between 'hands-on' and 'minds-on', that the 'Getting Practical' Continuing Professional Development (CPD) programme was designed and implemented. However, despite such good intentions, the evaluation of the programme (Abrahams & Reiss, 2012; Abrahams et al., 2014) found little change in teachers' actual practice in the classroom. Indeed, the final evaluation found there to be:

> no statistically significant change in the average amount of time teachers devoted, pre- and post-CPD training, to different aspects of their lessons, as would be expected if teachers had altered their practice to reflect their new ideas about effective practical work. (Abrahams et al., 2014, pp. 277–278)

One possible reason for this was that heavy teaching workloads made it particularly difficult for teachers to find the time required to develop new practical tasks based on the generic 'Getting Practical' ideas. As a result of this time pressure, what teachers told us they wanted, and what this book set out to provide, were clear examples of effective practical tasks that busy teachers could use in their teaching. It is important to make clear here that the effectiveness of a practical task is not an inherent property of the task itself, but rather is a measure of the extent to which what the students actually do with, and learn about, objects and ideas corresponds to what the teacher intends them to do with, and learn about, those objects and ideas. As such, the practical tasks presented in this book are not inherently effective; rather they have the potential to be effective *if* the teacher using them adopts the same learning objectives as those outlined by our contributing authors *and* they undertake the task in the manner laid out by that author.

One of the overarching features of the practical tasks presented in this book is the equitable division of lesson time between the domains of 'observables' and 'ideas' through the use of the 2 × 2 effectiveness matrixes. The use of this matrix, for each of the tasks, provides the teacher with an opportunity to consider what it is that the task has been designed to achieve, in terms of the intended learning objectives, and, as such, to take ownership of them so that those objectives become their own in terms of what they intend their students to 'do' and 'learn', not only in the domain of observables, but also in the domain of ideas. By breaking the objectives up into 'doing' and 'learning' in both domains, teachers will be guided to allocate time to each objective and, because the completed matrix provides evidence as to what is required of the pupils *if* the practical lesson is to be effective, teachers are encouraged to focus their attention on how best to achieve these aims.

Science education, as Millar (1991) has suggested, is 'irreducibly an interplay between experiment and theory, and so a total separation of theory and experiment is neither desirable nor possible' (p. 43). The practical tasks presented throughout this book involve just such interplay between experiment and theory *within* the context of a practical lesson and have been specifically designed to provide a bridge that links the domain of observables with the domain of ideas. However, while we have within these tasks devoted a greater proportion of class time to 'minds-on' work, this has necessitated a slight reduction in the amount of 'hands-on' work. This has been necessary as we have endeavoured to be realistic in terms of what pupils can be expected to achieve, *both* in terms of 'doing' and in terms of 'learning', in practical lessons (or parts thereof) that frequently last no more than 60 minutes and are unlikely, with arrival, registration and the need to pack away, to exceed 50 minutes.

We hope that by demonstrating this more equitable balance between 'minds-on' and 'hands-on' in the examples provided within this book, we have demonstrated how the overall effectiveness of practical work can be improved. By using these practical tasks with their students we hope that science teachers will better appreciate the central role that practical work can play as an effective bridge between the domain of observables and the domain of ideas. To maximize this, enhanced effectiveness will, we suggest, also require teachers to relinquish the 'discovery-based' view of learning, in which 'doing' and 'learning' about ideas are seen to emerge of their own accord simply from the successful production of a phenomenon, and embrace a hypothetico-deductive approach in which practical tasks have to be designed, as is the case for all of the practical tasks in this book, with the *explicit* aim of helping to scaffold pupils' efforts to form links between the two distinct domains of knowledge *within* the lesson.

One of the criticisms of the 'Getting Practical' project voiced by teachers was that while the generic ideas about a more equitable balance between 'hands-on' and 'minds-on', and the need to more effectively link what students did in practical lessons with the explanatory scientific ideas, made good sense, what they really wanted were actual examples of how to do this. This book was designed to redress this problem by providing teachers with examples of widely used practical tasks, across all three main sciences, that have been specifically redesigned in order to provide not only a more equitable balance between 'hands-on' and 'minds-on' but also to furnish the bridge between the domain of observables and that of ideas.

While we would like the resources provided in this book to be used and valued by science teachers, we also hope that those teachers will see these as exemplars from which they can, with growing confidence, move on to design their own potentially effective practical tasks. As such, we would like to end with a claim by Langeveld (1965) that states that '[e]ducational studies ... are a 'practical science' in the sense that we do not only want to know facts and to understand relations for the sake of knowledge, we want to know and understand in order to be able to act and act 'better' than we did before' (p. 4). It is therefore our hope that the educational studies that have been used to inform and support the design of the practical tasks presented in this book will enable teachers to act better than they did before in terms of how they use practical work and, in so doing, improve the learning of their students.

References

Abrahams, I. (2009). 'Does practical work really motivate? A study of the affective value of practical work in secondary school science'. *International Journal of Science Education*, 31 (17), 2335–2353.

Abrahams, I. (2011). *Practical Work in Secondary Science: A Minds-On Approach*. London: Continuum.

Abrahams, I., & Millar, R. (2008). 'Does practical work really work? A study of the effectiveness of practical work as a teaching and learning method in school science'. *International Journal of Science Education*, 30 (14), 1945–1969.

Abrahams, I., & Reiss, M. (2012). 'Practical work: Its effectiveness in primary and secondary schools in England'. *Journal of Research in Science Teaching*, 49 (8), 1035–1055.

Abrahams, I., & Saglam, M. (2010). 'A study of teachers' views on practical work in secondary schools in England and Wales'. *International Journal of Science Education*, 32 (6), 753–768.

Abrahams, I., Reiss, M., & Sharpe, R. (2011). 'Getting practical: Improving Practical Work in Science (IPWiS) project – The evaluation'. *School Science Review*, 93 (342), 37–44.

Abrahams, I., Reiss, M.J., & Sharpe, R. (2014). 'The impact of the "Getting Practical: Improving Practical Work in Science" continuing professional development programme on teachers' ideas and practice in science practical work'. *Research in Science & Technological Education,* 32 (3), 263–280.

Aiken, L.R., & Aiken, D.R. (1969). 'Recent research on attitude concerning science'. *Science Education*, 53, 295–305.

Arce, J., & Betancourt, R. (1997). 'Student-designed experiments in scientific lab instruction'. *Journal of College Science Teaching*, 27 (2), 114–118.

Ausubel, D.P. (1968). *Educational Psychology*. New York: Holt, Rinehart and Winston.

Bates, G.R. (1978). 'The role of the laboratory in secondary school science programs'. In M.B. Rowe (Ed.), *What Research Says to the Science Teacher* (pp. 55–82). Washington, DC: National Science Teachers Association.

Beatty, J.W. (1980). *School science, its organisation and practical work in the 11–13 Age Range*. Unpublished MSc dissertation. University of Oxford.

Beatty, J.W., & Woolnough, B.E. (1982). 'Practical work in 11–13 science: The context, type and aims of current practice'. *British Educational Research Journal*, 8, 23–30.

Bennett, J. (2003). *Teaching and Learning Science: A Guide to Recent Research and Its Applications*. London: Continuum.

Berry, A., Mulhall, P., Gunstone, R., & Loughran, J. (1999). 'Helping students learn from laboratory work'. *Australian Science Teachers' Journal*, 45 (1), 27–31.

Boud, D.J., Dunn, J., Kennedy, T., & Thorley, R. (1980). 'The aims of science laboratory courses: A survey of students, graduates and practising scientists'. *European Journal of Science Education*, 2, 415–428.

Brodin, G. (1978). 'The role of the laboratory in the education of industrial physicists & engineers. In J. Ogborn, Aims and organisation of the laboratory'. In J.G. Jones and J.L. Lewis, (Eds), *The Role of the Laboratory in Physics Education* (pp. 4–14). Birmingham: Goodman and Sons.

References

Chang, H.-P., & Lederman, N.G. (1994). 'The effects of levels of co-operation within physical science laboratory groups on physical science achievement'. *Journal of Research in Science Teaching*, 31, 167–181.

Clackson, S.G., & Wright, D.K. (1992). 'An appraisal of practical work in science education'. *School Science Review*, 74 (266), 39–42.

Connell, L. (1971). 'Demonstration and individual practical work in science teaching: A review of opinions'. *School Science Review*, 52, 692–702.

Dawe, S. (2003). *Practical work: The universal panacea?* Available online at http://www.bishops.k12.nf.ca/rriche/ed6620/practical.html.

Edwards, J., & Power, C. (1990). 'Role of laboratory work in a national junior secondary science project: Australian science education programme (ASSEP)'. In E. Hegarty-Hazel, (Ed.), *The Student Laboratory and the Science Curriculum*. (pp. 315–336) London: Routledge.

Fordham, A. (1980). 'Student-intrinsic motivation, science teaching practices and student learning'. *Research in Science Education*, 10, 108–117.

Gagné, R.M., & White, R.T. (1978). 'Memory structures and learning outcomes'. *Review of Educational Research*, 48, 187–222.

Gangoli, S.G., & Gurumurthy, C. (1995). 'A study of the effectiveness of a guided open-ended approach to physics experiments'. *International Journal of Science Education*, 17 (2), 233–324.

Gardner, P.L., & Gauld, C.F. (1990). 'Labwork and students' attitudes'. In E. Hegarty-Hazel (Ed.), *The Student Laboratory and the Science Curriculum* (pp. 132–158). London: Routledge.

Gauld, C.F., & Hukins, A.A. (1980). 'Scientific attitudes: A review'. *Studies in Science Education*, 7, 129–161.

Gott, R., & Duggan, S. (1995). *Investigative Work in the Science Curriculum*. Buckingham: Open University Press.

Gurumurthy, C. (1988). *A comparative study of the effectiveness of guided discovery approach of doing physics experiments versus instructed performance approach at pre-university level.* PhD Thesis. India: Mysore University.

Harlen, W., & Holroyd, C. (1997). 'Primary teachers' understanding of concepts of science: Impact on confidence and teaching'. *International Journal of Science Education*, 19 (1), 93–105.

Heaney, S. (1971). 'The effects of three teaching methods and the ability of young pupils to solve problems in biology: An experimental and quantitative investigation'. *Journal of Biological Education*, 5, 219–228.

Henry, N.W. (1975). 'Objectives for laboratory work'. In P.L. Gardner (Ed.), *The Structure of Science Education* (pp. 61-75). Hawthorn, Victoria: Longman.

Hewson, M., & Hewson, P. (1983). 'Effect of instruction using student prior knowledge and conceptual change strategies on science learning'. *Journal of research in Science Teaching*, 20 (8), 731–743.

Hidi, S., & Harackiewicz, J.M. (2000). 'Motivating the academically unmotivated: A critical issue for the 21st century'. *Review of Educational Research*, 70 (2), 151–179.

Hill, B.W. (1976). 'Using college chemistry to influence creativity'. *Journal of Research in Science Teaching*, 13, 71–77.

Hodson, D. (1989). *Children's Understanding of Science*. Auckland: University of Auckland Science and Technology Education Centre: Occasional Publications.

Hodson, D. (1990). 'A critical look at practical work in school science'. *School Science Review*, 70 (256), 33–40.

Hodson, D. (1991). 'Practical work in science: Time for a reappraisal'. *Studies in Science Education*, 19, 175–184.

Hodson, D. (1992). 'Redefining and reorientating practical work in school science'. *School Science Review*, 73 (264), 65–78.

Hodson, D. (1996). 'Practical work in school science: Exploring some directions for change'. *International Journal of Science Education*, 18 (7), 755–760.

References

Hofstein, A. (1988). 'Practical work and science education II'. In P. Fensham (Ed.), *Development and Dilemmas in Science Education* (pp. 189-217). Lewes: The Falmer Press.

Hofstein, A., & Lunetta, V.N. (1982). 'The role of the laboratory in science teaching: Neglected aspects of research'. *Review of Educational Research*, 52, 201–218.

House of Commons Science and Technology Committee (2002). *Third Report. Science Education from 14 to 19*. London: HMSO. Available online at http://www.publications.parliament.uk/pa/cm200102/cmselect/cmsctech/508/50802.htm.

Johnstone, A.H., & Wham, A.J.B. (1982). 'The demands of practical work'. *Education in Chemistry*, 19, 71–73.

Kempa, R.F., & Palmer, C.R. (1974). 'The effectiveness of video-tape recorded demonstration in the learning of manipulative skills in practical chemistry'. *Journal of Educational Technology*, 5 (1), 62–71.

Kerr, J.F. (1964). *Practical Work in School Science*. Leicester: Leicester University Press.

Kreitler, H., & Kreitler, S. (1974). 'The role of experiment in science education'. *Instructional Science*, 3, 75–88.

Langeveld, M.J. (1965). 'In search of research'. In *Paedagogica Europoea: The European Year Book of Educational Research* 1. Amsterdam: Elsevier.

Layton, D. (1990). 'Student laboratory practice and the history and philosophy of science'. In E. Hegarty-Hazel (Ed.), *The Student Laboratory and the Science Curriculum* (pp. 37-59). London: Routledge.

Lazarowitz, R., & Tamir, P. (1994). 'Research on using laboratory instruction in science'. In D.L. Gabel (Ed.), *Handbook of Research on Science Teaching and Learning* (pp. 94-128). New York: Macmillan.

Martin, M. (1979). 'Connections between philosophy of science and science education'. *Studies in Philosophy and Education*, 9 (4), 329–332.

Matthews, M.R., & Winchester, I. (1989). 'History, science and science teaching'. *Interchange*, 20, 1–15.

Millar, R. (1989). 'What is "scientific method" and can it be taught?' In J. Wellington (Ed.), *Skills and Processes in Science Education* (pp. 165-214). London: Routledge.

Millar, R. (1991). 'A means to an end: The role of process in science education'. In Woolnough, B.E. (Ed.), *Practical Science*. Milton Keynes: Open University Press.

Millar, R. (1998). 'Rhetoric and reality: What practical work in science education is *really* for'. In J. Wellington. (Ed.), *Practical Work in School Science: Which Way Now?* London: Routledge.

Millar, R. (2004). *The role of practical work in the teaching and learning of science*. Paper prepared for the meeting: High school science laboratories: Role and vision. Washington, DC: National Academy of Sciences.

Millar, R., & Driver, R. (1987). 'Beyond processes'. *Studies in Science Education*, 14, 33–62.

Millar, R., & Osborne, J. (Eds) (1998). *Beyond 2000: Science Education for the Future*. London: King's College.

Millar, R., Le Maréchal, J.-F., & Tiberghien, A. (1999). ' "Mapping" the domain: Varieties of practical work'. In J. Leach & A. Paulsen (Eds), *Practical Work in Science Education – Recent Research Studies* (pp. 33–59). Roskilde/Dordrecht, The Netherlands: Roskilde University Press/Kluwer.

Mulopo, M.M., & Fowler, H.S. (1987). 'Effects of traditional and discovery instructional approaches on learning outcomes for learners of different intellectual development: A study of chemistry students in Zambia'. *Journal of Research in Science Teaching*, 24 (3), 217–227.

Murphy, P.K., & Alexander, P. (2000). 'A motivated exploration of motivation terminology'. Quoted in S. Hidi and J. M. Harackiewicz, Motivating the academically unmotivated: A critical issue for the 21st century. *Review of Educational Research*, 70 (2), 151–179.

NSTA Commission on Professional Standards and Practices. (1970). *Conditions for good science teaching in secondary schools*. Washington, DC: National Science Teachers Association.

Osborne, J. (1998). 'Science education without a laboratory?' In J.J. Wellington (Ed.), *Practical Work in School Science: Which Way Now?* (pp. 156–173). London: Routledge.

Osborne, J., & Collins, S. (2001). 'Pupils' views of the role and value of the science curriculum: A focus-group study'. *International Journal of Science Education*, 23 (5), 441–467.

Osborne, J., Simon, S., & Collins, S. (2003). 'Attitudes towards science: A review of the literature and its implications'. *International Journal of Science Education*, 25 (9), 1049–1079.

Osborne, J.F., Driver, R., Simon, S., & Collins, S. (1998). 'Attitudes to science: Issues and concerns'. *School Science Review*, 79 (288), 27–34.

Pickering, M. (1987). 'Laboratory education as a problem in organization'. *Journal of College Science Teaching*, 16, 187–189.

Popper, K. (1989). *Conjectures and Refutations: The Growth of Scientific Knowledge*. London: Routledge.

Roberts, R., & Johnson, P. (2015). 'Understanding the quality of data: A concept map for "the thinking behind the doing" in scientific practice'. *The Curriculum Journal*, 26 (3), 345–369.

Shulman, L.D., & Tamir, P. (1973). 'Research on teaching in the natural sciences'. In R.M.W. Travers (Ed.), *Second Handbook of Research on Teaching* pp. 1098-1148. Chicago: Rand McNally and Co.

Simon, S. (2000). 'Student's attitudes towards science'. In M. Monk & J. Osborne (Eds), *Good Practice in Science Teaching: What Research Has to Say* (pp. 104-119). Buckingham: Open University Press.

Tamir, P. (1991). 'Practical work in school science: An analysis of current practice'. In B.E. Woolnough (Ed.), *Practical Science* (pp. 13-20). Milton Keynes: Open University Press.

Thompson, J.J. (Ed.) (1975). *Practical Work in Sixthform Science*. Oxford: Department of Educational Studies, University of Oxford.

Tiberghien, A. (2000). 'Designing teaching situations in the secondary school'. In R. Millar, J. Leach & J. Osborne (Eds), *Improving Science Education: The Contribution of Research* (pp. 27–47). Buckingham, UK: Open University Press.

Van den Berg, E., & Giddings, G. (1992). *Laboratory Practical Work: An Alternative View of Laboratory Teaching*. Western Australia: Curtin University, Science and Mathematics Education Centre.

Watson, R., & Fairbrother, R. (1993). 'Open ended work in science (OPENS) project: Managing investigations in the laboratory'. *School Science Review*, 75 (271), 31–38.

Watson, J.R., Prieto, T., & Dillon, J. (1995). 'The effect of practical work on students' understanding of combustion'. *Journal of Research in Science Teaching*, 32 (5), 487–502.

White, R.T. (1979). 'Relevance of practical work to comprehension of physics'. *Physics Education*, 14, 384–387.

White, R.T. (1988). *Learning Science*. Oxford: Blackwell.

White, R.T. (1996). 'The link between the laboratory and learning'. *International Journal of Science Education*, 18 (7), 761–774.

Windschitl, M., & Andre, T. (1998). 'Using computer simulation to enhance conceptual change: The roles of constructivist instruction and student epistemological beliefs'. *Journal of Research in Science Teaching*, 35 (2), 144–160.

Woolnough, B.E., & Allsop, T. (1985). 'Practical Work in Science'. Cambridge: Cambridge University Press.

Yager, R., Engen, H., & Snider, B. (1969). 'Effects of the laboratory and demonstration methods upon the outcomes of instruction in secondary biology'. *Journal of Research in Science Teaching*, 6, 76–86.

Young, M. (2007). *Bringing Knowledge Back In: From Social Constructivism to Social Realism in the Sociology of Education*. London: Routledge.

Index

Abrahams, I. 2, 5, 10, 12, 14, 17, 18, 20–2, 253, 255
absolute zero/Charles' law 230–2
acid-base titration 179
agar blocks, diffusion and surface area in 64–5
Aiken, D. R. 12
Aiken, L. R. 12
Alexander, P. 10
algal balls, photosynthesis using 79–81
Allsop, T. 8, 10, 14
alogen, reactive 101–3
amylase on starch 72–4
analogue metres 247
Andre, T. 10
animals
    cells, structure of 30–2
    respiration in 38–40
antiseptic growth 33–6
Arce, J. 10
Ausubel, D. P. 9, 11
average speed 184–6

bar magnet, magnetic field around 209–11
basalt 149
Bates, G. R. 15
Beatty, J. W. 7, 8, 10
Bennett, J. 7, 8, 10, 11, 13
Berry, A. 10
Betancourt, R. 10
biology
    breathing system, structure and function of 75–6
    Daphnia heart rate in response to caffeine 77–8
    diffusion and surface area in agar blocks 64–5
    effect of amylase on starch 72–4
    effect of antiseptic on microbial growth 33–6
    effects of evolution using model 94–6
    energy content of foods 66–8
    exercise on heart rate 36–7
    extracting DNA from plant tissue 49–51
    factors that promote decay 69–71
    measuring forces exerted by different muscles 41–2
    mitotic index 91–3
    nerve pathways on reaction times 43–5
    photosynthesis (*see* photosynthesis)
    plant species on school field 52–3
    respiration in plants and animals 38–40
    responses of woodlice using 56–8
    root tip preparation 91–3
    seeds dispersed by wind 54–5
    stomatal density on leaves 82–4
    structure of plant and animal cells 30–2
    transpiration rates from leaves 85–7
    turgor and plasmolysis in onion cells 88–90
    variation within and between species 46–7
black ink, colours in 98–100
Boud, D. J. 11
breathing system, structure and function of 75–6
Brodin, G. 6
Bunsen burner 224

caffeine, *Daphnia* heart rate in response to 77–8
candle 132–5
carbon
    and copper(II) oxide 119–20
    and iron(III) oxide 119
    and lead(II) oxide 120
    ores using 119–21
Chang, H.-P. 9
Charles' law 230–2
chemistry
    chemical reaction rate 155–8
    combustion products 132–5
    cracking hydrocarbons 169–72
    diffusion of ions in solution 126–8
    electricity from pairs of metals 162–4
    electrolysis of ionic compounds 159–61
    elements, mixtures and compounds 116–18
    emulsifiers 173–5
    extraction of metals 119–21
    iodine clock 165–8
    ionic solid 140–4
    Landolt Clock 165–8
    modelling formation of igneous rocks 148–51
    nylon rope, making of 176–8
    plants as indicators 122–5
    process of neutralisation 129–31
    rate of reaction 152–4
    reactive halogen 101–3
    reactive metal 111–15
    salts present in sea water 108–10
    separating colours in black ink 98–100

Index

substances cause hard water 104–7
thermal decomposition of copper carbonate 136–8
thermometric titration 179–81
transition metal ions as catalysts 145–7
chromatogram 98
circular motion 216–18
Clackson, S. G. 6, 9, 11, 22
Collins, S. 10
colours 207–8
in black ink 98–100
food 99
combustion products
analysis of 132–5
collecting 133
compounds 116–18
concentration of reactant 152–4
conduction, thermal 196–8
Connell, L. 12
converging lenses 239
copper carbonate, thermal decomposition of 136–8
copper coil 115
copper(II) oxide 119–20
cracking hydrocarbons 169–72
critical angle 233–5

Daphnia heart rate 77–8
Dawe, S. 11
decay factors 69–71
diffusion
in agar blocks 64–5
of ions 126–8
DNA extraction 49–51
Driver, R. 11
Duggan, S. 11

Edwards, J. 10
effective practical work 253–4
conclusions and implications for 27–8
'hands on' *and* 'minds on' model 18–20
post-training findings
doing with objects, materials and ideas 25
primary school impact 25–6
secondary school impact 26
pre-training observations
primary schools 22–3
secondary schools 23–4
using model in practice 20–2
efficiency 219–21
electric charge 249
electricity, from pairs of metals 162–4
electrodes
potential 162
S-shaped 159
electrolysis 249–51
equipment arrangement for 249
of ionic compounds in solution 159–61
with S-shaped electrodes 159

electromagnet 212–14
made with coil 212
electromagnetic induction 246–8
elements 116–18
emulsifiers 173–5
energy 224
content of foods 66–8
content of fuels 201–2
transfer 219–21
exercise on heart rate 36–7
extraction of metals 119–21

Fairbrother, R. 10
Faraday's Laws of Electrolysis 249
filters 207–8
food
colours 99
energy content of 66–8
Fordham, A. 12
forensic science variation 98–9
Fowler, H. S. 8
fuels, energy content of 201–2

Gagné, R. M. 14
Gangoli, S. G. 11
Gardner, P. L. 10, 13
garlic root tip squash 91
Gauld, C. F. 10, 13
Giddings, G. 9, 14
Gott, R. 11
granite 149
gravitational potential energy (GPE) 219–21, 223
Gurumurthy, C. 11

'hands on' *and* 'minds on' model 18–20
Harackiewicz, J. M. 10
hard water
vs soft water 104
substances cause 104–7
Harlen, W. 22
Heaney, S. 11
heart rate, exercise on 36–7
helical spring
force *vs* extension for 190–2
measuring extension of 190
Henry, N. W. 12
Hewson, M. 8
Hewson, P. 8
Hidi, S. 10
Hill, B. W. 11
Hodson, D. 8–14, 255
Hofstein, A. 9–12, 15
Holroyd, C. 22
Hooke's law 191
Hukins, A. A. 13
hydrocarbons
cracking 169–72
equipment set to 169–70

igneous rocks, formation of 148–51
incident rays 233
indicators, plants as 122–5
induction, electromagnetic 246–8
insulation, thermal 199–200
iodine clock 165–8
ionic compounds
    electrolysis of 159–61
    identifying 141
ionic solid, ions in 140–4
ions
    diffusion of 126–8
    in ionic solid 140–4
    metal 145–7
iron(III) oxide 119

Johnson, P. 1
Johnstone, A. H. 9

Kempa, R. F. 11
Kerr, J. F. 6–8, 10
Kreitler, H. 14
Kreitler, S. 14

Landolt Clock 165–8
Langeveld, M. J. 257
law of reflection 203–4
law of refraction 205–6
Layton, D. 13
Lazarowitz, R. 9, 10, 12–14
lead(II) iodide 126–8
lead(II) oxide 120
leaf, starch in 59–62
leaves
    stomatal density on 82–4
    transpiration rates from 85–7
Lederman, N. G. 9
lens
    converging 239
    focal length of 236–9
Lunetta, V. N. 9–12, 15

magnetic field around bar magnet 209–11
Martin, M. 13
mass 227–9
Matthews, M. R. 14
metals
    extraction of 119–21
    ions, transition 145–7
    reactive 111–15
    rods set up for heating 196
microbial growth 33–6
Millar, R. 9–11, 13–15, 18, 256
mitotic index 91–3
mixtures 116–18
model, effects of evolution using 94–6
Molten salol 148

Moon, change over time 193–5
motion graphs 184
moving objects, speed of 184–6
Mulopo, M. M. 8
Murphy, P. K. 10
muscles, measuring forces exerted by 41–2

nail varnish 83
neutralisation, process of 129–31
nylon rope
    extract and store 176
    greyish film of 176
    making 176–7

Ohmic resistor
    circuit diagram for 240
    potential difference and current
        characteristics for 240–2
onion cells 88–90
    plasmolysis in 88–90
    turgor in 88–90
ores using carbon 119–21
Osborne, J. 10, 255

pairs of metals, electricity from 162–4
Palmer, C. R. 11
personal power 222–3
photosynthesis
    by presence/absence of starch in leaf 59–62
    presence and absence of light on 79–81
    using algal balls 79–81
physics
    absolute zero/Charles' law 230–2
    appearance of Moon over time 193–5
    circular motion 216–18
    critical angle and total internal reflection 233–5
    efficiency and energy transfer 219–21
    electrolysis 249–51
    electromagnetic induction 246–8
    energy content of fuels 201–2
    filters and colours 207–8
    focal length of lens and making
        telescope 236–9
    helical spring, force and extension for 190–2
    law of reflection 203–4
    law of refraction 205–6
    magnetic field around bar magnet 209–11
    motion graphs 187–9
    Ohmic resistor 240–2
    personal power 222–3
    pressure law 227–9
    resistance of wire 243–5
    specific heat capacity 224–6
    speed of moving objects 184–6
    strength of a simple electromagnet 212–14
    thermal conduction 196–8
    thermal insulation 199–200

Index

Pickering, M. 10
plants
    cells, structure of 30–2
    as indicators 122–5
    respiration in 38–40
    species on school field 52–3
    tissue, extracting DNA from 49–51
plasmolysis in onion cells 88–90
polymerization 177
Popper, K. 13
post-training findings
    doing with objects, materials and ideas 25
    primary school impact 25–6
    secondary school impact 26
power 224
Power, C. 10
pressure law 227–9
pre-training observations
    primary schools 22–3
    secondary schools 23–4
primary schools 22–3
    impact 25–6
process of neutralisation 129–31
promote decay factors 69–71
    experimental set-up 69

rate of reaction 152–8
ray box 203
reactant, concentration of 152–4
reaction rate 152–4
    chemical reaction affect its 155–8
reaction times, nerve pathways on 43–5
reactive halogen 101–3
reactive metal 111–15
reflection, law of 203–4
refracted/reflected rays 233
refraction, law of 205–6
Reiss, M. 21, 29, 33, 253, 255
resistance of wire 243–5
Roberts, R. 1
rocks, igneous 148–51
root tip preparation 91–3

Saglam, M. 10
salol, crystal growth of 148
salts in sea water 108–10
school field, plant species on 52–3
science education, role of practical work
    in developing scientific attitudes 12–13
    enhancing learning of 8–9
    expertise of scientific method 13–14
    generic aims for use of 8
    in motivating students 10
    perspectives on nature and purpose of 14–15
    previous studies into 6–8
    in teaching laboratory skills 11–12
sea water, salts in 108–10

secondary schools 23–4
    impact 26
seeds, dispersed by wind 54–5
Sharpe, R. 21
Shulman, L. D. 12
Simon, S. 12
soft water, hard water *vs* 104
species, variation within and between 46–7
specific heat capacity 224–6
speed
    average 184
    of moving objects 184–6
S-shaped electrodes 159
starch
    effect of amylase on 72–4
    in leaf, photosynthesis by
        presence/absence of 59–62
stomatal density on leaves 82–4
'suck-back' prevention 172
surface area in agar blocks 64–5

Tamir, P. 9–10, 12–14
telescope 236–9
temperature 227–9
thermal conduction 196–8
thermal decomposition of copper carbonate 136–8
thermal insulation 199–200
    materials 199
thermometric titration 179–81
Thompson, J. J. 8, 10
Tiberghien, A. 19
total internal reflection 233–5
transition metal ions 145–7
transpiration rates from leaves 85–7
turgor in onion cells 88–90

universal indicator 129–31

Van den Berg, E. 9, 14
volume 227–9

water-based varnishes 83
water, fixed volume of 201
Watson, J. R. . 9
Watson, R. 10
Wham, A. J. B. 9
White, R. T. 6, 11, 14, 24
Winchester, I. 14
Windschitl, M. 10
wire, resistance of 243–5
woodlice using choice chambers 56–8
Woolnough, B. E. 8, 10, 14
Wright, D. K. 6, 9, 11, 22

Yager, R. 9
Young, M. 3

Milton Keynes UK
Ingram Content Group UK Ltd.
UKHW052252261123
433329UK00007B/198